GORDON · POLSON

FREDERICK

CASELY

· LEAL ·

ABERDEEN
1994

Bought 2nd hand at
Crathes Castle
15th February 2009
Donald Macpherson
7 Meikle Gardens, Westhill
Aberdeenshire

AN INTRODUCTION
TO HERALDRY

I.P.Elven Sculp.

Hugh *Clark,* C & G.

HERALDIC **ENGRAVER,**

& Editor of *the Concise*

History of Knighthood.

AN INTRODUCTION TO HERALDRY

BY

HUGH CLARK

WITH NEARLY ONE THOUSAND ILLUSTRATIONS

EIGHTEENTH EDITION

REVISED AND CORRECTED BY

J. R. PLANCHÉ
SOMERSET HERALD OF ARMS

TABARD PRESS
ROWMAN & LITTLEFIELD
1974

Published by Tabard Press Limited
East Ardsley, Wakefield
Yorkshire, England
and in the United States of America by
Rowman and Littlefield
Totowa, New Jersey

ISBN 0 85948 000 3
(Tabard)

ISBN 0-87471-462-1
(Rowman & Littlefield)

Please address all enquiries to Tabard Press Limited
(address as above)

Printed in Great Britain by
Redwood Press Limited, Trowbridge, Wiltshire

PREFACE

Two hundred years ago there appeared *A Short and Easy Introduction to Heraldry*, 'in which all the terms are displayed in a clear and alphabetical manner' by Hugh Clark and Thomas Wormull, Engravers. Wormull continued as co-editor until the eighth edition in 1812 and joined Clark in the publication of an Armorial Peerage in 1778 but not in the production of his illustrated *History of Knighthood* in two volumes in 1784.

Little is known about Clark or Wormull and neither appears to have been armigerous. They were pupils of that ingenious engraver, Barak Longmate who was also a competent heraldist. He died in 1793 and Hugh Clark inserted a memorial plate for him in the seventh edition of this work. His arms and those of J. R. Planché appear on the dust jacket of this book, together with the portrait of Clark by Elven.

This *Introduction to Heraldry* became a classic, running to thirteen editions—more than any other work on heraldry—before it was put into the hands of James Robinson Planché to produce a new edi-

tion. Planché, whose puns enlivened his panto-
mime 'The Sleeping Beauty', was born in London,
the son of a Huguenot watchmaker. He made his
name as a writer of stage burlesques, extravaganzas
and pantomimes and was musical director of the
Vauxhall Gardens. He designed stage costumes
and was costume director at Covent Garden and,
for a time, managed the Adelphi Theatre. He was a
competent antiquary and was appointed Rouge
Croix Pursuivant of Arms in 1854 and Somerset
Herald in 1866. In that year he edited the eighteenth edition of Hugh Clark's *Introduction to
Heraldry*, having made a considerable reputation
for himself as a scholar of armory through his own
book *The Pursuivant of Arms*; 'or, Heraldry founded
upon Facts', the first edition of which appeared in
1852.

Planché made a complete revision of Clark's
work. He omitted some exploded theories, corrected a few erroneous opinions and produced a
'trustworthy handbook to an Art as useful as it
is ornamental—to a Science, the real value of
which is daily becoming more apparent in this
age of progress and critical inquiry.' Clark's
Heraldry is certainly one of the classic books on
heraldry of all time and among the most reliable.
It will surely continue to run on for centuries to
come in new editions.

CANTERBURY 1972   CECIL R. HUMPHERY-SMITH

CONTENTS.

Contents.

Contents.   vii

Contents.

An Introduction to Heraldry.

HERALDIC devices, truly so called, make their first appearance in Europe in the middle of the twelfth century; and about one hundred years later we find Heraldry has become a science in high repute, without our being able to trace its intermediate progress, or discover the names of those who first laid down its laws, or subsequently promulgated them. The earliest Heraldic document, of which even a copy has come down to us, is a roll of arms, that is to say, a catalogue of the armorial bearings of the King of England, and the principal barons, knights, &c., in this country in the reign of Henry III., and, from internal evidence, supposed to have been originally compiled between the years 1240–1245. This transcript was made by Glover, Somerset Herald, in 1586, and is preserved in the College of Arms. Other rolls are to be found, both there and in the British Museum, of nearly the same date, but none earlier, and no work explanatory of the science has been yet discovered of a period anterior to

the reign of Edward III. It is not, therefore, our
intention to notice any of the various theories, either
ancient or modern, which have been advanced to
account for the origin of coat-armour, as they are
purely speculative—the most rational resting on no
contemporary authority. We shall confine ourselves to
the fact that in the reign of Henry III. armorial
ensigns had become hereditary, marks of cadency distinguished the various members of a family, and the
majority of the present Heraldic terms were already
in existence.

THE USE OF ARMS

at that period was to distinguish persons and property,
and record descent and alliance, and no modern invention has yet been found to supersede it. For this
reason alone, as we have remarked elsewhere, of all
ancient usages it is one of the least likely to become
obsolete. Hundreds of persons may be entitled to the
same initials, may possess precisely the same name;
but only the members of a particular family can lawfully bear certain armorial ensigns, and the various
branches of that family have their separate differences
to distinguish one from the other. After the lapse of
centuries, the date of a building, or the name of its
founder or ancient possessor, may be ascertained at the
present day, through the accidental preservation of a
sculptured coat of arms or heraldic encaustic tile; and
the careful study of early rolls of arms, enables us to
discover matrimonial alliances and family connexions,
of which no written record has been found, and thereby
not only to complete the very imperfect genealogies of

many of the bravest and wisest of our English nobility and gentry, but also to account for sundry acts, both public and private, the motives for which have been misunderstood, or altogether unknown to the biographer or the historian.

A few words on

THE ABUSE OF ARMS.

In the middle ages, it began by an unhappy ambition in the heralds to exalt their science in the eyes of the commonalty; and a less excusable desire to pander to the vanity of those who had inherited ancient armorial devices. On charges simple enough at the time they were assumed, the most preposterous stories were founded. The wildest legends, the most unsupported assertions were adopted and exaggerated, if they could by any possibility be connected with the arms on the shield, or the badge on the standard, till the characters, which were originally so clear that those who ran might read, were mystified and misrepresented beyond our power to decipher them by the light which has been left us.

With the increase of education, the absurdities became more and more apparent, and at length the study of Heraldry was pretty nearly abandoned as a silly and useless pursuit. The critical spirit of archæology has, within the last twenty years, done much to correct the prejudice; and the curious and important information to be derived from the study of armorial devices is rapidly becoming appreciated by even the general public.

The abuse of arms in modern days is constantly exhibited in the crests engraved on the plate and seals, or stamped on the note-paper, of thousands of persons

utterly unentitled, by ancient descent or modern grant,
to such insignia.

An erroneous impression, carefully fostered by certain advertising seal-engravers, exists amongst the
public, that all persons possessing the same name have
a right to bear the same arms.   Mr. Jones considers
himself justified in bearing the crest of Viscount Rane-
lagh ; Mr. Brown that of the Marquis of Sligo.   Mr.
Smith appropriates to himself the coat of Lord Car-
rington, and Mr. Robinson sees no just cause or im-
pediment to prevent his displaying that of Earl de
Grey and Ripon.

There are instances in which, not content with the
paternal coat of their noble namesake, persons have also
assumed the quarterings they have found marshalled
with it, and we remember having seen a baronet's
arms appropriated thus wholesale, including the distinguishing mark of his rank, the badge of Ulster ! Surely
even those who affect the greatest contempt for Heraldry,
will admit that if arms are to be borne at all, it should
be according to the laws of arms ; and that if the display of them be an empty vanity, it is a less creditable
vanity to parade as our own those which belong of
right to others.

The most useful purpose of Heraldry is also defeated
by this silly practice, as identification of family or
property is impossible under such circumstances.   Nor
is it scarcely possible for the more scrupulous, who
design coats or crests for themselves, to avoid inter-
fering, more or less, with recorded arms, either ancient
or modern, and thus equally, though more innocently,
contributing to the confusion.

Another abuse of arms is the common **custom of**

wives having their note-paper stamped with the crests appertaining to, or assumed by, their husbands. No lady is entitled to a crest (see under CRESTS), and the display of one by a female of any rank is an absurdity.

CLASSES OF ARMS.

Arms are usually divided by modern authorities into eleven classes.

1. Arms of Dominion.	7. Arms of Alliance.
2. Arms of Pretension.	8. Arms of Adoption.
3. Arms of Community.	9. Arms Paternal and Hereditary.
4. Arms of Assumption.	ditary.
5. Arms of Patronage.	10. Arms of Concession.
6. Arms of Succession.	11. Canting or Allusive Arms.

These may fairly be reduced to nine, and even less, as we shall show in our description of them.

ARMS OF DOMINION

are those which emperors and kings constantly bear, and which, being annexed to their territories, are stamped on their coins, and displayed on their colours, standards, banners, coaches, seals, &c.

ARMS OF PRETENSION

are those of kingdoms, provinces, or territories to which a prince or lord pretends to have some claim, and which he therefore adds to his own arms, although the land be possessed by some other prince or lord. Thus, the kings of England quartered the arms of France with those of England from the year 1330 (when Edward III. laid claim to that kingdom, as son to Isabella, sister of Charles the Handsome, who died without issue) till the year 1801, although at the latter date all

pretensions to France on the part of England had long
ceased. On the union of this kingdom with Ireland,
the arms of France were first omitted, and the ensign
of Ireland inserted in their stead. In like manner
Spain quarters the arms of Portugal and Jerusalem;
and Denmark those of Sweden.

ARMS OF COMMUNITY

are those of bishoprics, cities, universities, academies,
societies, companies, and other bodies corporate.

ASSUMPTIVE ARMS.

In the days of chivalry, according to Sir John Ferne,
it was considered lawful that the victor, upon making
captive any gentleman of higher degree than himself, might assume the shield of arms of his prisoner;
and the acquiring of coat-armour by such feats of
valour was esteemed highly honourable. As this practice has long been disused, if indeed it ever existed,
these so-called arms of assumption may be struck out
of the list.

ARMS OF PATRONAGE

are, in one sense, such as governors of provinces, lords
of manors, patrons of benefices, add to their family
arms, as a token of their rights and jurisdiction; in
another, they are part of the arms of such lords,
assumed by and added to the paternal arms of persons
holding lands in fee under them. Thus, as the earls
of Chester bore garbs, many gentlemen of the county
bore the same ensign; and numerous instances of this
kind of bearing may still be adduced in England,
Scotland, and, indeed, in most parts of Europe.

ARMS OF SUCCESSION

are those taken up by such as inherit certain lands, manors, &c., either by will, entail, or donation; and which they bear instead of, or quarter with, their own arms.

ARMS OF ALLIANCE

are such as, when heiresses marry into families, are taken up by their issue, to show their descent paternal and maternal; and by this means the memory of many ancient and noble families, extinct in the male line, is preserved and conveyed to posterity; which is one of the principal reasons of marshalling several coats, pertaining to distict families in one shield.

ARMS OF ADOPTION.

Already described as arms of succession. They are called "of adoption" because the last of a family may by will adopt a stranger to possess his name, estate, and arms, and thereby continue the name and coat of his family in the world after his decease. The present custom for persons adopted, is to apply to the Crown for a Royal license to empower them to fulfil the will of the testator, or to the Parliament for an Act.

ARMS PATERNAL AND HEREDITARY

are such as are transmitted from the first possessor to his son, grandson, great-grandson, &c. In such case they are arms of a perfect and complete nobility, begun in the grandfather, or great-grandfather (as heralds say), growing in the son, complete in the grandson, or rather great-grandson; from which rises the distinction of gentleman of blood in the grandson, and, in the great-grandson, gentleman of ancestry.

ARMS OF CONCESSION

are augmentations granted by the sovereign, of part
of his ensigns or regalia, to such persons as he pleaseth
to honour therewith. Henry VIII. honoured the arms
of *Thomas Manners* (whom he created Earl of Rut-
land) with an augmentation, on account of his being
descended from a sister of King Edward IV. His
paternal arms were, *or, two bars azure, a chief gules.*
The augmentations were, the *chief quarterly, azure and
gules ;* on the first, *two fleurs de lis in fess, or ;* on the
second, *a lion passant gardant. See Plate XI. n.* 3. The
same monarch also granted, as an augmentation of
honour, to Lady Jane Seymour, *a pile gules, charged with
three lions passant gardant, or,* to be marshalled with
her paternal coat ; and many similar instances might
be adduced of our sovereigns giving special proof of
their favour by granting arms of concession by their
royal warrant, recorded in the College of Arms. But
these augmentations did not always consist of part of
the royal bearings. Thus, the arms granted in 1692 to
Sir Cloudesley Shovel were *gules, a chevron ermine, in
chief two crescents argent, in base a fleur de lis or ;* to denote
three victories gained by him, two over the Turks, and
one over the French : Lord Heathfield was permitted to
assume a fortress, to commemorate his gallant defence
of Gibraltar. The arms of many other of our heroes,
naval and military, as Nelson, Collingwood, Wel-
lington, may also be referred to, as justly bearing these
augmentations of honour (called by the French heralds
armes de concession), although we cannot too strongly
express our disapprobation of the wretched taste and
unheraldic character of the augmentations themselves.

CANTING ARMS.

Canting or allusive arms are coats of arms whose figures allude to the names, professions, &c., of the bearer; as *a trevet*, for Trevet; *three herrings*, for Herring; *a camel*, for Camel; *three covered cups*, for Butler; *a pine tree*, for Pine; *three arches*, for Arches; *three harrows*, for Harrow, &c. Such arms have been ignorantly described by some writers as of an inferior order, whereas there can scarcely be a greater proof of their antiquity and highly honourable character.

We will now proceed to the study of *the points of the escutcheon, metals, colours, furs, partition lines, ordinaries, charges, and distinctions of houses.*

It is highly necessary, before a person attempt to blazon a coat of arms, that he should be well acquainted with the terms and rules laid down in the following tables, which may be acquired by a little practice and application.

THE ESCUTCHEON.

The shield or escutcheon (from the Latin word *scutum*, a hide, of which shields are supposed to have been originally made,) represents the defensive implement of that name used in war, and on which armorial ensigns were originally borne. The ground or surface of it is called the *field*, and here are depicted the figures which make up the coat of arms.

The field of the escutcheon is divided into nine integral parts, used to mark the position of the bearings. They are termed the *points* of the escutcheon, and are clearly illustrated in Table I.

It should be particularly observed, that the side of the escutcheon which is opposite to the left hand of

the person looking at it is the *dexter* or right side
of the escutcheon, and that opposite the right hand
the *sinister* or left side. Great care should also be
taken to understand the points; for the very same
figures placed differently constitute distinct and different arms.

TABLE I.

POINTS OF THE ESCUTCHEON.

The dexter,
or
right-hand
side of the
escutcheon.

A	B	C
	D	
	E	
	F	
G	H	I

The sinister,
or
left-hand
side of the
escutcheon.

A Dexter chief.
B Middle chief.
C Sinister chief.
D Honour point.
E Fess point.
F Nombril point.
G Dexter base.
H Middle base.
I Sinister base.

Note.—The *chief* is the top or chief part of the escutcheon,
marked A, B, C; the base is the lower part of the escutcheon,
marked G, H, I.

TABLE II. (Plate II.)

TINCTURES AND FURS.

The tinctures or colours generally used in the science of heraldry are *red, blue, black, green,* and *purple;* termed in this science *gules, azure, sable, vert,* and *purpure. Yellow* and *white,* termed *or* and *argent,* are metals :

NAMES.				COLOURS.
Or	.	.	.	Gold, or yellow.
Argent	.	.	.	Silver, or white.
Gules	.	.	.	Red
Azure	.	.	.	Blue.
Sable	.	.	.	Black.
Vert	.	.	.	Green.
Purpure	.	.	.	Purple.

Colours and metals, when engraved, are known by dots and lines; as OR, the metal gold, is known by dots; ARGENT, which signifies white, or the white metal silver, is always left plain; GULES, is expressed by lines perpendicular from top to bottom; AZURE, by horizontal lines from side to side; SABLE, by horizontal and perpendicular lines crossing each other; VERT, by diagonal lines from right to left; PURPURE, by diagonal lines from left to right. See the examples Table II (Plate II.) S. Petrasancta, an Italian herald, about two centuries ago, is said to have been the first who thought of expressing the tinctures by lines and points.

English heralds admit of two other colours, namely, orange, called *tenné,* and blood-colour, called *sanguine ;*

though their is no instance of their occurrence in British bearings. If used, *tenné* should be expressed by diagonal lines from left to right, crossed by horizontal lines; and *sanguine*, by lines crossing each other diagonally from left to right and from right to left.

FURS.

Furs are not only used for the linings of robes and garments of state, the linings of the mantle, and other ornaments of the shield, but also in the coat-armours themselves. They originally were limited to *ermine* and *vair*, but later heralds have added *ermines, erminois, erminites, pean, vair-en-point, counter-vair, potent-counter-potent.* All these may be seen under each head in the Dictionary of Terms; but for illustration we have selected only the most common in use: viz.,

Ermine,	Ermines,	Erminois,
Vair,	Counter-vair,	Potent.

ERMINE is described by sable spots on a white field, the tail terminating in three hairs: see Table II., n. 1.

ERMINES is a field black, with white spots, n. 2.

ERMINOIS is a field gold, with black spots, n. 3.

VAIR is white and blue, represented by figures of small escutcheons, ranged in a line, so that the *base argent* is opposite to the *base azure*, n. 4.

COUNTER-VAIR is when escutcheons of the same colour are placed *base* against *base* and *point* against *point*, n. 5.

POTENT-COUNTER-POTENT is a field covered with figures like crutch-heads, termed potents *counter placed*, n. 6, potent being the old word for a crutch.

TABLE III. (Plate III.)

PARTITION LINES.

SHIELDS are divided by lines, called *partition lines,* which are distinguished by different names, according to their different forms. These lines are either straight or curved. The straight lines are perpendicular, horizontal, diagonal dexter, and diagonal sinister; termed *per pale, per fess, per bend,* &c., as explained below. The shield is said to be *party,* or divided, by these lines; as thus :—

PARTY PER PALE, *or impaled* is the field divided by a perpendicular line, as Pl. III., n. 1.

PARTY PER BEND is a field divided by a diagonal line from the dexter chief to the sinister base, as n. 2.

PARTY PER BEND Sinister is precisely the reverse of the above; the partition line running from the sinister chief to the dexter base, instead of from the dexter to the sinister.

PARTY PER FESS is a field equally divided by a horizontal line, as n. 3.

PARTY PER CHEVRON is a field divided by such a line as helps to make the chevron, as n. 4.

PARTY PER CROSS, *or quarterly,* is a field divided by two lines, the one perpendicular, the other horizontal, crossing each other in the centre of the field, as n. 5.

PARTY PER SALTIRE, is a field divided by two diagonal lines, dexter and sinister, crossing each other in the centre of the field, as n. 6.

The curved lines of partition are the *engrailed, invecked, wavy or undée, nebulé, embattled, raguly, indented, dancetté,* and *dove-tail.* See examples conspicuously engraved in Pl. III.

TABLE IV.   (PLATE IV.)

ORDINARIES.

ORDINARIES are certain charges which, by their ordinary and frequent use in a shield of arms, are become most essential to the science of Heraldry: viz., the *chief, pale, bend, bend sinister, fess, bar, chevron, cross, and saltire ;* with their diminutives or subordinaries, the *fillet, pallet, endorse, garter, cost, ribbon, baton, closet,* &c., as in Pl. IV.

THE CHIEF is formed by a horizontal line, and contains in depth the third of the field, as n. 1. Its diminutive is termed a *fillet,* and does not exceed one-fourth of the chief. The line may be indented, wavy, &c.; but this must be noticed in the blazonry.

The PALE consists of two perpendicular lines, drawn from the top to the base of the shield, and occupying one-third of its centre, as n. 2.

The pale has two diminutives—the half of the pale is called a *pallet,* as n. 3; and the half of the pallet is called an *endorse,* as n. 4.

The BEND is formed by two parallel lines, drawn from the dexter chief to the sinister base, as n. 5. It contains a fifth part of the shield in breadth, if uncharged, and a third part if charged.

The bend has four diminutives, the *bendlet,* n. 6; the *garter,* n 7; the *cost* (called when in pairs *cottices*), n. 8;

and *ribbon,* which is always couped, or cut off straight, at the ends, n. 9.

The BEND SINISTER, which passes diagonally from the sinister chief to the dexter base of the shield, as n. 10. The Bend Sinister has two diminutives; the *scarp,* which is half the bend, as n. 11 ; and the *baton,* which is half of the scarp, and couped at the ends, as n. 12.

The FESS is formed by two horizontal lines across the shield : it occupies the third part of the field, and is always confined to the centre, as n. 13.

The BAR is formed of two horizontal lines, and contains the fifth part of the field, as n. 14. The Bar is distinguished from the Fess, by being never borne single : it has two diminutives; the *closet,* which is half the bar, n. 15 ; and the *barrulet,* which is half the closet, n. 16.

The CHEVRON is formed of two lines placed in the form of a pyramid, like two rafters of a house joined together, and descending in form of a pair of compasses to the extremities of the shield, n. 17. The Chevron has two diminutives ; the *chevronel,* which is half the chevron, n. 18 ; and the *couple-close,* which is half the chevronel, n. 19.

The CROSS. The Cross is formed by the meeting of two perpendicular with two horizontal lines near the fess point, where they make four right angles : the lines are not drawn throughout, but discontinued the breadth of the cross, n. 20.

The SALTIRE is formed by the bend-dexter and bend-sinister crossing each other at right angles, n. 21.

The PILE is composed of two lines which form a long wedge, n. 22.

The QUARTER is formed of two lines, one perpendicular, the other horizontal, taking up one-fourth of the field, and is always placed in the chief, n. 23.

The CANTON is a square figure like the *quarter*, but possessing only the third part of the chief, n. 24.

TABLE V. (PLATE V.)

AMONG OTHER SUB-ORDINARIES ARE THE FOLLOWING:—

A GYRON is a triangular figure, composed of two lines, one diagonally from the dexter chief angle to the centre of the shield; the other drawn horizontally from the dexter side of the shield, and meeting the other line in the centre of the field, as n. 1.

FLANCHES are formed by two circular lines, and are always borne double, as n. 2.

The LABEL, though used as a distinction of houses, is placed by Holme as an ordinary, from its being variously borne and charged, n. 3.

The ORLE is an inner border of the same shape as the escutcheon, but does not touch the extremities of the shield, the field being seen within and round it on both sides, as n. 4.

The TRESSURE is a diminutive of the Orle, half its breadth, and is generally borne flory and counter-flory, n. 5.

The FRET is composed of six pieces, two of which form a *saltire*, and the other four a *mascle*, which is placed in the centre. The saltire pieces must be interlaced over and under the pieces that form the mascle, as n. 6.

The INESCUTCHEON is a small escutcheon borne

within the shield, in the middle of a coat, or in chief. If there be more than one in a coat, they are usually called escutcheons, n. 7.

The CHAPLET is always composed of four roses only, all the other parts being leaves, n. 8.

A BORDER *or Bordure* is a bearing that goes all round and parallel to the boundary of the shield in form of a hem, and contains the fifth part of the field, n. 9.—When a border is plain, as in the example, it need not be termed *plain,* as it is always understood so in the science ; viz., *argent, a border azure ;* but if the border be engrailed, indented, &c., you must express it : viz., *argent, a border engrailed azure.* See the two examples, n. 10 and 11. In blazon, borders always give place to the *chief,* the *quarter,* and the *canton ;* as, for example, *argent, a border gules, a chief azure ;* therefore, the chief is placed over the border, see Pl. xxxix., n. 2. So that in coats charged with either a *chief, quarter,* or *canton,* the border goes round the field until it touches them, and there finishes, see Pl. xxxix., n. 3 ; but in respect to all other ordinaries, the border passes over them, Pl. xxxix., n. 4.

In a coat which has a border impaled with another, be it either the man's or the woman's, the border must terminate at the impaled line, see Pl. xxxix., n. 5. This method is also to be observed in impaling a coat that has either a single or double tressure, as Pl. xxxix., n. 6.

A BORDER ENGRAILED. This border is bounded by small semicircles, the points of which enter the field, as n. 10.

A BORDER INDENTED is the same in shape as the partition line indented, n. 11.

A BORDER QUARTERLY is a border divided into four

equal parts by a perpendicular and horizontal line, as n. 12.

A BORDER GOBONY *or compony* is a border composed of one row of squares (*of two colours*), and no more, as n. 13.

A BORDER COUNTER-COMPONY is a border composed of two rows of squares, as n. 14.

A BORDER CHECKY is a border composed of three rows of squares, as n. 15.

A BORDER VAIR. Vair is represented by the figures of little escutcheons reversed, ranged in a line so that the *base argent* is opposite to the *base azure*, as n. 16.

PALY is a field divided into four, six, or more (even number of) parts, by perpendicular lines, consisting of two colours; the first beginning with *metal*, and the last consisting of *colour*, as n. 17.

BENDY is a field divided into four, six, or more (equal) parts diagonally, from the dexter to the sinister, or from sinister to dexter, and consisting of two colours, as n. 18.

BARRY is a field divided by horizontal lines, into four, six, or more (equal) parts, and consisting of two tinctures, as n. 19.

BARRY PILY of eight pieces or and gules, as n. 20.

In paly, bendy, and barry, the number of divisions is always even, and to be specified ; as four, six, eight, ten, or twelve, viz., *Paly of six, barry of six, bendy of six, barry pily of eight, or and gules.* See the examples, **T.** 5,

LOZENGY is a field or bearing covered with lozenges of different tinctures alternately, as *lozengy, argent and azure,* n. 21.

CHECKY is a field or bearing covered with small squares of different tinctures alternately, as n. 22. When on ordinaries, it always consists of three or more rows.

GYRONNY is a field divided into six, eight, ten, or twelve triangular parts, of two or more different tinctures, and the points all meeting in the centre of the field, as n. 23.

FRETTY consists of eight, ten, or more pieces, each passing to the extremity of the shield, and interlacing each other, as n. 24.

TABLE VI. (PLATE VI.)

CROSSES.

A CROSS. The Cross is one of the ordinaries before mentioned. It is borne *indented, engrailed,* &c., as well as *plain ;* but when *plain,* as the example, n. 1, *a cross* only is mentioned, which is understood to be plain.

A CROSS MOLINE signifies a cross which turns round both ways at the extremities, as n. 2.

A CROSS FLORY. This signifies the ends of the cross to terminate in fleurs-de-lis, as n. 3.

A CROSS PATONCE. This cross terminates like the bottom of the fleurs-de-lis, as n. 4.

A CROSS POTENT. This cross terminates like the head of a crutch, which anciently was called a potent, as n. 5.

A CROSS PATTÉE, or spread out, is one which is small in the centre, and so goes on widening to the ends, which are very broad, as n. 6.

A CROSS AVELANE, so termed from its parts resembling the *nux avellanœ,* filbert, or hazel-nut, as n. 7.

A Cross Botonné, *or budded,* is so termed because its extremities resemble buds of flowers. The French, with greater propriety, call it *croix trefflée,* on account of its nearer resemblance to the trefoil; n. 8.

A Cross Pommée signifies a cross with a ball at each end; from *pomme,* an apple. See n. 9.

A Cross Croslet is a cross crossed again at the extremities, at a small distance from each of the ends, as n. 10.

A Cross Croslet Fitchy. So termed when the under-limb of the cross ends in a sharp point, as n. 11.

A Cross of four Pheons. That is, *four Pheons in Cross,* their points all meeting in the centre, as n. 12.

A Cross of four Ermine Spots, *or four Ermine Spots in Cross,* their tops meeting in the centre point, as n. 13.

A Cross Milrine. So termed as its form is like the mill-ink, which carries the millstone, and is perforated as that is. See n. 14, 15.

A Cross Rayonnant is a cross from the angles of which issue rays, as n. 16.

Charges.

Charges are any figures whatever borne in an escutcheon.

A Lozenge. The shape is the same with that of a pane of glass in old casements, as n. 17. In this form the arms of maidens and widows should be borne. The true proportion of the Lozenge is to have its width three-fourths of its height.

A Fusil. The Fusil differs from the Lozenge, being longer and more acute. See the difference in n. 17 and 18.—*Note.* If a Fusil is four inches in height, it must be but one inch and three-quarters in width, and so in proportion to any other height.

The Mascle is formed like the Lozenge, but is exactly square, and the centre is perforated, as example, n. 19.

A Water Bouget was a vessel anciently used by soldiers for carrying water in long marches, n. 20.*

A Trefoil, or three-leaved grass, as n. 21.

A Quatrefoil, or four-leaved grass, as n. 22.

A Cinquefoil, or five-leaved grass. This charge is very frequent in armoury, n. 23.

A Rose in Heraldry is always represented full-blown, with its leaves expanded, seeded in the middle, with five green barbs, as n. 24.

TABLE VII. (Plate VII.)

CHARGES (*continued*).

A Mullet, n. 1. Some have confounded stars and mullets together, which is easily rectified, by allowing mullets to consist of five points, and stars to be of six, eight, or more points.

An Estoile, or star of six waved points. See n. 2.

A Gal-Trap; an instrument of iron composed of four points, so that whichever way it lies on the

* There are various forms of it; the one here referred to though strictly heraldic, bearing little resemblance to the article it professes to represent.

ground, one point is always upwards; they were used to impede the enemy's cavalry in passing fords, morasses, &c.   See n. 3.

A PHEON is the iron part of a dart with a barbed head, n. 4.

An ANNULET, or Ring.   See n. 5.

A CRESCENT, or Half Moon, has the horns turned upwards.   See n. 6.

An INCRESCENT is a Half Moon with the horns turned to the dexter side.   See n. 7.

A DECRESCENT is a Half Moon with the horns turned to the sinister side.   See n. 8.

A CHESS-ROOK, a piece used in the game of chess, as n. 9.

A FOUNTAIN is drawn as a roundle *barry wavy of six, Argent and Azure,* as n. 10.

A REST.   This figure by some is termed a rest for a horseman's lance; others describe it as a musical instrument called a clarion, n. 11.

A PORTCULLIS; used in fortifying the gateways of a city, town, or castle, as n. 12.

A MANCHE; an old-fashioned sleeve of the 12th century, with long cuff dependant, as n. 13.   This charge is represented in forms as various as that of the Water-Bouget.

A GARB signifies a sheaf of any kind of grain, as n. 14.—If it be a sheaf of wheat, it is sufficient to say a garb; but if of any other grain, it must be expressed.

A MARTLET; a bird shaped like a martin, but represented without legs, as n. 15.

BAR-GEMEL signifies two bars placed near and parallel to each other, as n. 16.—*Note.* Gemels are much narrower than bars, and are always borne in couples.

A CATHERINE-WHEEL; named from St. Catherine, whose limbs were broken in pieces by its iron teeth, n. 17.

An ESCARBUNCLE; supposed to represent the rays of a precious stone (the carbuncle), and drawn by the ancient heralds, as n. 18. It is composed of an annulet in the centre, from which issue eight or more sceptres.

A PELICAN. The Pelican in heraldry is generally represented with her wings indorsed, her neck em-bowed, and pecking at her breast, as n. 19. When in her nest, feeding her young, it is termed in blazon, a *Pelican in her piety.*

A PHŒNIX is an imaginary bird, like an eagle in shape, and in heraldry is always represented in flames, so that seldom more of the bird is seen than what is in the example, n. 20.

An ANTELOPE; a well-known slender-limbed animal of the deer kind, with two straight taper horns: it is drawn according to nature, as n. 21.

AN HERALDIC ANTELOPE. This imaginary animal is represented with a body like a stag, with a unicorn's tail, a tusk issuing from the tip of the nose, a row of tufts down the back part of the neck, and the like tufts on his tail, chest, and thighs, as n. 22.

A COCKATRICE is also a chimerical figure; its wings, beak, legs, comb, wattles, and spurs, partake of the fowl, and its body and tail of the dragon, as n. 23.

A WYVERN. This figure also is of heraldic crea-tion: it differs from the cockatrice in its head, and is without a comb, wattles, or spurs, as n. 24, and is dis-tinguished from the dragon by only having two legs.

TABLE VIII. (Plate VIII.)

CHARGES *(continued)*.

A Dragon is an imaginary beast with four legs, drawn by heralds as the example, n. 1.

A Harpy is a poetical monster, composed of the head and breasts of a woman, joined to the body of a vulture, as n. 2.

An Heraldic Tiger, so termed from being different from the tiger of nature, owes its origin to the ancients, who represented it like the example, n. 3.

Billets are oblong squares, and are generally supposed to be letters made up in the form of the example, n. 4, or blocks of wood, as there is an instance of a Billet raguly in the coat of Billettes and of Billety in that of *de la Plaunch.*

A Cannet; a term for a duck without beak or feet, as n. 5. This is only used in foreign arms.

An Allerion is an eagle displayed, without beak or feet, as n. 6.

A Welk; the name of a shell fish. See n. 7.

Guttes signify drops of anything liquid, and are represented as n. 8. As these drops differ in colour, they receive different terms. Being much used in English heraldry, it is necessary to introduce them; viz.—

When they are		they are termed		and meant to be like	
Or,		Guttes d'or,		Drops of gold,	
Argent,		Guttes d'eau,		Drops of water,	
Vert,		Guttes d'olive,		Drops of oil of olive	
Azure,		Guttes de larmes,		Drops of tears,	
Sable,		Guttes de poix,		Drops of pitch,	
Gules,		Guttes de sang,		Drops of blood.	

The French heralds use none of the above variations, but say gutté (*i. e.*, dropped) of such a colour.

ROUNDLES are round figures; if of metal, as the bezant and plate, they are to be flat; if of colour, they are drawn globular, and termed according to the colour or metal they are composed of. See Pl. VIII., n. 9 to 15; viz.—

When they are		they are termed	
	Or,		Bezants,
	Argent,		Plates,
	Vert,		Pommes,
	Azure,		Hurts,
	Sable,		Pellets,
	Gules,		Torteaux,
	Purpure,		Golpes.

If there be two, three, or more in a coat, counterchanged, being of any colour or metal, they retain the name of roundle.—*Note.* Foreigners term the round figures, when of metal, bezants; when of colour, torteaux; viz., *Bezants d'or,* or *d'argent, torteaux de gules, d'azure, de sable,* &c.

CHARGES, AND THEIR VARIOUS HERALDIC TERMS.

COUPED. A term for any charge in an escutcheon that is borne *cut* evenly off, as the example; viz., *A Lion's Head Couped,* n. 16.

ERASED. A term for anything torn or plucked off from the part to which nature had fixed it. The part torn off must be drawn jagged, as the example; viz., *A Lion's Head Erased,* n. 17.

DEMI signifies the half of anything; viz., *A Demi-Lion,* n. 18.

DORMANT, or sleeping; viz., *A Lion dormant,* with its head resting on its fore-paws, as n. 19.

COUCHANT, lying or squatting on the ground, with

the head upright; viz., *A Lion Couchant.* See
n. 20.

SEJANT. A term for any beast *sitting* in the position
of the example; viz., *A Lion Sejant,* n. 21.

PASSANT. A term for any beast when in a walking
position; viz., *A Lion Passant,* n. 22.

STATANT. A term for a beast standing, with all
four legs on the ground, as n. 23.

TABLE IX. (PLATE IX.)

PASSANT-GARDANT. A term for a beast when walking with his head *affronté,* or looking full-faced, as
example, n. 1.

RAMPANT. A term for lions, bears, tigers, &c., when
standing erect on their hind legs. *A Lion Rampant,*
n. 2.

RAMPANT-GARDANT signifies a beast standing on his
hind legs, looking full-faced, as example, *A Lion Rampant-Gardant,* n. 3.

RAMPANT-REGARDANT. A term for a beast standing
upon his hind legs, looking towards his tail; viz , *A
Lion Rampant-Regardant,* as n. 4.

RAMPANT-COMBATANT. A term for beasts fighting,
or rampant face to face, as the example, *Two Lions
Rampant-Combatant.* See n. 5.

SALIANT. A term for beasts of prey when leaping
or springing forward, as the example, n. 6.

ADDORSED signifies beasts, birds, or fish turned back
to back, as the example, *Two Lions Rampant Addorsed.*
See n. 7.

COUNTER-PASSANT; for two beasts, as lions, &c,.

when walking different ways, the one to the dexter, the other to the sinister, as the example, n. 8.

COUNTER-SALIANT. A term for two beasts when leaping different ways from each other, as the example, *Two Foxes Counter-Saliant in Saltire, the dexter surmounted of the sinister*, n. 9.

COUNTER-TRIPPING. This term is given when two rams, deer, &c., as the example, are tripping, the one passing one way and the other another. See n. 10.

SEJANT ADDORSED. A term for two animals sitting back to back, as the example, n. 11.

PASSANT-REGARDANT. A term for a beast when walking with its head looking behind, n. 12.

AT GAZE. The stag, buck, or hind, when looking *affronté*, or full-faced, it is said to be at Gaze, n. 13. All other beasts, when in this attitude, are termed Gardant.

TRIPPING. A term which signifies a stag, antelope, or hind, &c., when walking, as n. 14.

SPRINGING. This term is used for beasts of chase, in the same sense as Saliant is for beasts of prey, n. 15. This term is likewise used for fish when placed in bend.

COURANT. A term for stag, horse, or greyhound, or any other beast, represented running, as the example, n. 16.

LODGED. This term is for stags, &c., when at rest, lying on the ground, n. 17. Beasts of chase are said to be lodged; beasts of prey, when lying down, are termed couchant.

CABOSSED. This term is used to express the head of a stag or other animal drawn full-faced, and without any part of the neck being visible, n. 18.

CLOSE. This term is for the wings of birds (of flight) when they are down and close to the body, n. 19. But must not be used to the peacock, dung-hill-cock, nor to any others that are not addicted to flight.

RISING. A term for birds when in a position as if preparing to fly, as n. 20.

DISPLAYED. The term is used for the wings of eagles, and all other birds, when they are expanded, as n. 21.

VOLANT. Thus we term any bird that is represented flying, as n. 22.

DEMI-VOL. A term for a single wing, n. 23.

INDORSED. A term for wings when placed back to back, as n. 24.

TABLE X. (PLATE X.)

ERECT signifies anything perpendicularly elevated, as the example : viz., *Two wings conjoined and erect ;* that is, the points of the wings are upwards, n. 1. This charge is also called a VOL.

INVERTED. This example is the reverse position of the former, the points of these being downwards : viz., *Two wings conjoined and inverted*, n. 2.—*Vide* LURE.

NAIANT. A term for fish when borne horizontally across the field as swimming, as n. 3.

HAURIANT signifies the fish to be erect, or breathing, as the example, n. 4.

RESPECTING. A term for fish, or birds, when placed upright, and apparently *looking* at each other, as n. 5.

NAIANT EMBOWED. This term is used for the dolphin, to signify the crookedness of his motion when swimming, as the example, n. 6.

DEMI-LION PASSANT is one half of a lion in a walking position, as n. 7.

DEMI FLEUR-DE-LIS is the half of a fleur-de-lis, as n. 8, also as Pl. VII., n. 24.

ISSUANT, or issuing, signifies coming out; as from the bottom of the chief in the example, n. 9, or from clouds as Pl. XIX., n. 23.

ROUSANT signifies heavy birds, as if preparing to fly, with the wings indorsed, as n. 10.

SLIPPED. A term for a flower, branch, or leaf, when plucked from the stock, and not cut off, n. 11.

TIRRET. A modern term d rived from the French, for *manacles,* or handcuffs, n. 12.

The following twelve examples are introduced for the instruction of the learner, as he should be well acquainted with the difference of the two monosyllables in *blazon,* viz., *on* and *in;* which, by observing, he will see makes a great difference in a coat of arms—the *former* expressing the bearing to be placed on one of the ordinaries; the *latter* as if the bearings were left remaining, but the ordinaries taken away.

ON A CHIEF.

13. Argent *on a chief,* gules, three lozenges, or,

IN CHIEF.

14. Argent, three lozenges *in chief,* gules.

ON A PALE.

15. Argent *on a pale,* azure, three plates.

IN PALE.

16. Argent, three hurts *in pale.*

ON A BEND.

17. Gules, *on a bend,* argent, three mullets, azure.

IN BEND.

18. Argent, three mullets *in bend,* sable.

ON A FESS.

19. Argent, *on a fess,* vert, three trefoils, or,

IN FESS.

20. Argent, three trefoils, *in fess,* vert.

ON A CROSS.

21. Purpure, *on a cross,* argent, five crescents, gules.

IN CROSS.

22. Argent, five crescents *in cross,* gules.

ON A SALTIRE.

23. Azure, *on a saltire,* argent, five torteaux.

IN SALTIRE.

24. Argent, five torteaux *in saltire.*

Rules of Blazoning.

THIS science, according to the *Notitia Anglicana,* teaches how to describe the things borne in proper terms, according to their several gestures, positions, and tinctures; and how to marshal or dispose regularly divers arms on a field, in which particular care must be observed, because the adding or omitting any part is oftentimes an alteration of the coat.

In blazon the following rules must be carefully followed :—

First, in blazoning a coat, you must always begin with the field; noticing the lines wherewith it is divided, whether *per pale, per fess, per bend,* &c., as also the difference of those lines, whether *indented, engrailed,* &c. ; then proceed to the next immediate charge. By an immediate charge is meant that which lies next the field, and nearest the centre; this must be first named; and then those which are more remote : for example, *azure, a crescent, between three stars argent;* thus the *crescent* is first named, as being next the centre of the field. See Pl. XII., n. 21.

If a coat consist of two colours only, as the coat of Robinson, you are to blazon it *vert, a chevron, between three bucks standing at gaze, or;* which implies that both the chevron and bucks are *or.* See Pl. XIV., n. 15.

When colour and metal are placed several times one upon the other, as Pl. XI., n. 13, *Azure, on a chevron, between three besants, as many pallets, gules.* Here the *chevron* is named *first* after the field, because it is nearest the centre; and as the *pallets lie upon the chevron*, so they are most remote from the *field*, and must be last named. But when bearings are described without expressing the point of the escutcheon where they are to be placed, they are then understood to possess the centre of the shield : for instance, *argent, a lion rampant, gules;* but if I say, *argent, a lion rampant in base, gules*, it must be placed in the base part of a shield, which is the bottom.

A repetition, in blazoning a coat, of such words as *of, on, and, with*, is accounted a great fault, or indeed of any words, for tautology should be particularly avoided ; as, for example, *or, on a saltire azure, nine lozenges of the first;* and not, *or, on a saltire azure, nine lozenges or;* because the word *or* is then named twice. But be careful that, by endeavouring to be concise, you are not ambiguous, and that you omit nothing which ought to be mentioned.

It is a general rule in English Heraldry, *that metal shall never be placed upon metal, nor colour upon colour;* but examples are frequently found in foreign courts, particularly German.

CHARGES.

In blazoning of charges, be they of what nature or kind soever, whether animate or inanimate, if you perceive them to be of the natural and proper colours of the creatures or things they represent, you must always term them *proper*, and not argent, or, gules, or by the like terms of this science.

ORDINARIES.

In blazoning of ordinaries formed of straight lines, you must only name the ordinary, without making mention of the straightness of the line whereof it is composed; for example, Pl. IV., n. 5, *Argent, a bend azure;* but if the ordinary, &c., should be *engrailed, wavy, nebuly, embattled,* it must not be omitted: for example, Pl. XI., n. 12, *ermine, on a chevron engrailed, azure, three estoiles argent.*

ANIMALS.

The teeth, claws, or talons of lions, tigers, bears, leopards, boars, wolves, dragons, and all ravenous beasts, are called their arms, because they are weapons of defence and offence. When these are of a different tincture from their bodies, the colour must be named; and when their tongues are of the colour of their arms, they are said to be *langued,* as a lion *argent, armed and langued, gules.* The claws and tongue of a lion are always gules, unless the field or charge be gules; then they must be azure.

Among such beasts as by nature are milder, and by custom more sociable, may be reckoned the bull, ox, goat, ram, &c., which are endowed by nature with weapons, as horns, which, together with their hoofs, are very often of a colour different from their bodies; we then say *armed* and *hoofed,* or *unguled,* of such or such tinctures.

Deer, being by nature timorous and without courage, are supposed to wear their lofty antlers, not as weapons, but ornaments; therefore, in blazon, we say *attired.*

As to the dog, there are various kinds, bred up to divers exercises and games; so that the first consideration is, what kind of dog is borne, as greyhounds, spaniels, talbots, &c.; what sport he seems fitted for; and hence the particular terms of *beating, coursing, scenting*, &c., are very proper if they be found in gestures suitable to their several exercises.

Nisbet says, when animals are painted upon banners, they must look to the staff; when upon caparisons and other horse furniture, they ought to look to the head of the horse that bears them; and so of all things whose parts are distinguished by *ante* and *post*.

BIRDS.

In blazoning birds of prey, as the eagle, vulture, hawk, kite, owl, &c., all whose weapons, viz., beaks and talons, are termed arms, we say *armed and membered* so and so, when they differ in colour from the body.

But when you meet with swans, geese, ducks, cranes, herons, cormorants, &c., which are a kind of river-fowl, and have no talons, instead of armed, you must say *beaked and membered;* the last term signifying the leg of any fowl, as the feet of swans, geese, ducks, &c., are webbed, and in some measure resemble the palm of a man's hand; so in blazon they are sometimes termed *palmipedes.*

In blazoning the cock, you must say *armed, crested, and jelloped; armed* signifies his *beak and spurs; crested,* his *comb;* and *jelloped,* his *wattles:* when his comb, beak, wattles, and spurs, are of a different tincture from his body, then in blazon they must be named; for instance, *azure, a cock argent, armed, crested, and jelloped, gules.*

As to the falcon, this bird is borne in the same postures as the eagle, and described in the same terms, except when with *hood, bells, virols* (or rings), *and leashes.* In blazon he is said to *be hooded, belled, jessed, and leashed,* and the colours thereof must be named ; *pouncing* is a term given when he is striking at his prey.

Edmonson remarks, that when small birds are borne in coat-armour, they are most usually drawn in the form and shape of blackbirds, although they are represented in all the different colours and metals of heraldry, and, consequently, no distinction of species is made : therefore, in blazon they are called by the general terms of birds only. Hence, then, when you find birds mentioned in a blazon without expressing the sort they are of, they must always be drawn as blackbirds in shape.

FISHES.

Nearly every variety of fish is used in heraldry—the dolphin occupying the principal position, like the lion among animals, and the eagle among birds ; the others are chiefly used to designate the name of the bearer, as in the names of Herring, Roach, Pike, Sal mon, &c., and the kind of fish intended may generally thus be ascertained. The heraldic terms peculiar to fish are *hauriant,* with their heads raised upright or breathing (Pl. xvi., 21 and 23); *naiant* or in their swimming position (Pl. xvi., 20), and *embowed* applied exclusively to the curved position of the dolphin (Pl. xvi., 17, 18, 22). Occasionally we meet with the terms *allumé* when their eyes are bright, and *pamé* when their mouths are open. When the kind of fish is not named, the ordinary shape is implied, similar to a dace or herring.

When the fins of fishes are of a different tincture from their bodies, they are then said to be *finned of such a colour*, naming it, *as a dolphin proper finned or.*

HEAVENLY BODIES.

Should the bearing be of any heavenly body, such as a planet, &c., your first consideration is, in what state or condition such planet appears to be : as the sun, *whether in his meridian or eclipse;* or the moon, *whether in her increase or decrease,* &c.; then give your description in proper astronomical terms : for it is a rule that all blazons are the more elegant when expressed in the proper terms of the several arts or sciences which the figures to be described are of, or belonging to; yet you must take care not to omit any *armorial term necessary to be used.* Thus, in the coat of St. Clere, Pl. XIII., n. 3, *azure, the sun in his meridian, proper,* the word *proper* must not be omitted.

TREES AND VEGETABLES.

When you meet with any kind of tree, or any vegetable, or their parts, you must observe, first, in what condition it seems to appear, as whether *spread or blasted;* what kind of tree, *whether bearing fruit or not;* if a part only, *what part;* whether the *trunk, branches, fruit, or leaves;* if the former, whether *standing or not;* if not, in what manner it seems to have been *felled;* whether *eradicated* or torn up by the roots; see Pl. XIII., n. 22. If the bearing consist of members, as its *branches, fruit, or leaves only,* whether *with fruit or withered;* or simply alone, *whether slipped,* as Pl. XVIII., n. 9, 10; *pendent* (drooping) or *erect;* which last holds goods for all kinds of flowers or grain, when borne simply, or on their stalks.

MAN AND HIS PARTS.

Man, and the parts of his body, are frequently charges in coat-armour; as to which these considerations follow. First, as is said of other things, whether he is borne *whole, or in part;* if whole, *in what kind of gesture or action;* also, *whether naked or habited;* if the latter, after what manner, as *whether rustic, in armour, or in robes.*

When the temples of a man or woman are encircled with *laurel, oak, ivy,* &c., you are to call it *wreathed* with *laurel, oak,* or *ivy.*

Examples of Blazonry.

Having now explained rudimentally the terms, &c., of the science, and concisely enumerated the rules of blazon, we proceed to illustrate the theory by examples, which, if carefully examined, one by one, cannot fail to prove of the highest utility to the young student.

Blazoning of Plate XI.

1. Argent, on a chief gules, two mullets pierced or; name, *St. John.*
2. Argent, a fess, and in chief three lozenges sable; name, *Aston.*
3. Or, two bars azure, a chief quarterly, azure and gules, on the first two fleurs-de-lis, or; the second, a lion, passant-gardant of the last; the third as the second; the fourth as the first; name *Manners.*

N.B. Of the first is of the colour or metal of the field, which is always first mentioned.

Note. The term *on the first* is to be understood on the field of the first quarter; *the second* is the field of the second quarter charged *of the last,* that is, of the last-mentioned colour or metal, which is *or; the third as the second, the fourth as the first,* which signifies the third quarter like the second, and the fourth quarter like the first.

4. Gules, a chief argent; on the lower part thereof a cloud, the sun's resplendent rays issuing thereout proper; name, *Leeson.*

5. Ermine, on a canton sable, a harp argent; name, *Fraunces.*

6. Argent, on a quarter gules, a spear in bend or; name, *Knight.*

7. Argent, on a fess sable, three mullets, or ; name, *Clive.*

8. Azure, a fess super-embattled, between six estoiles or; name, *Tryon.*

9. Or, on a fess, between two chevrons sable, three cross-croslets of the first; name, *Walpole.*

10. Argent, a fess and canton conjoined gules; name, *Woodvile.*

11. Ermine, three lozenges conjoined in fess, sable; name, *Pigot.*

12. Ermine, on a chevron engrailed azure, three estoiles argent; name, *Smyth.*

13. Azure, on a chevron or between three besants, as many pallets gules; name, *Hope.*

14. Ermine, a chevron couped sable ; name, *Jones.*

15. Azure, a chevron engrailed, voided plain, or ; name, *Dudley.*

16. Sabl a chevron cotised between three cinquefoils, or , name, *Renton.*

17. Gules, a chevron between ten cinquefoils, four and two, in chief; one, two and one in base, argent; name, *Berkley.*

18. Sable, two lion's paws issuing out of the dexter and sinister base points, erected chevronwise, argent, armed gules; name, *Frampton.*

19. Sable, a bend or, between six fountains; name, *Stourton.*

20. Argent, on a bend gules, cotised sable, three pair of wings conjoined and inverted of the first; name, *Wingfield.*

21. Sable, a bend flory counter-flory, argent; name, *Highlord.*

22. Sable, a bend and chief or; name, ———

23. Argent, two bends raguled sable, the lower one rebated at the top; name, *Wagstaff.*

24. Sable, four lozenges in bend between two plain *cotises* argent; name, *Puckering.*

25. Argent, three bugle-horns in bend gules, garnished and stringed vert; name, *Hunter.*

26. Vert, on a pale radiant or, a lion rampant sable; name, *O'Hara.*

27. Argent, on a pale, between two leopards' faces sable, three crescents or; name, ———.

28. Argent, a pale and chief sable; name, *Mendorf.*

29. Sable, a key erected in pale or, between two pallets erminois; name, *Knot.*

30. Argent, three pallets wavy gules; name, *Downes.*

31. Gules, three tilting-spears, erect in fess or, heads argent; name, *Amherst.*

32. Azure, three leopards' faces in pale or; name, *Snigg*

33. Argent, on a pile engrailed azure, three crescents of the first; name, *Dallison.*

34. Sable, a pile argent, surmounted of a chevron gules; name, *Dyxton.*
35. Argent, three piles, one issuant out of the chief between two others reversed, and issuing from the base, sable; name, *Hulse.*

BLAZONING OF PLATE XII.

1. Sable, on a cross within a border, both engrailed or, five pellets; name, *Greville.*
2. Gules, a cross of lozenges between four roses argent; name, *Packer.*
3. Argent, a cross sable, edged with a tressure of half fleurs-de-lis, between four mullets pierced of the second (that is, of the second colour mentioned, which is sable); name, *Atkins.*
4. Or, a cross vert, on a bend over all gules, three fleurs-de-lis of the first; name, *Beringer.*
5. Azure, five escalop shells in cross or; name, *Barker.*
6. Sable, a shin-bone in pale, surmounted of another in fess argent; name, *Baines.*
7. Ermine, on a cross quarter, pierced, argent, four millrinds sable; name, *Turnor.*
8. Party per fess, sable and argent, a pale, counterchanged; on each piece of the first a trefoil slipped of the second; name, *Simeon.*
9. Or, on a saltire raguly gules, five cross-croslets fitchy of the first; name, *Rich.*
10. Gules, a saltire between four crescents or; name, *Kinnard.*
11. Gyrony of four, argent and gules, a saltire between as many cross-croslets, all counterchanged; name, *Twisden.*

12. Gules, a saltire, or, over all a cross engrailed ermine; name, *Prince.*

13. Party per saltire, gules and or, in pale two garbs, and in fess as many roses, all counterchanged; name, *Hilborne.*

14. Sable, two shin-bones, in saltire, the sinister surmounted of the dexter; name, *Newton.*

15. Gules, five marlions' wings inverted in saltire argent; name, *Porter.*

16. Or, three closets wavy, gules; name, *Drummond.*

17. Azure, two bars counter-imbattled ermine; name, *Burnaby.*

18. Or, two bars-gemel sable, in chief, three pellets; name, *Hildesley.*

19. Argent, three bars-gemel azure, on a chief gules, a barrulet indented or; name, *Haydon.*

20. Sable three leopards' faces jessant fleurs-de-lis or; name, *Morley.*

21. Azure, a crescent between three mullets argent; name, *Arbuthnot.*

The following fourteen coats are collected to show how useful the points of the escutcheon are in blazon, which the learner will find very essential in his practice of this science.

22. Sable, three swords barwise, in pale, their points towards the sinister part of the escutcheon argent, the hilts and pommels or; name, *Rawlyns.*

23. Gules, three swords, barwise, their points towards the dexter part of the shield, hilted or; name, *Chute.*

24. Gules, three swords, conjoined at the pommels in the centre, their points extended into the corners of the escutcheon argent; name, *Stapleton.*

25. Sable, three swords, their points meeting in base argent, hilted or ; name, *Paulet* or *Powlet.*

26. Or, three swords, one in fess surmounted of the other two in saltire, points upwards, between a dexter hand in chief, and a heart in base gules ; name, *Ewart.*

27. Sable, three swords in pale, two with their points downward, and the middlemost upward ; name, *Rawline.*

28. Azure, three swords, one in pale, point upward, surmounted of the other two, placed in saltire, points downward, argent ; name, *Norton.*

29. Sable, a fess or, between two swords ; that in chief point upwards, the other downwards, both in pale argent, hilted of the second ; name, *Gwyn.*

30. Azure, one ray of the sun issuing out of the dexter corner of the escutcheon, in bend proper; name, *Aldam.*

31. Azure, a pile inverted in bend sinister, or; name, *Kagg.*

32. Argent, a triple pile, flory on the tops, issuing out of the sinister base in bend, towards the dexter corner, sable ; name, *Wroton.*

33. Sable, a goshawk close, argent, standing upon a perch, fixed in base, jessed and belled or; name, *Weele.*

34. Gules, a bend wavy argent, in the sinister chief point, a falcon standing on a perch or ; name, *Hawkeridge.*

35. Or, a dexter arm embowed, issuant from the sinister fess-point out of a cloud proper, holding a cross-croslet fitchy, azure.

BLAZONING OF PLATE XIII.

1. Gules, three lions' gambs erased argent; name, *Newdigate.*

2. Party per saltire, sable and ermine, a lion rampant or, armed and langued gules; name, *Grafton.*

3. Azure, the sun in his meridian, proper; name, *St. Clare.*

4. Argent, a lion rampant gules, debruised by a fess azure, between three estoiles issuing out of as many crescents of the second; name, *Dillon*, of Ireland.

5. Argent, on a chevron sable, between three oak-leaves proper, as many besants on a chief gules, a sea-mew between two anchors erected of the first; name, *Monox.*

6. Quarterly, first and fourth azure, a pale argent, second and third gules, a bend argent.

7. Sable, four pallets ermine; name, *Humphrey.*

8. Or, six annulets, three, two, and one, sable; name, *Lowther.*

Note.—When six things are borne, *three, two*, and *one*, it is unnecessary to mention their position.

9. Gules, nine arrows or, each three, two saltirewise, and one in pale, banded together with a ribbon, feathered and headed argent; name, *Biest.*

10. Gules, five cross-croslets fitchy in saltire, between four escalop-shells in cross or; name, *Tonnson.*

11. Azure, three hautboys between as many cross-croslets or; name, *Bourden.*

12. Azure, a salamander or, in flames proper; name, *Cennino.*

13. Party per chevron, argent and gules, a crescent counterchanged; name, *Chapman.*

14. Party per saltire, or and sable, a border counterchanged; name, *Shorter.*

15. Quarterly or and azure, a cross of four lozenges between as many annulets counterchanged; name, *Peacock.*

16. Argent, a chevron gules, between three scorpions reversed sable; name, *Cole.*

17. Argent, on a fess, between six martlets gules, three cinquefoils of the field; name, *Washbourne.*

18. Sable, three scaling-ladders in bend argent; name, *Shipstowe.*

19. Sable, a falcon or, his wings expanded, trussing a mallard argent, on a chief of the latter, a cross botoné gules; name, *Madden.*

20. Argent, on a chevron azure, between three trefoils slipped, party per pale gules and vert, as many besants; name, *Row.*

21. Gules, three dexter arms conjoined at the shoulders, and flexed in triangle, or, with the fists clenched towards the points of the shield proper; name, *Tremaine.*

22. Gules, the trunk of a tree eradicated (torn up by the roots) and couped in pale, sprouting out two branches argent; name, *Borough.*

23. Gules, a cherub, having three pair of wings, whereof the uppermost and lowermost are counterly crossed, and the middlemost displayed, or; name, *Buocafoco.*

24. Argent, a man's heart gules, within two equilateral triangles interlaced; name, *Villages.*

25. Gules, three besants figured; name, *Gamin.*

26. Argent, a chevron voided, azure, between three flames of fire proper; name, *Wells.*

27. Sable, chevron rompu, enhanced between three mullets or; name, *Sault.*

28. Sable, a chevron engrailed, ermine, between three annulets argent; borne by the *Rev. Charles Davy*, of One-house, Suffolk.

29. Azure, a bull's head couped affronté, argent, winged and armed or; name, *Hoast*, of Holland.

30. Or, three stars issuing out of as many crescents gules; name, Bateman, *Visc. Bateman.*

31. Sable, a chevron or, between three attires of a stag fixed to the scalp, argent; name, *Cocks, Lord Somers.*

32. Argent, a man's heart gules, ensigned with an imperial crown or, on a chief azure, three mullets of the field; name, *Douglas*, of Scotland. The reason of this singular charge is, that one Douglas was sent on a pilgrimage to the Holy Land, A.D. 1328, with the heart of *Robert Bruce*, King of Scotland, which, by order of that prince, was to be and is now buried there.

33. Argent, on a bend gules, between three pellets, as many swans proper, rewarded with a canton sinister azure, thereupon a demi-ram mounting argent, armed or, between two fleurs-de-lis of the last, over all a baton dexter-wise, as the second in the canton; this is the arms of *Sir John Clarke.* The canton was the arms of the *Duke of Longueville*, and was given as a reward to *Sir John Clarke*, for his taking in lawful war *Lewis of Orleans, Duke of Longueville, prisoner* at the battle of the Spurs, near Terouane, August 16, *anno* Hen. VIII. 5.

34. Azure, three sturgeons naiant in pale argent, and debruised by a fret of eight pieces or; name, *Stourgeon.*

35. Or, three dice sable each charged with an ace argent; name, *Ambesace.*

Blazoning of Plate XIV.

1. Argent, a saltire gules, between four wolves' heads couped proper; name, *Outlawe.*

2. Gules, three demi-lions rampant, a chief or; name, *Fisher.*

3. Argent, a fess sable, between three lions' heads erased gules, langued azure; name, *Farmer.*

4. Gules, a lion couchant between six cross-croslets, three in chief, and three in base barwise, argent; name, *Tynte.*

5. Azure, a lion passant, between three estoiles argent; name, *Burrard.*

6. Argent, a chevron gules, between three lions passant-gardant sable; name, *Cooke.*

7. Party per chevron, vert and or, in chief a rose or, between two fleurs-de-lis argent; in base a lion rampant-regardant, azure; name, *Gideon.*

8. Party per pale, argent and sable, a lion rampant or, within a border of the field, engrailed and counter-changed; name, *Champneys.*

9. Argent, a lion sejant azure, between three torteaux.

10. Argent, a lion saliant, in chief three pellets.

11. Gules, a lion rampant-gardant, double-queuée (or queue fourchée) or, holding in his paws a rose-branch proper; name, *Masters.*

The term *queuée* applies to the tail of a beast, and the term *fourchée* denotes its being forked, as the example.

12. Or, a pale between two lions rampant sable ; name, *Naylor*.

13. Argent, three bars wavy azure, over all a lion rampant of the first ; name, *Bulbeck.*

14. Argent, a chevron between three bucks tripping sable, attired or ; name, *Rogers.*

15. Vert, a chevron between three bucks standing at gaze or ; name, *Robinson.*

16. Argent, a bend engrailed azure, between two bucks' heads cabosed sable ; name, *Needham.*

17. Argent, three greyhounds current in pale sable, collared or ; name, *Moore.*

18. A hart cumbent upon a hill in a park paled, all proper ; the arms of the town of Derby.

19. Argent, three moles sable, their snouts and feet gules ; name, *Nangothan.*

20. Gules, three conies sejant within a bordue engrailed argent ; name, *Conisbie.*

21. Argent, a chevron gules between three talbots passant sable ; name, *Talbot.*

22. Or, a chevron gules between three lions' paws erased and erected sable ; name, *Austen*, of Kent, baronet.

23. Argent, two lions' gambs erased in saltire, the dexter surmounted of the sinister, gules.

24. Sable, three lions' tails erect and erased argent ; name, *Corke.*

The two Plates XV. and XVII., are introduced to show the student of heraldry the concise and easy method which is in practice among heralds, heraldic painters, and engravers, of tricking coats of arms.

Made use of in the heraldic sketches * and blazons of
Plates XIV. and XVI.

O			Or,
A			Argent,
G			Gules,
B			Blue,
V	} stands for {		Vert,
P			Purpure,
S			Sable,
Ppr			Proper,
Er			Ermine.

ABBREVIATED BLAZON OF PLATE XIV.

1. A, a saltire G, between four wolves' heads couped
   Ppr.
2. G, three demi-lions couped A, a chief O,
3. A, on a fess S, between three lions' heads erased G,
   langued B.
4. G, a lion couched between six cross-croslets, three
   in chief, and as many in base A.
5. B, a lion passant, between three estoiles A.
6. A, a chevron G, between three lions passant-gar
   dant S.
7. Party per chevron, V and O, in chief a rose O, between two fleurs-de-lis A, in base a lion rampant-
   regardant B.
8. Party per pale, A and S, within a bordure of the
   same engrailed and counterchanged, a lion
   rampant O.
9. A lion sejant B, between three torteaux.
10. A lion saliant Ppr. and in chief three pellets.

* Coats thus sketched are by heralds said to be "in trick."

11. G, a lion rampant-gardant double queuée O, hold-
    ing in his paws a rose-branch Ppr.
12. O, a pale between two lions rampant S.
13. A, three bars wavy B, over all a lion rampant of
    the first.
14. A, chevron between three bucks tripping S, at-
    tired O.
15. V, a chevron between three bucks standing at
    gaze O.
16. A, a bend engrailed B, between two bucks' heads
    caboshed S.
17. A, three greyhounds current in pale S, collared of
    the first.
18. A hart cumbent upon a hill in a park paled, all Ppr.
19. A, three moles, S, their snouts and feet G.
20. G, three conies sejant, within a bordure engrailed A.
21. A, a chevron G, between three talbots passant S.
22. O, a chevron G, between three lions' paws erased
    and erect S.
23. A, two lions' gambs erased in saltire, the dexter
    surmounted of the sinister G.
24. S, three lions' tails erect and erased A.

BLAZONING OF PLATE XVI.

1. Argent, a heron volant, in fess azure, membered or,
   between three escalops, sable ; name, *Herondon.*
2. Or, three kingfishers proper ; name, *Fisher.*
3. Or, three eagles displayed gules; name, *Eglefelde.*
4. Azure, a bend engrailed between two cygnets royal
   argent, gorged with ducal crowns, strings reflexed
   over their backs, or; name, *Pitfield.*
5. Azure, a pelican with wings elevated and vulning

E

her breast argent, between three fleurs-de-lis, or;
name, *Kempton.*

6. Azure, three doves rising argent, their wings gules,
and crowned with ducal coronets or; name,
Baylie.

7. Argent, on a pile gules, three owls of the field;
name, *Cropley.*

8. Argent, three eagles' heads, or, erased sable; name,
Yellen.

9. Argent, three peacocks in their pride proper; name,
Pawne.

10. Or, three swallows close sable; name, *Watton.*

11 Azure, on a bend cotised argent, three martlets
gules; name, *Edwards.*

12. Ermine, on two bars gules, three martlets or; name,
Ward.

13. Argent, on a fess between three trefoils azure, as
many swans' heads erased of the first, beaked
gules; name, *Baker.*

14. Argent, on a pale azure, three pair of wings conjoined and elevated of the first; name, *Potter.*

15. Argent, six ostrich-feathers, three, two, and one,
sable; name, *Jarvis.*

16. Argent, a chevron between three eagles' legs
erased sable, their talons gules; name, *Bray.*

17. Azure, a dolphin naiant embowed or, on a chief of
the second, two saltires coupled gules; name,
Frankland.

18. Or, three dolphins hauriant embowed azure; name,
Vandeput.

19. Sable, a dolphin naiant, embowed, vorant a fish
proper; name, *James.*

20. Argent, three eels naiant in pale, sable; name, *Ellis.*

21. Or, three chalbots hauriant gules ; name, *Chalbots.*
22. Argent, on a bend azure, three dolphins naiant of the first ; name, *Franklyn.*
23. Sable, a chevron ermine, between three salmons hauriant argent; name, *Ord.*
24. Argent, a chevron engrailed sable, between three sea-crabs gules ; name, *Bridger.*

ABBREVIATIONS OF PLATE XVII.

1. A, a heron volant, in fess B, membered O, between three escalops S.
2. O, three kingfishers Ppr.
3. O, three eagles displayed G.
4. B, a bend engrailed between two cygnets royal A, gorged with ducal crowns, strings reflexed over their backs O.
5. B, a pelican with wings elevated, and vulning her breast A, between three fleurs-de-lis O.
6. B, three doves rising A, their legs G, and crowned with ducal coronets O.
7. A, on a pile G, three owls of the field.
8. A, three eagles' heads erased S, armed O.
9. A, three peacocks in their pride Ppr.
10. O, three swallows close Ppr.
11. B, on a bend cotised A, three martlets G.
12. Er. on two bars G, three martlets, O.
13. A, on a fess between three trefoils B, as many swans' necks erased of the first, beaked G.
14. A, on a pale B, three pair of wings conjoined and elevated of the first.
15. A, six ostrich-feathers S.
16. A, a chevron between three eagles' legs erased *à la cuisse* (cuisse *signifies the thigh*) S, their talons G.

17. B, a dolphin naiant embowed O, on a chief of the second two saltires G.
18. O, three dolphins hauriant B.
19. S, a dolphin naiant, vorant a fish Ppr.
20. A, three eels naiant in pale S.
21. O, three chalbots hauriant G.
22. A, on a bend B, three dolphins of the first.
23. S, a chevron Er. between three salmons hauriant A.
24. A, a chevron engrailed S, between three sea-crabs G.

BLAZONING OF PLATE XVIII.

1. Gules, on a bend sinister argent, three of the celestial signs, viz. Sagittarius, Scorpio, and Libra, of the first.
2. Ermine, three increscents gules; name, *Symmes.*
3. Azure, the sun, full moon, and seven stars or, the two first in chief, the last of orbicular form in base; name, *Johannes de Fontibus.*
4. Argent, on a chevron gules, between three crescents sable, a mullet for difference or; name, *Withers.*
5. Argent, two bars sable, between six estoiles, three, two, and one, gules; name, *Pearse.*
6. Argent, issuant out of two petit clouds in fess azure, a rainbow in the nombril point, a star, proper.
7. Azure, a blazing star, or comet, streaming in bend proper; name, *Cartwright.*
8. Azure, a fess dancetté or, between three cherubim's heads argent, crined of the second; name, *Adye.*
9. Argent, three woodbine-leaves bend-wise proper, two and one; name, *Theme.*

10. Or, three woodbine-leaves pendant azure; name, *Gamboa*.

11. Azure, issuant out of a mount in base three wheat-stalks bladed and eared, all proper; name, *Garzoni*.

12. Or, on a mount in base, an oak acorned proper; name, *Wood*.

13. Argent, three starved branches slipped sable; name, *Blackstock*.

14. Argent, three stocks or stumps of trees, couped and erased sable; name, *Retowre*.

15. Or, on a bend sable, three clusters of grapes argent; name, *Maroley*.

16. Gules, a bend of the limb of a tree, raguled and trunked argent; name, *Penruddock*.

17. Barry of six pieces, or and sable, over all a pale gules, charged with a woman's breast distilling drops of milk proper; name, *Dodge*.

18. Argent, an arm sinister, issuing out of the dexter point, and extended towards the sinister base, in form of a bend gules; name, *Cornhill*.

19. Argent, three sinister hands couped at the wrist gules; name, *Maynard*.

20. Or, a man's leg couped at the midst of the thigh azure; name, *Haddon*.

21. Sable, a chevron between three children's heads couped at the shoulders argent, crined or, enwrapped about the necks with as many snakes proper; name, *Vaughan*.

22. Argent, on a chevron gules, three men's skulls of the first; name, *Bolter*.

23. Or, a king enthroned on his seat, royal azure crowned, sceptred, and invested of the first; the

cape of his robe ermine.   These are the arms of
the city of Seville, in Spain.

24. Gules, three demi-savages, or wild men argent, holding clubs over their right shoulders or; name,
Basil Woodd.

Blazoning of Plate XIX.

1. Party per pale indented, or and gules; name,
   Birmingham.
2. Party per chevron nebuly, sable and or, three panthers' heads erased counterchanged; name, *Smith.*
3. Party per fess dancetté, or and azure, two mullets
   pierced counterchanged; name, *Doubleday.*
4. Party per bend crenellé, or imbattled argent and
   gules; name, *Boyle.*
5. Party per bend sinister, ermine and ermines, a lion
   rampant or; name, *Trevor.*
6. Party per saltire, argent and or, four eagles in cross
   sable; name, *Barnsdale.*
7. Quarterly, per pale dove-tailed, gules and or; name,
   Bromley.
8. Azure, a fess wavy, argent, in chief three stars;
   name, *Jenkinson.*
9. Argent, a double tressure-flory counter-flory, over
   all a fess imbattled counter-imbattled gules;
   name, *Miller.*
10. Argent, on a fess raguly azure, three fleurs-de-lis
    or; name, *Atwood.*
11. Azure, two bars indented or, a chief argent; name,
    Stoner.
12. Or, a fess dancetté sable; name, *Vavasour.*
13. Argent, on a fess engrailed gules, three leopards'
    faces or; name, *Barbon.*

14. Argent, a fess invecked, between three torteaux.

15. Azure, a fess nebuly, between three crescents ermine ; name, *Weld*.

16. Azure, a saltire quarterly quartered, or and argent, is the arms of the episcopal see of Bath and Wells.

17. Or, a fess checky argent and azure; name, *Stewart*

18. Gules, a chevron counter-compony argent and sable, between three fleurs-de-lis or; name, *Shirley*.

19. Quarterly, first and fourth argent, a chevron gules between three torteaux; second quarterly; first, argent, a bend gules; second, argent, a fess azure; third, argent, a chevron sable; fourth, argent, a pale vert; third, argent, a fess between three billets gules.

20. Ermine, two flanches azure, each charged with three ears of wheat couped or; name, *Greby*.

21. Or, a buffalo's head caboshed sable, attired argent, through the nostrils an annulet of the last, ducally crowned gules, the attire passing through the crown ; is the arms of Mecklenburg.

22. Or, a buffalo's head in profile sable, armed argent, ducally crowned gules; is the arms of the barony of Rostock in Mecklenburg.

23. Gules, an arm embowed, in armour to the wrist, issuing from clouds on the sinister side, and holding between the finger and thumb a gem-ring all proper, round the arm at the elbow a ribbon tied azure; is the arms of the county of Schwerin in Germany.

24. Argent, a wheel of eight spokes, gules; is the arms of the Bishop of Osnaburgh.

Marshalling.

Marshalling coats of arms is the art of disposing several, or more than one, of them in one escutcheon, and of distributing their parts and contingent ornaments in proper places. Coats of arms are thus marshalled on various accounts: viz. to show descent, marriage, alliance, adoption, or the gift of the sovereign.

Such coats as betoken marriage represent either a match single or hereditary. By a single match is meant the conjoining of the coat-armours of a man and woman, descended of distinct families, in one escutcheon pale-wise; the man bears his coat on the dexter side of the escutcheon, and the sinister part for the woman. See the example, Pl. xl, n. 3.

Sometimes in blazon the man and woman are called *baron* and *femme*. There are three rules to be observed in impaling the arms of husband and wife: *First*, the husband's arms are always to be placed on the right side as *baron*, and the wife's on the left as *femme*. *Secondly*, that no husband can impale his wife's arms with his own on a surcoat of arms, ensign, or banner, but may use them impaled on domestic utensils. *Thirdly*, that no husband impaling his wife's arms with his own can surround the shield with the order of the Garter, or with any other order.

When a man marries an heiress and has issue by her, it is in his choice whether he will still bear her coat impaled, or in an escutcheon of pretence upon his own ; because he pretendeth (God giving life to such his issue) to bear the same coat of his wife to him and to his heirs.

Moreover the heir of these two inheritors shall bear the hereditary coats of his father and mother to himself and his heirs quarterly : the father's in the first and fourth, the mother's in the second and third quarters, to show that the inheritance, as well of the possessions, as of the coat-armours, are invested in them and their posterity. See Pl. xiii., n. 6. If the wife be no heir, neither her husband nor child shall have further to do with her coat, than to set up the same in their house pale-wise, to show the father's match with such a family.

Concerning the bearing of several coat-armours pale-wise in one escutcheon (according to *Gerard Leigh*), viz. the marshalling of divers femmes with one baron, he says : "If a man marry two wives, the first shall be placed on the sinister side of the chief part, and the second's coat on the base impaled with the husband." Pl. xl., n. 5.

Arms of a man and his three wives; the first two tierced in chief with his own, and the third in base. Pl. xl., n. 6.

Arms of a man and his four wives; the two first tierced in chief, and the third and fourth in base. Pl. xl., n. 7.

Arms of a man and his five wives ; his own in the middle, with his first three on the dexter side, and the fourth and fifth on the sinister. Pl. xl., n. 8.

Arms of a man and his six wives; his own in the middle, with his first three on the dexter side, and the other three on the sinister. Pl. XL., n. 9.

Arms of a man and his seven wives; his own in the middle, with his first four on the dexter side, and the other three on the sinister. Pl. XL., n. 10.*

ARMS OF A WIDOW.

A widow is to impale the arms of her late husband on the dexter side of the paternal coat of her ancestor, upon a lozenge. Pl. XL., n. 11.

ARMS OF A MAIDEN, OR DOWAGER LADY OF QUALITY.

If a maiden, or dowager lady of quality, marry a commoner, or a nobleman inferior to her in rank, their coats of arms must be set side by side in two separate escutcheons. If the lady be privileged to retain her title and rank, she must continue her arms in a maiden or widow's escutcheon, which is a lozenge, placed on the sinister side of her husband's; the arms ornamented according to her title. See Pl. XLI., n. 16.

ARMS OF A WIDOW AND HEIRESS.

The arms of a widow, being an heiress, are to be borne on an escutcheon of pretence, over those of her late husband, in a lozenge. Pl. XL., n. 12.

* These five last rules and examples have been retained as part of the original work; but if ever they were in practice they are now discarded. The object of Heraldry is distinctness. No person save an adept in the art could tell, from such marshalling whether they were the coats of different wives, or quarterings brought in by one heiress.—EDITOR.

ARMS OF A WIFE AND TWO HUSBANDS.

Of a wife and her two husbands: the arms of the first husband in chief; the arms of the second husband in base, impaled on the dexter side of her own. See Pl. xl., n. 13.*

ARMS OF A BACHELOR.

Whilst he remains such, he may quarter his paternal coat with other coats, if any right to him belongs; but may not impale it till he is married. Pl. xl., n. 1.

ARMS OF A MAID.

She is entitled to bear the coat of her father in a lozenge. See Pl. xl., n. 2. If her father bore any difference in his coat, the same ought to be continued; for by that mark will be known what branch she descends from.

All co-heiresses convey also to their husbands a right of bearing their arms on an escutcheon of pretence, the same as an heiress.

If all the brothers die without issue, and leave sisters behind, as they are co-inheritors of the land and estate, so shall they be of the coat-armour also, without any distinction at all to either of them; because by them the name of the house cannot be preserved, being all reckoned but as one heir.

Anciently women of noble descent used to bear their fathers' arms on their *mantles*, to show their descent.

* This also is now discarded, as a widow marrying a second husband loses all title to the arms of the first as well as to his name.—EDITOR.

The ancient heralds tell us, when the arms are the same, both on the *mantle* and *kirtle*, they are then those of their fathers; and when there are arms on the *mantle* different from those on the under habit, the *kirtle*, she is then a wife : those on the *mantle* belong to her husband, who is a cloak to shroud the wife from all violence, and the other on the *kirtle* belonged to her father.

ARMS OF A BISHOP.

Such as have a function ecclesiastical, and are pre ferred to the honour of pastoral jurisdiction, are said to be knit in nuptial bands of love and care for the cathedral churches whereof they are superintendents; therefore their paternal coat is marshalled on the left side of the escutcheon, giving the pre-eminence of the right side to the arms of their see; as the example, Pl. XLI., n. 13. Deans of Cathedrals, Masters of Colleges and similar institutions, impale their arms in a like manner, with those of the Societies over which they preside.

ARMS OF A KNIGHT OF THE GARTER, AND HIS LADY.

When married, the arms of his wife must be placed in a distinct shield, because his own is surrounded with the ensign of that order; for though the husband may give his equal half of the escutcheon and hereditary honour, yet he cannot share his temporary order of knighthood with her, except she be sovereign of the order. Pl. XLI., n. 14. This rule applies to all the orders of knighthood.

ARMS QUARTERLY,

Is when a shield is divided into many parts, then it shows the bearer's alliance to several families : and it is to be observed, that in all marshalled arms, quarterly with coats of alliance, the paternal coat is always placed in the first quarter; as Pl. xiii., n. 6.

When a coat is borne with four or more quarterings, and any one or more of those quarterings are again divided into two or more coats, then such a quarter is termed a *grand quarter*, and is said to be quarterly or counter-quartered. Pl. xix., n. 19.

Quartered arms were borne by Eleanor, queen of Edward I., and Isabella, queen of Edward II.; but the first English king who quartered arms was *Edward III.*, who bore England and France in right of his mother *Isabel*, daughter and heir of *Philip IV.* of France, and heir also to her three brothers, successively kings of France, which the same king afterwards changed to France and England upon his laying claim to the said kingdom; and about the end of his reign his subjects began to imitate him, and quartered the arms of their maternal ancestors; the first of whom is said to be Hastings, Earl of Pembroke.

ARMS OF A BARONET.

The arms of Sir George Beaumont, of Stoughton, Leicestershire, baronet: *azure*, semée of fleurs-de-lis, a lion rampant *or*, in a canton *argent*, a sinister hand couped at the wrist and erect, *gules;* are given at Pl. xli., n. 15.

The canton charged with the hand, is the arms of the province of Ulster in Ireland, and was given by King James the First as a badge or augmentation of honour to all baronets. It may be placed as in the above example, or in an escutcheon, and is generally borne in the most convenient part of the shield, so as not to cover any principal charge.

ARMS OF A COMMONER AND LADY.

If a commoner marry a lady of quality, he is not to impale her arms with his own ; they are to be set aside of one another in separate shields, as the lady still retains her title and rank: therefore her arms are placed as the example, Pl. XLI., n. 16.

MARSHALLING BORDERED COATS.

When a coat of arms, surrounded with a border, is marshalled pale-wise with another, then that part of the border which is next the coat impaled with it must be omitted.   See Pl. XL., n. 14.   But if a bordered coat be marshalled with other coats quarterly, then no part of the border must be omitted.   See Pl. XL., n. 15.

Exterior Ornaments.

THE exterior ornaments of the escutcheon are the helmet, mantling, wreath, crest, badge, motto, supporters, crown, or coronet.

HELMETS.

The helmet being placed at the top of the escutcheon, claims our first attention.   These pieces of armour for the head have varied in different ages and countries, both in form and the materials of which they were made, and in English Heraldry they vary according to the rank of the bearer.   See Pl. XLII.

First, The full-faced helmet with six bars, all of gold, for the sovereign and princes of the blood.

Second, The full-faced helmet with five bars; the helmet steel, and the bars and breast part gold; for dukes and marquesses.

Third, A profile or side-faced helmet of steel; the bars, bailes, or grills, and ornaments gold; for earls, viscounts, and barons. Pl. XLII., n. 2.

Fourth, A full-faced helmet of steel, with its beaver or vizor open; for baronets and knights. Pl. XLII., n. 3.

Fifth, A profile or side-faced helmet of steel, with the vizor shut; for an esquire. Pl. XLII., n. 4.

If two helmets are placed on one shield, they are usually set face to face, in imitation of the Germans, who sometimes place ten or more helmets on a shield, and in such case set the centre helmet affrontée, and those on each side looking towards that in the centre.

MANTLING.

The mantling was anciently fixed to the helmet, from which it depended behind with escalloped or jagged edges and tassels.

Mantlings are also used like cloaks to encompass the whole achievement, the ornaments flowing from the helmet being called lambrequins.

According to the modernized mode of bearing mantles, those of the sovereign are supposed to be of gold doubled with ermine; those of the peers, crimson velvet folded, and ermine inside; and those of knights and gentlemen, crimson velvet doubled with white satin.

Mr. Edmondson, in his Complete Body of Heraldry, says, in the year 1760 he proposed to several of the peers, to paint on their carriages their arms placed in mantles of crimson, with their edges thrown back so as to show their doublings and linings, which should be of ermine, and containing a number of rows of ermine spots, equal to those of the guards on their coronation robes, expressing their respective degrees : viz. a baron, *two rows ;* a viscount, *two and a half ;* an earl, *three ;* a marquis, *three and a half ;* a duke, *four,* &c.

" This proposal," he adds, " having met with general approbation, was carried into execution, and had the desired effect of showing the distinction between the several degrees of our nobility ; after which I formed mantles for the knights companions of the several orders, taken from the mantles and robes which they wear at their installations."

The lambrequin should be of the principal colour in the arms, and the lining of the principal metal. Considerable fancy and taste may be displayed in these ornaments, which were often powdered with the badges of the family. Some fine examples may be seen in the Garter Plates of the 15th century.

THE WREATH.

The wreath is placed over the helmet as a support for the crest. It is composed of two rolls of silk twisted together, and of the colours or metal of the arms. If one of the rolls be metal, the other must be of the principal colour of the arms ; but when there is no metal in the arms, then one of the rolls should be of the colour of the field, and the other part of the colour of the immediate charge.

In the middle ages, no man, who was under the degree of a knight, had his crest set on a wreath.

THE CREST

The crest is the highest part of the ornaments of a coat of arms, and is placed on the wreath, unless it is issuant from a coronet, or standing on a *chapeau*, in either of which cases, the wreath is dispensed with. Crests appear on the helmets of Knights as early as the 13th century; and after the institution of the order of the Garter, and in imitation of King Edward the Third, who was the first king of England that bore a crest on his helmet, all knights companions of the order began to wear crests. This practice soon became more general, until at length they were assumed discretionally by all who considered themselves as legally entitled to bear arms.

BADGES.

Badges were anciently placed on banners, ensigns, caparisons, and the breasts or shoulders of private soldiers, servants, and attendants; and that without any wreath, or other thing, under them. They were much worn from the reign of King Edward the First, until that of Queen Elizabeth, when they grew into disuse.

Gerard Leigh says, the badge was not placed on a wreath in the time of Henry the Fifth; and it never should be so borne.

The Earl Delawarr bears the *crampette* and *impaled rose;* and the Lord Abergavenny bears the *portcullis* and *rose*, which were ancient badges. For further particulars refer to the articles BADGES, in the DICTIONARY OF TECHNICAL TERMS.

MOTTO.

The motto, *mot, word, legend, saying,* or *epigraph,* added or appropriated to arms, not being hereditary may be taken, changed, varied, or relinquished, when and as often as the bearer thinks fit; and may, with impunity to the assumer, be the same as is used by other families. Many still in use have been originally war-cries.

SUPPORTERS.

Supporters are exterior ornaments, placed at the sides of the escutcheon to support it. Menestrier and others say, that supporters had their origin from tilts and tournaments, wherein the knights caused their shields to be carried by servants or pages, under the disguise of lions, bears, griffins, Moors, &c., who also held and guarded the escutcheons, which the knights were obliged to expose to public view some time before the lists were opened.

Supporters have formerly been taken from such animals or birds as are borne in the shields, or had been introduced by the early engravers as ornaments on the seals, and at the present day they are occasionally chosen as bearing some allusion to the services of those whose arms they support.

It does not appear to have been customary with our ancestors to change or alter their family supporters; neither is it a practice used in our days, except in some singular instances, and then it has been done under the sanction of the royal sign-manual, &c.

The practice of the sovereigns of England granting supporters to the peers of each degree, seems to have commenced in the reign of King Henry the Eighth, as did that of granting the like ornaments to the arms of the knights of the Garter and of the Bath.

Supporters do not appear to the arms of the kings of England before the time of Richard II.; but a lion, *or*, and an eagle or falcon *proper* have been assigned to the arms of Edward III. The arms of Richard II. are seen accompanied rather than supported by two white harts, collared and chained *or;* and in Westminster Hall, by angels. A lion and an antelope, and sometimes an antelope and a swan, have been assigned to Henry IV. and Henry V., but upon no very reliable authority. Examples of the arms of Henry VI. appear supported by two antelopes *argent*, also, others, with a lion for the dexter, and a panther, antelope, or heraldic tiger for the sinister supporter. The arms of Edward IV. are painted in a contemporary MS. in the British Museum, supported by two white lions. He is said also to have used a lion, *or*, for the dexter and a bull *sable* for the sinister supporter. Of Edward V., there is no example. Richard III. seems to have generally used two boars *argent*. Henry VII. a dragon *gules* and a greyhound *argent*, a lion, *or*, and a dragon *gules*, and occasionally two greyhounds *argent*.

Henry VIII. generally a lion *or*, and a dragon *gules*. Sometimes the red dragon on the dexter side, and a white bull, greyhound, or cock on the sinister.

Edward VI., lion *or*, and dragon *gules*.

Mary, lion *or*, and dragon *or*, or a greyhound *argent*. When impaled with the arms of her husband, King Philip of Spain, the shield is supported by an eagle and a lion.

Elizabeth used the lion and dragon both *or*, and sometimes, in lieu of the dragon, the greyhound *argent.*

On the accession of James I., one of the silver unicorns at that time used as supporters to the royal arms of Scotland supplanted the dragon and greyhound of the Tudors, and since that period the supporters of the royal arms of the United Kingdoms have remained unchanged, being, dexter a lion rampant, gardant, *or* imperially crowned proper. Sinister, a unicorn, *argent,* armed, unguled, and crined, *or*, gorged with a coronet composed of crosses-pattée, and fleurs-de-lis, having a chain affixed thereto, all of the last, passing between the forelegs, and reflexed over the back.

The Nova-Scotia baronets are, by their patents of creation, allowed to carry supporters, notwithstanding that privilege was not granted to the English baronets, at the time of the institution of their dignity. Some of the English baronets now bear supporters, but it is by virtue of a royal licence obtained for that special purpose.

The kings of arms in England are not authorized to grant supporters to any person under the degree of a knight Grand Cross of the Bath, unless they receive a royal warrant directed to them for that purpose; and yet Lyon king of arms of Scotland may, by virtue of his office, grant supporters without such royal warrant, within the kingdom of Scotland, and has frequently put that power in practice.

The eldest sons of peers, above the degree of a baron, bear their fathers' arms and supporters with a label, and use the coronet belonging to their father's second title, if he has one; but all younger sons bear their arms with proper differences, and use no coronet or supporters.

𝔥𝔞𝔱𝔠𝔥𝔪𝔢𝔫𝔱𝔰.—Pl. xx.

By the following rules may be known, upon sight of any hatchment, what the person was wnen living, whether a private gentleman, or a nobleman; whether a married man, bachelor, or widower; a married woman, maid, or widow, &c.

BACHELOR.

When a bachelor dies, his arms and crest are painted single or quartered, but never impaled; the ground of the hatchment under the shield is all black.

MAIDEN.

When a maiden dies, her arms (but no crest) must be placed in a lozenge, and may be single or quartered, with the ground under the escutcheon all black, as the former.

MARRIED MAN.

When a married man dies, his arms are impaled with his wife's; the ground of the hatchment under his side of the shield in black, the ground under his wife's side in white; the black side signifies the husband to be dead, and the white side denotes the wife to be living.

MARRIED WOMAN.

When a married woman dies, her arms are impaled with her husband's (but no crest); the ground of the hatchment under her side of the shield is black, that of her husband white; which signifies the wife to be dead, and the husband living.

WIDOWER.

When a widower dies, his arms are impaled with those of his deceased wife, with his crest; the ground of the hatchment to be all black.

WIDOW.

When a widow dies, her arms are impaled with her husband's in a lozenge (but no crest); the ground of the hatchment to be all black.

When a man is the last of a family, the death's head supplies the place of a crest, denoting that death has conquered all.

When a woman is the last of a family, her arms are placed in a lozenge, with a death's head on the top.

OTHER DISTINCTIONS.

The peer is distinguished by his coronet and supporters.

The baronet by his peculiar badge.

The knight-companion by the motto of his order.

The bishop by the mitre.

Heraldry,

In Conjunction with Architecture.

THE revival of the various styles of architecture, which prevailed in Britain from the Norman Conquest to the reign of James the First, has rendered the study of the heraldic ornaments, which formed so prominent a feature in the ecclesiastical structures of the fourteenth and fifteenth centuries, an object of interest to all engaged in the erection or decoration of churches or other public buildings; particularly as a taste prevails for that style of architecture where heraldic figures were most lavishly applied in external and internal decoration.

Those who assert that Heraldry as a science was little known previous to the Crusades, are in some degree borne out in their statements, by the total absence of heraldic ornament in the ecclesiastical and castellated structures erected during the eleventh and twelfth centuries, in the Anglo-Norman style of architecture. That this omission was not caused by the inability of the sculptors of that period, is proved by the elaborate carvings exhibited in the semicircular doorways and windows, the highly wrought and diversified capitals, to which may be added the sculptured figures which may be seen at the present time at Iffley, Malmesbury, and many other places. Heraldic ornaments formed no part of the decoration of the buildings first erected in the Lancet or Early English style of architecture; but at a later period, when this style of building became more extended, and the simple pointed or lancet-shaped windows were superseded by the introduction of windows divided by mullions, and other deviations from the original simplicity of this beautiful style of architecture, Heraldic ornaments were introduced. The large shields on the side walls of the nave of Westminster Abbey, erected during the reign of Henry III., A.D. 1249, may be cited as one of the early introductions of Heraldry as an adjunct to architecture.

When the Early English style had become so altered by the introduction of exuberant ornament, and by large pointed arched windows divided by mullions, terminating in flowing tracery filling up the heading of the windows, by an almost infinite variety of graceful curves, the boldness and elegance of the embellishments introduced into the structures erected about the time of Edward III., A. D. 1327—1377, demanded a distinct title; and is now designated the Decorated style of architecture.

In this splendid era of English architecture, Heraldry became a distinguished feature, particularly in its application to sepulchral monuments. One of the earliest and most beautiful altar tombs erected in the Decorated style is that of Queen Eleanor, the lamented consort of Edward the First, in St. Edward's Chapel, Westminster. Each side of the tomb is divided by small buttresses into six compartments, having angular canopies ornamented with crockets and finials; each compartment contains a shield of arms, sculptured as suspended from an oak or vine branch : a representation of one compartment is given in the annexed engraving. The charges on the shields, which are repeated alternately, are those of England, three lions passant-gardant, Castile and Leon quarterly ; first and fourth, a castle, and second and third, a lion rampant. This was the paternal shield of arms of the deceased Queen, which she inherited from her father, Fer-  dinand the Third, who quartered the arms of two kingdoms, viz., Castile and Leon, in one shield. This is said to be the earliest instance of two coats of arms being borne quarterly ; and the example was followed by Edward the Third, when he quartered the arms of France with those of England—the third shield for Ponthieu, viz., three bendlets within a bordure. These Heraldic symbols sufficiently declare to posterity the title and connexions of the deceased Queen, and supply the place of a long pompous inscription.

During the reign of Edward the Third, chivalry, and, consequently, Heraldry, became the ruling fashion of the time. Every person who could rank above a yeoman desired to obtain those heraldic honours which could alone be granted by the Earl Marshal and the King-at-Arms. Those who were allowed to bear coats of arms sought every opportunity of displaying them on their banners, habiliments, and

the furniture of their apartments. The contributor to
the foundation of a religious establishment was in

some measure rewarded by
having his arms emblazoned
in a conspicuous part of the
building; and these assumed
the appearance of architectural ornaments by filling up
the spandrils or spaces between the arches (as represented in the annexed engrav-
ing), which would otherwise have presented too much of
the plain surface of the wall. Shields of arms are thus
disposed in the nave and transepts of York Minster.

In some instances, Heraldic ornaments formed part of the decorations introduced in the capitals. The annexed cut is taken
from a column in Bloxham Church,
Oxon. It is said to represent
Saint George. The cross is em-
blazoned on his shield, and on the pennon attached to
the lance. The arms in the annexed cut form part of

the pierced work that supports the
transom beams in the Chapter-house
of Exeter Cathedral.

Not only did the shields and the
charges upon them become architectural ornaments, but the badges and
devices of the king and nobility were
admitted in the decoration of corbels, cornices, and
capitals.

The recumbent figures of knights upon altar-tombs

were generally sculptured in complete armour, with their arms emblazoned on the shield. In some instances, the arms are emblazoned in their proper tinctures and metals. The sculptured figure ascribed to Geoffrey Magnaville, Earl of Essex, in the Temple Church, is said to be the earliest instance of the arms being placed in the shield ; but there exists much difference of opinion both as to date and identity of this effigy.

The splendid windows of the Decorated style were filled with stained and painted glass, which admitted shields of arms to be emblazoned in their proper colours. Whole-length and kneeling male and female figures are frequently seen in ancient windows. The figure of the knight is usually depicted with his arms emblazoned on his surcoat or tabard; the dame or lady is frequently habited in garments bearing heraldic charges ; on the fore part of the close robe that covers her body was emblazoned her paternal arms, and the charges she was entitled to assume in her own right. This dress was called the kirtle. The mantle worn over her shoulders was considered typical of honour and protection, and on this garment the arms of her husband were emblazoned.

We have now to glance at Heraldry as an adjunct to architecture, when the flowing tracery of the Decorated style gave place to the latest style of English architecture, now called the Perpendicular. This transition took place about the end of the fourteenth century. Heraldry before this period was only admitted as a portion of the architectural ornament ; but, from the exuberant display of symbolic figures, and

the almost entire absence of other ornaments, it became
an integral part of the architectural character ; and it
has always been a matter of surprise, when looking at
the stately buildings erected under the auspices of the
Tudors, that the architecture of this period did not
obtain the title of the Heraldic style.   England contains two buildings in the Perpendicular style, which
for architectural splendour are unequalled in Europe,
or perhaps in the world.   One is King's College Chapel,
at Cambridge ; the other Henry the Seventh's Chapel,
at Westminster.   It is not our province to dilate upon
the beauties of either of these splendid structures,
farther than to notice the gorgeous display of Heraldry
that pervades them.

The west and south entrances of King's College
Chapel are enriched with bold carvings of the badges
of King Henry the Seventh, in whose reign they were
erected ; but, as the Royal badges will again come
under notice, when describing the chapel at Westminster, we will at once enter King's College Chapel ;
and no person ever glanced his eye over the wonders
around and above him, without being awe-struck at the
daring of the architect that could plan, and the builders
that could erect such a structure.   The whole of the
lower part of the Chapel beneath the windows is
divided into panels, and every panel is filled with the
arms of the king who erected the building.   The engraving on p. 77 is a representation of his arms and supporters : they fill three large compartments under
each window.   The immense pendants hanging from
the gorgeous roof are ornamented with the rose, the
royal badge of both the king and queen at this period.

The   gateway   towers   of Christ's   and St. John's

Colleges have a noble display of Heraldry in the arms, supporters, badges, &c., of their noble foundress, Margaret, Countess of Richmond.

ARMS OF HENRY VIII.

The entrance gateway tower of Trinity College was originally the entrance to King's Hall, founded by Edward III., in 1337, and is decorated with the arms of that monarch and his six sons, a blank shield representing William of Hatfield, who died in his infancy. Henry VIII. refounded the college, and changed its name, and as his statue occupies a niche over these arms, they have sometimes been erroneously assigned to him and his family.

We have now to notice Henry the Seventh's Chapel at Westminster. Mr. Brayley, in his history of this splendid structure, observes : " There is no other edifice in the kingdom in which external ornaments have been spread over its surface with such exuberant luxuriance. It would seem, indeed, as though the architect had intended to give to stone the character of embroidery, and inclose its walls within meshes of lacework : with the exception of the plinth, every part is covered by sculptural decorations ; the buttress towers are crested by ornamental domes, and enriched by niches and elegant tracery. The cross springers are crossed with airy forms, and the very cornices and parapets are charged even to profusion with armorial cognizances." If we were to notice the application of the arms, badges, animals, &c., which decorate the exterior of this building, it would occupy a much larger volume than the one that contains these brief remarks. We must,

therefore, proceed to the interior; and we are arrested
on our very entrance to this gorgeous temple by the
display of Heraldic devices on the brazen gates. The
central gates are divided into sixty-eight perforated
compartments of an oblong figure, each of which contains a badge of different members of the Houses of
York and Lancaster. Among others is the well-known
badge of Edward the Fourth, viz., the falcon with an
open fetter-lock, the portcullis chained and crowned,
three fleurs-de-lis, a root of daisies intersecting a coronet ;
the letters H. R. in a knot : but we dare not loiter at
the entrance. On each side of the Chapel are the
elegantly-carved stalls, now appropriated to the Knights
of the Bath, each surmounted by a canopy of delicate
tabernacle-work, no two being alike. The helmets,
swords, and banners of the knights would add to the
splendour of any other place, but here appear mean
compared to the gorgeous architecture above and
around them. The cornices are formed by demi-
angels, supporting the royal badges. Dragons, greyhounds, and lions, supporting shields, intermixed with
beautiful foliage, form the ornaments of the arches of
the ceiling, filled up with fan-tracery, from which hang
pendants, &c.

Following are representations of some of the Royal
badges found in this Chapel :—

1. The badge of York—the white rose
crowned. In some instances, this rose is
parted per pale argent and gules, showing
the union of the houses of York and Lancaster ;—the latter having adopted the red
rose as its badge.

The fleur-de-lis crowned—the badge of France.

The portcullis crowned and chained—the ancient badge of the Beauforts; used by Henry the Seventh, as a descendant from that family.

The letters H. R. in a knot is worked into the open work of the compartments of the centre gates of the Chapel, and also in the sculptured cornices. Knots were frequently used as badges to distinguish different families : see Pl. xv., No. 31 to 35.

The Broom - plant — planta-genista — was the badge of the Plantagenets, in allusion to their name. The annexed example is from the cornice in Westminster Hall.

King's College Chapel, and the Chapel at Westminster, were both completed in the reign of Henry the Eighth, and were the last efforts of English Pointed

architecture. The Reformation put a stop to archi
tectural splendour in the construction of buildings for
divine worship, and Heraldry no longer held its place
in connection with architecture. The discovery of the
art of printing had enabled the publishers to produce
translations of the classic authors. The architecture
of Greece and of Rome, in addition to their inherent
beauty, had all the charms of novelty. English architecture was neglected ; and the mansions of the nobility
and gentry erected during the reign of Elizabeth, all
show the hold that the classic orders had obtained at
that time, though the builders were unacquainted with
the means of applying them correctly. By the accidental mixture of the panelled work of the Tudors
with the Greek columns and entablatures, producing
that style of building called Elizabethan, Heraldry
was partially admitted into the heterogeneous yet
picturesque masses erected during the reign of the
Virgin Queen and her successor. Inigo Jones and Sir
Christopher Wren, by introducing the classic orders in
their purity and beauty, put an end to the incongruities
of the Elizabethan style ; and from this period to the
latter end of the reign of George the Third, churches,
palaces, and public buildings, that had any pretensions
to architectural elegance, were all erected in the classic
orders.

Architects of the present day prove, by many of
their works, that they have caught the spirit of the
ancient masters, and heraldry has again become an
important adjunct to architecture : it is especially
noticeable in the decorative features of Sir Charles
Barry's New Palace of Westminster.

A Dictionary of Technical Terms

A—ACH.

A. The heraldic abbreviation of ARGENT. AR. is never used, as it is liable to be mistaken for Az. (Plates XV. & XVII.)

ABASED, or ABAISSÉ, signifies that a chevron, fess, or other ordinary, is placed lower than its usual position.

ABATEMENTS are certain marks of disgrace, added to arms, for some dishonourable action committed by the bearer; but as there is now not an instance of such dishonourable bearings, we shall not insert them; especially as a person not being obliged to make use of arms, it cannot be supposed that any one would voluntarily exhibit a mark of infamy to himself and family.

ACCOMPANIED. Sometimes used for *between*, as a cross accompanied by four crescents.

ACCOSTED signifies side by side, as Guillim blazons the arms of Harman; viz. Azure, a chevron, between six rams, *accosted*, counter-tripping, two, two, and two. See Pl. IX., n. 10.

ACCRUED, full grown; applied to trees.

ACHIEVEMENT (French *achèvement* the performance of an action, *achever*, to perform), the escutcheon containing the ensigns armorial granted to any man for the performance of great actions. This word is corrupted to HATCHMENT. *Vide* p. 69.

ACORNED. This term is for an oak-tree, or branch, with acorns on it.

ADDITIONS. See AUGMENTATIONS.

ADDORSED, ADOSSÉ, or ADOSSED, signifies turned back to back. Pl. IX. n. 7. *Two lions rampant addorsed.*

ADUMBRATION is the shadow only of any bearing, outlined and painted of a colour darker than the field.

AFFRONTÉ, front-faced, full-faced; as, a *savage's head affronté.* Pl. XL., n. 24. This term is also occasionally used in the same sense as gardant; as, a *lion sejant affronté.*

AISLÉ, winged, or having wings.

À LA CUISSE (French), at the thigh: erased or couped *à la cuisse.*

ALANT, a mastiff-dog with short ears. It was one of the supporters to the arms of *Lord Dacre.*

ALLERION is an eagle without beak or feet. Pl. VIII., n. 6.

ALTERNATE, ALTERNATELY, by turns, one after another, applying to the positions of quarterings, &c., that succeed one another by turns.

AMBULANT, walking; the same as passant.

AMETHYST, the name of a precious stone of a violet colour, formerly used in blazoning the arms of peers instead of purpure.

AMPHISIEN COCKATRICE. See BASILISK.

ANCHOR is the emblem of Hope, and taken for such in a spiritual as well as a temporal sense; hope being, as it were, the anchor which holds us firm to our faith in all adversities. When used as a bearing, it is drawn without a cable, unless it be mentioned in the blazonry. Pl. XXVII., n. 10.

ANCHORED, or ANCRED, a cross so termed; as the four

extremities of it resemble the fluke of an anchor. Pl. xxxvi., n. 33.

ANGLES, two angles interlaced saltierwise; at each end an annulet. Pl. xl., n. 3. *Three pairs* of these are borne by the name of *Wastley.*

ANIMÉ. See INCENSED.

ANNODATED, another term for *nowed;* bent in the form of the letter S. The serpents round the caduceus of Mercury may be said to be annodated.

ANNULET, a ring. Leigh supposes annulets to be rings of mail, which was an armour of defence long before the harness of steel was invented. An annulet is the mark of difference assigned to the fifth son. Pl. vii., n. 5.

ANSHENT, or ANCIENT, a small flag or streamer, set up on the stern of a ship, or on a tent. The guidon used at funerals was also called an *anshent.*

ANTÉ, or ENTÉ, irgrafted, or pieces let one into another, like dovetail. See Pl. xix., n. 7.

ANTELOPE is an animal of the deer kind; his horns are almost straight, tapering gradually from his head up; a long and slender neck, feet, legs, and body, like a deer. Pl. vii., n. 21, and n. 22, is termed an heraldic antelope.

ANVIL, the iron block used by smiths, is represented in heraldry as Pl. xxx., n. 6. *Party per chevron, argent and sable, three anvils counterchanged;* name, *Smith,* of Abingdon, Berks.

APAUMÉE is the hand open, with the full palm appearing, the thumb and fingers at full length. See Pl. xxxv., n. 32 and 33.

ARCHDUKE'S CROWN. A circle of gold, adorned with eight strawberry-leaves, and closed by two arches of gold set with pearls. meeting in a globe crossed, like the emperor's. The cap scarlet. Pl. xlv., n. 16.

ARCH, as in architecture, is borne in Heraldry either double or single, and should be drawn on, or supported by pillars; see Pl. xli., n. 3.

ARCHED, or ARCHY, bowed or bent in the form of an arch.

ARGENT is the French word for silver, and in Heraldry is white: in heraldic sketches it is abbreviated to A. Silver was formerly used, but from its soon turning black, white was substituted. Pl. ii.

ARM. This part of the human body is frequently and variously borne, both as a charge and for a crest; as, an *arm erect, couped at the elbow.* Pl. xl., n. 17.

Arm in armour, embowed proper, couped at the shoulder, grasping an arrow. Pl. xl., n. 22. *Three dexter arms conjoined at the shoulders, and flexed in triangle, with the fists clenched.* Pl. xl., n. 2. *Two arms in armour, embowed, supporting a pheon.* Pl. xl., n. 23.

ARMED signifies the horns, hoofs, beak, or talons, of any beast or bird of prey (being their weapons), which, when borne of a different tincture from that of their bodies, are described as being *armed* so and so.

ARMING BUCKLE, a buckle in the shape of a lozenge. See Pl. xxviii., n. 9.

ARRACHÉ, the French term for ERASED.

ARRONDIE signifies round or circular. See Pl. xxxvii., n. 31.

ARROWS are frequently used in heraldry, and are usually borne barbed and flighted, *i. e.* feathered. See one, Pl. xxiv., n. 8. In English heraldry (it is exactly the reverse in French) the arrow is always represented with its barb or point downwards, unless otherwise expressed. Arrows, when in bundles or parcels, are usually termed *sheaves*, and are understood, unless a greater number be mentioned, to consist of three only, one in pale (upright), and two others in saltier (crossing it), bound together, or banded. It is not uncommon, however, to have five or seven in a sheaf; but the number, if more than three, must be specified.

ASCENDANT, rising, or issuing upward; sometimes applied to smoke, flame, rays, or beams.

ASPERSED, by some authors used instead of *strewed* or *powdered*.

Ass (the) is frequently borne in heraldry. Pl. XXVI., n. 7. *Argent, a fess between three asses passant, sable;* name, *Askewe.*

ASSIS signifies sitting, or *sejant:* the example is a lion assis affronté, or *sejant gardant.* Pl. XXXI., n. 6.

ASTEROIDS, stars resembling planets : see ESTOILES.

ASSURGENT, rising out of the sea.

ASTROLABE, an instrument for taking the altitude of the sun or stars at sea.

ASSYRIAN GOAT. See INDIAN GOAT.

AT BAY. A stag *at bay,* is used to express the position of a stag when standing on the defensive, with his head downwards, to meet the onset of dogs and huntsmen.

ATHELSTAN'S CROSS. *Party per saltire, gules and azure, on a besant, a cross botonné or.* Arms invented by later heralds for King Athelstan, who expelled the Danes, subdued the Scots, and reduced this country to one monarchy. Pl. XXXIX., n. 14.

ATTIRED, a term used when speaking of the horns of a stag, buck, goat, or ram, &c. When of different tinctures from their bodies, it must be mentioned.

ATTIRES, a term for the horns of a stag or buck: see the attires of a stag affixed to the scalp   Pl. XXXI., n. 33.

AVELLANE, a cross, so called because the quarters of it resemble a filbert-nut.   Pl. VI., n. 7.

AUGMENTATIONS signify particular marks of honour, granted by the sovereign for some heroic or meritorious act.   They are usually borne either on an escutcheon, or a canton, as by the baronets of England.   See Pl. XLI., n. 15.   When augmentations are borne on a chief, fess, canton, or quarter, the paternal coat keeps its natural place, and is blazoned first.   See the arms of *Manners.*   Pl. XI., n. 3.

AURÉ, dropped with gold ; the same as *Guttée d'or.*

AYLETS, or sea-swallows, represented sable, beaked and legged, gules ; some term them Cornish choughs.

AZURE is the colour blue, and in engraving this colour is expressed by horizontal lines from the dexter to the sinister side of the shield.   To avoid mistakes in the abbreviations of Argent and Azure, the letter B is always used to signify the latter.   (See Plates II., XV., XVII.)

BADGE.   A device or cognizance embroidered upon the sleeves of servants and followers, or on the backs and breasts of the soldiery and yeomen of the guard, &c.

King Henry II. is said to have first used a badge in this country.   It is stated to have been an *escarbuncle*, the cognizance of the House of Anjou, he being the son of the Empress Maud, daughter of Henry I., and of Plantagenet, Earl of Anjou, but there is no contemporary authority for it.   A star between the horns of a crescent is seen upon the great seals of Richard I.,

John, and Henry III., a rose *or*, stalked proper is
attributed to Edward I. A castle is seen on the great
seal of Edward II. Edward III. used for a badge,
rays of the sun descending from clouds *argent*, also
an ostrich feather all *gold*. His son, Edward the Black
Prince, bearing it *argent* and John of Gaunt *ermine*. The
badge of Richard II. was a *white hart, lodged, with a
crown round his neck, and chained, or ;* he bore, also, *the
sun in his splendour*. Henry IV. bore, on a sable
ground, *three ostrich feathers, erm.* ; also a *fox's tail
dependant, ppr*. He also bore the *red rose*, which he
inherited from his grandfather, Henry, first Duke of
Lancaster. In his single combat with Mowbray, Duke
of Norfolk, he exhibited the *swan and antelope*, while
the Duke had *mulberry-leaves* for his badge, in allusion
to his name of Mowbray. The badges of Henry V. were
a *burning cresset* and a *fleur-de-lis crowned*. Henry VI.
chose a *panther*, semée of roundles, and also two
ostrich feathers in saltier. Edward IV. took the *white
rose*, to which, after the battle of Mortimer's Cross,
where he thought he saw three suns conjoined, he
added *golden rays*. Another badge of this monarch was
a *falcon in a fetterlock*. Richard III. used the *white
rose in the sun*, in imitation of his brother, and a *white
boar*. Henry VII. adopted the portcullis of the House
of Lancaster, and a rose, per pale *white* and *red :* afterwards, he placed the white rose within the red one.
Henry VIII. continued this badge ; but with him the
party-coloured rose was frequently rayonnée and
crowned. Queen Elizabeth took a *phœnix in flames*,
with the motto, *semper eadem*. Her other badge was a
falcon or, crowned *or*, holding a sceptre of the *second*,
and standing on the stump of a tree, between two

gr)wing *branches of white and red roses ;* which badge had been given to her mother, Anne Boleyne, by Henry VIII.

Among the most celebrated of the badges borne by nobles, was *the bear and ragged staff* (which still exists as an inn sign) of the great Earl of Warwick, derived from the Beauchamps. The *white hart* of Richard II., and the *silver swan* of the House of Lancaster, are also still frequently met with as signs to inns, though their origin is seldom thought of. Few of the ancient cognisances are now generally remembered, except the roses of York and Lancaster, and the three feathers borne in a coronet by the Princes of Wales since the reign of Henry VIII. ; which latter have, without interruption, continued from the time of their first assumption to be a favourite ornament of royalty.

The Badge of England (proper) is a rose, white and red, ensigned with the royal crown.

The Badge of Scotland is a thistle, ensigned with the royal crown.

The Badges of Ireland are,—1. A harp *or*, stringed *or*, ensigned with the royal crown :—2. The trefoil or shamrock, similarly ensigned.

All of these may be said to be the badges of the *United Kingdom*, and are now represented at Pl. XLIII., n. 1, conjointly.

The Badge of Wales is a dragon passant, wings elevated, *gu.*, on a mount *vert*. It was first adopted by King Henry VII.

The Badge of Ulster (which is the distinguishing mark borne in the paternal coat of English baronets, commonly called " the bloody hand " in the arms of baronets,) is on a shield, or canton, *argent*, a sinister hand erect and apaumée, *gu.*

The Badge of Nova Scotia is, *or*, a saltier, *az.*, thereon an escutcheon of the arms of Scotland, ensigned with an imperial crown, and encircled with the motto, *Fax mentis honestæ gloria.*

BADGER. Otherwise called a *brock*, is borne as a crest by several families, as a play upon their name; as Broke, Brook, Brooks, Brokelsby, Badger, &c. See Pl. xxx., n. 13.

BAG OF MADDER. This is a charge in the dyers' arms. Pl. xxxviii., n. 1.

BAILLONNÉ. A term used to express a lion rampant, holding a staff in his mouth. Pl. xxxii., n. 15.

BALISTA. An engine used by the ancient Greeks and Romans for throwing stones at the time of a siege. It is otherwise called a swepe, and is represented as engraved. Pl. xxxiv., n. 17.

BALL TASSELLED, Pl. xxx., n. 12. *Argent, a chevron, between three balls sable, tasselled or;* name, *Ball*, of Devonshire.

BALL, fired proper. See FIRE-BALL.

BANDÉ, a French term for *bend*, implying the *bend dexter.*

BANDED: when anything is tied round with a band of a different tincture from the charge, as a garb, wheatsheaf, or sheaf of arrows, it is said to be *banded;* for example, *A garb azure, banded or.*

BANDEROLLE, a streamer, or small flag, affixed by lines or strings, immediately under the crook on the top of the staff of a crosier, and folding over the staff.

BANNER, a square flag, standard, or ensign, carried at the end of a lance.

BANNER, *disveloped*. This term is used for an ensign, or colours, in the army, being open and flying; as Pl. xxv., n. 1.

BAR is less than the fess, and is a diminution, containing a fifth part of the field, and is borne in several parts of the field; whereas the fess is confined to the centre. Pl. iv., n. 14.

BARBED. The green leaves or petals which appear on the outside of a full-blown rose are in heraldry called barbs, and are thus blazoned : a rose, gu., *barbed* and seeded ppr.

BARBED ARROW, an arrow whose head is pointed and jagged.

BARBED AND CRESTED ; a term occasionally used for the comb and gills of a cock, if of a different tincture from the body; but the usual term is *combed and wattled*.

BARBED, or BARBÉE, a cross so termed, as its extremities are like the barbed irons used for striking fish. Pl. xxxvii., n. 14.

BAR-GEMEL, from the Latin *gemelli*, twins, signifies a double bar, or two bars placed near and parallel to each other. Pl. vii., n. 16.

BARON and FEMME is used in blazoning the arms of a man and his wife marshalled together side by side. *Baron* expresses the husband's side of the shield, which is the dexter ; *femme*, the sinister. See Pl. xl., n. 3. Achievements.

BARON'S CORONET. See CROWNS and CORONETS, and Pl. xliii., n. 10.

BARNACLE, a large water-fowl resembling a goose ; and by the Scots called a *Cleg Goose*. Pl. xxv., n. 11. The barnacle has a flat broad bill, with a hooked point; the fore-part of the head is white, with a bead of black between the eyes; the neck and fore-part of the breast are black, the belly is white and brown, the thighs blackish, the back black and brown, the tail black : the wings black, brown, and ash colour. *Argent, a fess, between three barnacles, sable;* name, *Bernake,* of Leicestershire.

BARNACLES, an instrument which farriers fix to the upper lip of a horse, to keep the animal quiet while they bleed, or perform any other operation. Pl. xxxiv., n. 35. *Argent, three barnacles, gules;* name, *Barnack,* of Leicestershire.

BARRULET is a diminutive, and the fourth of the bar, or twentieth part of the field. Pl. iv., n. 16.

BARRULY. See BARRY.

BARRY is a field divided by horizontal lines into four, six, or more equal parts counterchanged, and is termed Barry of six, eight, ten, or twelve; it being necessary to specify the number. Pl. v., n. 19. *Barry of six, or, and azure;* name, *Constable.*

BARRY-BENDY is a field equally divided into four, six, or more equal parts by lines, from the dexter chief to the sinister base, and from side to side interchangeably varying the tinctures. Pl. xxxviii., n. 20.

BARRY-BENDY SINISTER, by some authors termed *Barry indented.*

BARRY-INDENTED, *or barry of six, argent, and sable indented one in the other;* name, *Gise.* Pl. xxxviii., n. 19.

BARRY-PILY of eight pieces *gules,* and *or;* name, *Holland.* Pl. v., n. 20.

BASE is the bottom or lower part of the shield, marked with the letters G, H, I, on the diagram, page **10.**

IN BASE is the position of anything placed in the lower part of the shield.

BASILISK, an imaginary animal, represented like the fictitious heraldic cockatrice, and with the head of a dragon at the end of its tail. It is called the *Amphisien Cockatrice*, from having two heads. Pl. xxv., n. 13.

BASKET. See WINNOWING BASKET.

BASNET. The name of a head-piece worn in the 14th and 15th centuries, sometimes without and sometimes under the heaume or helmet. *Argent, a chevron, gules, between three helmets proper ;* name, *Basnet.*

BAT. See RERE MOUSE.

BATON. See BATTON.

BATTERING-RAM. An ancient engine made of large pieces of timber, fastened together with iron hoops, and strengthened at one end with an iron head, shaped and horned like that of a ram, from whence it took its name. It was hung up by two chains, and swung forwards and backwards, by numbers of men, to beat down the walls of a besieged town or city. Pl. xli., n. 7. *Argent, three battering-rams, barwise proper, headed azure, armed and garnished or ;* name, *Bertie.*

BATTLE-AXE was a weapon anciently used in war, having an axe on the one side, whence it takes the name, and a point on the other ; as also a point at the end, so that it could be used to thrust or cleave. Pl. xxvii., n. 21. *Argent three battle-axes sable ;* name, *Gyves* or *Hall.*

BATTLED ARRONDIE signifies the battlement of a town &c., to be circular on the top.

BATTLED-EMBATTLED is one battlement upon another and is a line of partition. Pl. xxxv., n. 28.

BATTON, BASTON, or BATON, signifying a staff or

truncheon, is generally used as a rebatement on coats of arms to denote illegitimacy. Pl. IV., n. 12. It is also, however, frequently adopted as a crest, without any reference to illegitimacy; as, *an arm embowed, holding a baton,* and many others.

BEACON. In ancient times, upon the invasion of an enemy, beacons were set on high hills, with an iron pot on the top, wherein was pitch, hemp, &c., which, when set on fire, alarmed the country, and called the people together. In the eleventh year of the reign of Edward III., every county in England had one. Pl. XXXIV., n. 16.

Prior to King Edward, the fire-beacons were made of large stocks of wood. *Sable, three beacons fired or, flames proper;* name, *Dauntre.*

BEAKED. A term for the bills of birds, which, when borne of a different tincture from their bodies, are said to be *beaked* of this or that colour.

BEAR, the well-known beast of prey so called, is common in coats armorial and crests. Pl. XXXI., n. 9. *Or, a bear passant, sable;* name, *Fitzourse.*

BEARING signifies any single charge of a coat of arms; but if used in the plural, the word is understood to describe the whole coat armorial. See CHARGES.

BEAVER, or VISOR, is that part of the helmet which defends the sight, and opens in the front of the helmet.

BEAVER, an amphibious animal, noted for its extraordinary industry and sagacity, is naturally very frequently met with in heraldry. *Argent, a beaver erected sable, devouring a fish proper, armed gules;* this coat is in a window of New-Inn Hall, London. Pl. XXVI., n. 9.

BEE-HIVE and BEES. Bees are most wonderful and

profitable insects; they have two properties of the best
kind of subjects; they keep close to their king; and
are very industrious for their livelihood, expelling all
idle drones. In heraldry they are much used, to represent industry. *Argent, a bee-hive beset with bees,
diversely volant, sable;* name, *Rooe.* Pl. xxvi., n. 21.

BELFRY, that part of the steeple or tower of a church
in which the bells are hung, is occasionally met with as
a bearing.

BELLED, having bells affixed to some part. See the
example. *A hawk rising jessed and belled.* Pl. ix., n. 20.

BELLOWS. This useful utensil, when borne in
heraldry, is drawn erect, as represented Pl. xxx., n. 9.

BELLS. Used as the proclaimers of joyful solemnity,
and designed for the service of God, by calling the
people to it, are in heraldry termed CHURCH-BELLS, to
distinguish them from those which are tied to the legs
of hawks or falcons. See Pl. xxviii., n. 23.

BEND, one of the honourable ordinaries, is formed by
two diagonal lines drawn from the dexter chief to the
sinister base, and contains the third part, if charged;
and uncharged, the fifth of the field. Pl. iv., n. 5.

BEND SINISTER is the same ordinary, but drawn from
the sinister chief to the dexter base, or from *left to right.*
Pl. iv., n. 10.

PARTY PER BEND SINISTER, argent and gules.
Pl. xxxix., n. 1.

IN BEND is when things borne in arms are placed
diagonally, from the dexter chief to the sinister base.
See Pl. x., n. 18, and Pl. xi., n. 25.

BENDS ENHANCED. See ENHANCED.

PER BEND is when the field, or charge, is equally
divided by a line drawn diagonally from the dexter

chief to the sinister base; *party per bend, or and vert;* name, *Hawley.* Pl. III., n. 2.

BENDLET, is one of the first of the diminutives of the bend, and is in size half the breadth of a bend. Pl. IV., n. 6.

BENDY is when a field, or charge, is divided bendwise into four, six, eight, ten, or more equal parts diagonally. *Bendy of six, argent and azure;* name, *John de St. Philibert.* Pl. V., n. 18. *A border bendy, argent and gules.* Pl. XXXVIII., n. 15.

BESANTS, or BEZANTS, are roundlets of gold without any impression, so called from the ancient gold coin of Byzantium, now Constantinople (the value of one being 375*l.* sterling, according to Kent in his abridgment of Guillim), and supposed to have been introduced in arms by those who were in the Crusades. Pl. VIII., n. 9.

Similar figures, when party-coloured, or when the colour is not known, are called under the general term of *roundles.*

BEZANTY CROSS, a cross composed of bezants. Pl. XXXVI., n, 18. *Bezanty,* or *bezantée,* is also a term when the field of the escutcheon, or any particular charge, is indiscriminately strewed with bezants, their number or position not being specified.

BICAPITATED, having two heads. Pl. XXXII., n. 19.

BICORPORATED, having two bodies. Pl. XXXII., n. 22.

BILLETS are oblong squares, by some taken for pieces of wood, and by others supposed to be letters made up in that form. Pl. VIII., n. 4.

BILLETY signifies a field (*charge or supporters*) strewed with billets when they exceed ten, otherwise their number and position must be expressed.

BIPARTED, so cut off as to form an indent showing

two projections: differing from *erased*, which signifies torn off, and shows three jagged pieces.

BIRD-BOLT, a blunt-headed arrow used for shooting birds with a cross-bow, and variously borne with one, two, or three heads. Pl. xxxiv., n. 26, 27. As the number of heads varies, it should always be specified when there are more than one. *Gules, three bird-bolts, argent;* name, *Bottlesham. Argent, three triple-headed bird-bolts, sable;* name, *Risdon.*

BLADED. This term is for the stalk or blade of any kind of grain or corn, represented in arms, *borne* of a different *colour from the ear,* or fruit.

BLAZON. A term derived from the German word *Blasen,* which signifies the blowing of a horn; it was introduced in heraldry from an ancient custom of the heralds. It was the practice when knights attended jousts or tournaments, to blow a horn, announcing their arrival. This was answered by the heralds, who then described aloud, and recorded the arms, borne by each knight. Hence originated, it is presumed, the word BLAZON, or BLAZONRY, which signifies the describing in proper terms all that belongs to coats of arms. See RULES, &c.

BLUE-BOTTLE is a flower of the cyanus. Pl. xxv., n. 20. *Argent, a chevron, gules between three blue-bottles or, slipped vert;* name, *Cherley.*

BOAR. This animal, when used in heraldry, is always understood to be the wild boar, and is represented as Pl. xxxi., n. 20. *Argent, a boar passant, gules, armed or;* name, *Trewarthen.*

BOLT-IN-TUN is a bird-bolt in pale piercing through a tun, as Pl. xxiv., n. 22; it is properly rebus of the name Bolton, rather than a heraldic charge.

BOLTANT, or BOLTING, a term occasionally used to describe the position of hares or rabbits in *springing forward* when first disturbed from their burrows.

BONNET, a cap of velvet worn within a coronet.

BORDER, or BORDURE. Borders were anciently used for distinguishing one part of a family from the other, descended of one family and from the same parents. When used as a distinction of houses, the border must be continued all round the extremities of the field, and should always contain the fifth part thereof. Pl. v., n. 9.

But, if a coat be impaled with another, either on the dexter or sinister side, and hath a border, the border must finish at the impaled line, and not be continued round the coat. See an example, Pl. XL., n. 14; also Pl. XXXIX., n. 5.

In Blazon, *borders* always give place to the chief, the quarter, and the canton: as, for example, *argent, a border ingrailed gules, a chief azure :* and, therefore, the chief is placed over the border, as the quarter and canton likewise are. In coats charged with a chief, quarter, or canton, the border goes round the field until it touches them, and there finishes; but with respect to all other ordinaries, it passes over them.

	Plate	No.
Border Enaluron	3	9
Border Enurney	3	10
Border Quarterly	3	11
Border Verdoy	3	12
Border Entoyre	3	13
Border Diapered	3	14
Border Bendy	3	15

Boss of a bit, as borne in the arms of the Lorimers' or Bit-makers' Company. Pl. XXIV., n. 23.

BOTEROLL, according to the French heralds, is a tag

of a broadsword scabbard, and is esteemed an honourable bearing. See Pl. xxiv., n. 24.

The crampette, which is the badge of the Right Hon.
Earl *Delawarr*, is supposed by Edmondson to be meant
for the same ornament of the scabbard. See the two
examples, Pl. xxiv., n. 20 and n. 24.

Botonny, or Botoné, a Cross. This term is given
because its extremities resemble the trefoil. Pl. vi., n. 8.

Bottom, a trundle or quill of gold thread. See
Trundle. *Argent three bottoms, in fess gules, the thread
or ;* name, *Hoby*, of Badland. See Pl. xxv., n. 19.

Bourchier Knot is a knot of silk tied as the example,
Pl. xxxii., n. 32. This knot was a cognisance of Archbishop Bourchier, and a representation of it is still preserved in several of the apartments of Knole House, in
Kent, which was formerly the property and residence
of the archbishop.

Bowen's Knot. See Pl. xxxviii., n. 7. *Gules, a
chevron, between three such knots, argent ;* name, *Bowen.*

Bows. See Pl. xxxii., n. 29. *Ermine three bows
bent in pale gules ;* name, *Bowes.*

Brasses are sepulchral engravings on large or small
brass plates let into slabs in the pavement of ancient
churches, portraying the effigies of illustrious persons ;
the greater part of the figures as large as life. The
various colours for the dresses, armours, and coats of
arms, in many instances, were laid on in enamel ; the
attitudes are well drawn ; and the lines of the dresses
are made out with a precision which is truly surprising.
We refer for proof to the abbey church of St. Alban's,
and St. Margaret's church, King's Lynn.

Braced, *fretted* or *interlaced*, signifies figures of the
same sort interlacing one another, as the example

Argent, three chevronels interlaced *in base, gules.* Pl. xxx., n. 30.

BRANCHES, slips and sprigs of shrubs, &c., frequently occur in coat armour. The *slip* should consist of three leaves; the *sprig*, of five; and the *branch*, if fructed, of four — or if unfructed, of nine leaves.

BRASSARTS, or BRASSETS, pieces of armour for the arms.

BREASTPLATE. See CUIRASS.

BRETESSÉ is embattled on both sides equal to each other. See an example, Pl. XL., n. 6.

BRIDGES, as borne in arms, are of various forms, depending chiefly on the number of arches, which should be particularly specified, as in the following example :—*Or, on a bridge of three arches in fess gules, masoned sable, the stream transfluent proper, a fane argent;* name, *Trowbridge,* of Trowbridge. This seems to have been given to the bearer as an allusion to his name, *quasi Throughbridge,* with respect to the current of the stream passing through the arches. Pl. XVI., n. 22.

BRIGANDINE or BRIGANTINE. See HABERGEON.

BRISÉ. See ROMPU.

BRISTLED, the term used in blazonry to express the hair on the neck and back of a boar.

BROAD ARROW, differs from the pheon, by having the inside of its barbs plain, as Pl. XXV., n. 21.

BROAD AXE, as borne in arms, is represented, Pl. XXXII., n. 12. *Gules three broad-axes, argent, a demi fleur-de-lis, joined to each handle within-side, or, between as many mullets pierced of the last;* name, *Tregold.*

BROCHES are instruments used by embroiderers, and are borne in the arms of the Embroiderer's Company. Pl. XXIV., n. 5.

BROGUE, a kind of shoe, borne as depicted Pl. xxxiv., n. 9. *Gules, a chevron between three brogues or ;* name, *Arthure.*

BRONCHANT. See OVER-ALL.

BRUNSWICK, CROWN OF. Pl. xlv., n. 19.

BRUSKE. See TENNE.

BUCKETS are used in heraldry of various forms, but most frequently as Pl. xxiv., n. 7. *Sable, a chevron between three well-buckets, argent ;* name, *Sutton.* They are sometimes borne with feet, as the example, *Argent, a well-bucket sable, bailed and hooped or ;* name, *Pemberton,* Pl. xxxvi., n. 30.

BUCKLER, or SHIELD.

BUCKLES. The buckle of a military belt or girdle, is a bearing both ancient and honourable. See Pl. xxviii., n. 9. The shape of buckles, as borne in a coat, must be described, whether *oval, round, square,* or *lozengy,* as they are various.

BUFFALO, a species of wild bull. Pl. xxxiii., n. 14.

BUGLE-HORN, or HUNTING HORN, is a frequent bearing in heraldry. When the *mouth* and *strings* of this instrument are of different tinctures from the horn, then in blazon they must be named ; and when it is adorned with rings, then it is termed *garnished.* Pl. xxvii., n. 23.

BULL (the) is common in coat armour. *Ermine, a bull passant gules ;* name, *Bevile.*

BULL'S HEAD, caboshed. Pl. xxxi., n. 27.

BUR, was a broad ring of iron, behind the hand, on the spears anciently used at tiltings.

BURGONET, a steel cap, formerly worn by foot soldiers in battle. Pl. xxv., n. 3.

BUBLING-IRON, an instrument used by weavers, and

borne in the arms of the Weavers' Company of Exeter,
Pl. xxv., n. 5.

BUST, affronté, signifies the head, neck, and part of
the shoulders, and the full face. See Pl. xl., n. 24 ;
also a *bust, in profile*, Pl. xl., n. 25.

BUSTARD, a kind of wild turkey, rarely met with in
England, and in heraldry depicted as Pl. xxxiii., n. 13.

CABOSHED, or CABOSED (Spanish), is when the head
of a beast is cut close off behind the ears, and full-
faced, having no neck left to it. Pl. ix., n. 18.

CADENCY, distinction of houses.

CALTRAP. See GALTRAP.

CALVARY, a CROSS, represents the cross on which
our Saviour suffered on Mount Calvary, and is always
set upon three steps, termed grieces. According to
Morgan, the three steps signify the three qualities
whereby we mount up to Christ, *Faith, Hope,* and
Charity. See Pl. xxxvi., n. 19. *Gules, a cross on three
grieces or ;* name, *Jones,* of Denbighshire.

CAMEL, the well-known animal so called. *Azure, a
camel argent ;* name, *Camel.* Pl. xxxi., n. 23.

CAMELOPARDALIS, CAMELOPARD, or GIRAFFE. See
Pl. xxv., n. 2.

CANDLESTICK. This example is blazoned in the arms
of the Founders' Company. *A taper candlestick.* See
Pl. xxxvii., n. 10.

CANNETS, a term for ducks, when they are represented
without beak or feet. See Pl. viii., n. 5. *Argent, a chevron
gules, between three cannets sable ;* name, *Dubuisson.*

CANTON, so called, because it occupies but a corner
of the field, is either dexter or sinister, and is the third
of the chief. Pl. viii., n. 24. *Argent, a canton sable ;*
name, *Sutton.*

CANTONNED, signifies a cross between four figures.

CAP or BONNET. See Pl. XXXVI., n. 11. *Argent, three such caps sable, banded or;* name, *Capper*, of Chester.

CAP OF MAINTENANCE or DIGNITY, is made of crimson velvet lined and turned up with ermine, worn by nobility: such a cap was sent by Pope Julius the Second, with a sword, to King Henry the Eighth; and Pope Leo the Tenth gave him the title *Defender of the Faith*, for his writing a book against Martin Luther. Pl. XLIII., n. 13.

CAPARISONED, the term used to describe a war-horse completely furnished for the field.

CARBUNCLE. See ESCARBUNCLE.

CARDINAL'S HAT. Pope Innocent IV. ordained, that Cardinals should wear red hats, whereby he would signify that those that entered into that order ought to expose themselves, even to the shedding of their blood and hazard of their lives, in defence of ecclesiastical liberty. *Argent, a cardinal's hat, with strings pendent and plaited in knots, the ends meeting in base, gules;* these are the arms of *Sclavonia.* Pl. XXVII., n. 11.

CASQUE. See HELMET.

CASTLE. *Or, a castle triple-towered gules, the port displayed of the first, leaved argent.* Pl. XXXIX., n. 19.

Whatever tincture the castle is of, if the cement of the building is of another colour from the stones, then the building, being argent, is said to be *masoned* of such a colour, as *sable*, &c. When the windows and ports of castles are of a different tincture from the field and building, the windows and ports are supposed to be shut, and must be so expressed in the blazon; if the windows and ports are of the tincture of the field, so that the field is seen through them, then they are supposed to be open ; if the port is in form of a portcullis, it is to be named in the blazon. *Note.*—The difference between a tower and a castle is this : the tower stands without walls to its sides, but a castle extends from side to side, as the example. See a tower, Pl. xxxix., n. 20, which points the difference.

CAT. This domestic animal is used as a crest and supporter, but rarely as a bearing in arms.

CAT-A-MOUNTAIN, a wild cat. Pl. xxvi., n. 16. These cats being always painted *gardant*, the word *gardant* need not be used in the blazon.

CATERFOIL. See QUATREFOIL.

CATHERINE-WHEEL, so called from St. Catherine the Virgin (who suffered martyrdom in Alexandria under the Emperor Maximinus), who had her limbs broken in pieces by its iron teeth. Pl. vii., n. 17. *Azure, a Cathe-rine-wheel argent ;* name, *Wegirton.*

CENTAUR. See SAGITTARIUS.

CERCELÉE, or RECERCELÉE, (a CROSS,) signifies one circling, or curling at the ends, like a ram's horn. Pl. xxxvi., n. 4.

CHAINS are borne frequently and in various forms, especially as appendant to dogs and other animals. They are often, too, borne independent of any other charge : see, for instance, a *circle of chains,* Pl. xxx., n. 22. Or, as in the arms of Navarre, formerly quartered by the kings of France, " Na Varra," signifying a chain. Pl. xxix., Fig. 12.

CHAIN-SHOT. Some have taken this to be the head of a club called holy-water sprinkler, others to be balls of wildfire, generally supposed to be chain-shot, which is two bullets with a chain between them; their use is, at sea, to shoot down yards, masts, or rigging of ships. *Azure, three chain-shots or ;* this coat was borne by the *Earl of Cumberland,* next to his paternal coat. Pl. xli., n. 8.

CHAMBER-PIECE, a term for a short piece of ordnance, without a carriage. Pl. xxiv., n. 6.

CHAPEAU. See CAP OF MAINTENANCE.

CHAPERON, or CHAPERONE (French), a hood, and by metonymy applied to the little shields containing armorial bearings, placed on the heads of horses drawing hearses at pompous funerals.

CHAPLET, a garland, or head-band of leaves and flowers. Pl. v., n. 8. A chaplet of roses, in heraldry, is always composed of four roses only, all the other parts being leaves. *Argent, three chaplets vert;* name, *Richardson,* of Shropshire.

CHAPOURNET, a corruption of the French word, *cha-peronet,* which signifies a little hood.

CHARGES are all manner of figures or bearings what-soever, borne in the field of a coat of arms, which are by custom become peculiarly proper to the science.

CHARGED. Any ordinary or figure, bearing any other device upon it, is said to be charged therewith; *azure, a saltire argent, charged with another gules.* Pl. xli., n. 4.

CHARLEMAGNE'S CROWN. This crown, which is divided into eight parts, is made of gold, weighing fourteen pounds, and is still preserved at Nuremberg. Pl. xlv., n. 5. The fore part of the crown is decorated with twelve jewels, all unpolished. On the second quarter, on the right hand, is our Saviour sitting between two cherubs, each with four wings, whereof two point up·

ward, and two downward; and under, this motto, *Per me Reges regnant.* The third part on the same side has only gems and pearls. On the fourth part is King Hezekiah sitting, holding his head with his right hand; and by his side Isaiah the prophet, with a scroll, whereon is this motto, *Ecce adjiciam super dies tuos* 15 *annos:* also over the heads of these figures, *Isaias Propheta, Ezechias Rex.* The fifth part, which is behind, contains jewels semée. The sixth part has the effigy of a king crowned, and a scroll in his hand, with these words, *Honor Regis judicium diligit:* and over his head, *Rex David.* The seventh part is only of gems; but the eighth has a king sitting, with his crown upon his head, and on a scroll which he holds in both hands is this motto, *Time Dominum, & Regem amato:* as likewise over his head, *Rex Solomon.*

On the top of this crown is a cross, the fore part of which contains seventeen jewels, and in the top of the cross are these words, IHS *Nazarenus Rex Judæorum;* as also in the arch or semicircle, these, *CHVONRADUS, DEI GRATIA ROMANORUM IMPERATOR AUG.*, which shows that the semicircle was added after Charlemagne's time, by the Emperor Conrad.

CHECKY, or CHEQUÉ, is a term used when the field, or any charge, is composed of small squares of different tinctures alternately, as Pl. v., n. 22.

CHERUB'S HEAD is a child's head between two wings displayed. See Pl. xxxiii., n. 2.

CHESS ROOK, a figure used in the game of chess. Pl. vii., n. 9, *ermine, three chess-rooks, gules;* name, *Smert.* See another shape, Pl. xxxiii., n. 3.

CHEVAL-TRAP. See GAL-TRAP.

CHEVRON is an ordinary representing the two rafters

of a house, joined together in chief, and, descending in the form of a pair of compasses to the extremities of the shield, contains the fifth of the field. *Gules, a chevron argent;* name, *Fulford.* Pl. IV., n. 17. Also Pl. XXXIX., n. 7 ; name, *Twemlow.*

PER CHEVRON is when the field or charge is divided by such a line as helps to make the chevron, *party per chevron, argent and vert,* Pl. III., n. 4.

CHEVRONEL is a diminutive of, and in size half, the chevron. Pl. IV., n. 18. When there are more than one chevron on a coat, and placed at equal distances from each other, they should be called chevronels : but if they are placed in *pairs,* they are called *couple-closes. Ermine, two chevronels azure;* name, *Bagot.*

CHEVRONNY is the parting of a shield into several equal partitions chevronwise. See Pl. XLI., n. 10.

CHEVRONS BRACED. See BRACED.

CHEVRONS COUCHED signifies lying sidewise. Pl. XXXVIII., n. 16.

CHEVRONS CONTREPOINT signifies standing one upon the head of another. Pl. XXXVIII., n. 17.

CHIEF is an ordinary formed by a horizontal line, and occupies the upper part of the shield, containing in depth the third of the field : it is so termed because it has place in the chief or principal part of the shield. Pl. IV., n. 1.

IN CHIEF is a thing born in the chief part or top of the escutcheon. See Pl. XI., n. 2, viz., *argent, a fess, in chief three lozenges sable* ; name, *Ashton.*

CHIMÆRA, a fabulous monster, feigned to have the head of a lion breathing flames, the body of a goat, and the tail of a dragon; because the mountain Chimæra, in Lycia, had a volcano on its top, and nourished lions; the middle part afforded pasture for goats, and the bottom was infested with serpents. Pl. XXIX., n. 9.

CHIMERICAL. A term applied to such figures as have no other existence but in the imagination. See Pl. XL., n. 20, T. 7, n. 22. n. 23, n. 24.

CHURCH-BELLS. See BELLS.

CIMIER, the French word for *crest.*

CINQUEFOIL. The Five-leaved Grass, so called, which is a common bearing, usually drawn or engraved with the leaves issuing from a kind of ball as a centre point. Pl. VI., n. 24. *Or, a cinquefoil sable*; name, *Brailford*, of Derby

CIRCLE of CHAINS, Pl. XXX., n. 22.

——— of GOLD, Pl. XXXVIII., n. 9.

CIRCULAR WREATH. See Pl. XXXVIII., n. 6.

CIVIC CROWN was a garland composed of oak-leaves and acorns, and given by the Romans as a reward to any soldier that saved the life of a Roman citizen in an engagement. This was reckoned more honourable than any other crown, though composed of better materials. Plutarch says the reason why the branches of the oak should be made choice of before all others is, that the oaken wreath being sacred to Jupiter, the great guardian of the city, they might think it the most proper ornament for him who preserved a citizen. The most remarkable person upon record for obtaining these rewards, was one C. Siccius (or Sicinius) Dentatus : who had received in the time of his military service eight crowns of gold ; fourteen *civic crowns*, three *mural*, eighty-three golden *torques* or collars, sixty golden *armillæ* or bracelets, eighteen *hastæ puræ*, or fine spears of wood, and seventy-five *phaleræ*, or suits of rich trappings for a horse.

CLAM, a Scotch term for an escalop or cockle-shell.

CLARION, or CLARICORD. See REST.

CLECHÉ, or CLECHÉE, a French term, applied to any ordinary which is so completely perforated, that its edges only are visible.

CLECHÉ, A CROSS (voided and pometté), is one which spreads from the centre towards the extremities, then ends in an angle in the middle of the extremity, by lines drawn from the two points that make the breadth till they join. Pl. xxxvii., n. 17.

CLEG GOOSE. See BARNACLE.

CLINCHED signifies the hand to be shut, as Pl. xl., n. 17.

CLOCKS, when used in arms, are drawn as table-clocks. In that in the arms of the Clockmakers' Company, the feet are four lions couchant, and it is ensigned with a regal crown.

CLOSE, when the wings of a bird are down, and close to the body. Pl. ix., n. 19. The term is used for horse barnacles when they are not extended: also to denote a helmet with the visor down, as Pl. xlii., n. 4.

CLOSE-GIRT, is said of figures habited, whose clothes are tied about the middle.

CLOSET is a diminutive of the bar, being the same figure to one half of its breadth. Pl. iv., n. 15.

CLOSING TONGS, a tool used by the founders, and made part of their crest. Pl. xxiv., n. 9.

CLOUDS frequently occur in arms, with devices issuing therefrom, and surrounding charges.

CLYMANT, a term sometimes used to describe a goat when reared on its hind legs: see SALIENT.

CO-AMBULANT, passant or walking together.

COBWEB and SPIDER, *a cobweb, in the centre a spider.*
Pl. xxxix., n. 10   This is the arms of *Cobster.*

COCK. In heraldry, the cock is always understood
to be the dunghill cock, unless otherwise expressed,
and is represented as Pl. xxxi., n. 14. *Azure, three
cocks, argent, armed, crested, and jelloped, proper ;* name,
Cokaine.

COCKATRICE, an imaginary monster, which in his
wings and legs partakes of the fowl, and in his tail of
the snake, Pl. vii., n. 23. *Sable, a cockatrice or, combed
gules ;* name, *Bothe.*

COCKATRICE DISPLAYED, Pl. xxxviii., n. 26. *Sable, a
cockatrice displayed argent, crested, membered, and jelloped,
gules ;* name, *Buggine.*

COCKE, a term used by Leigh for a chess-rook.

COGNIZANCE. This term is frequently but very in-
accurately used to signify the crest. Crests were only
worn by such as had superior military command, in
order that they might be the better distinguished in an
engagement, and thereby rally their men, if dispersed ;
whereas *Cognizances* were badges which subordinate
officers, and even soldiers, bore on their clothes or
arms for distinction-sake ; see BADGES.

COLLARED signifies any animal having a collar about
his neck.

COLOURS, and metals, when engraved, are known by
dots and lines : as OR, the metal gold, is known in
engraving by small dots or points ; ARGENT, a metal
which is white, and signifies silver, is always left
plain ; GULES, is expressed by lines perpendicular from
top to bottom ; AZURE, by horizontal lines from side to
side ; SABLE, by horizontal and perpendicular lines
crossing each other ; VERT, by hatched lines from right

to left diagonally ; PURPURE, by hatched lines from the sinister chief to the dexter base, diagonally. The metals or and argent are allowed precedency to colours. Pl. II.

Some of those fantastic writers of the 15th and 16th centuries, who have thrown such discredit upon the science they intended to support, promulgated the absurd opinion that colours, especially when compounded, were originally intended to signify certain virtues in the bearer, viz., *gules* with *or* signifies desire to conquer, with *argent* revenge, with *vert* courage in youth, &c.

Some, also, that Gentlemen, Esquires, Knights, and Baronets' arms should be blazoned by *metals* and *colours ;* Barons, Viscounts, Earls, Marquises, and Dukes, by *precious stones ;* Sovereign Princes, Kings, and Emperors, by *planets.* Premising that such ideas are purely visionary, and the practice of such rules mere affectation, we subjoin a table illustrating the subject —

COLOURS'	Which are termed in Heraldry,	NAMES.	STONES.	PLANETS.	VIRTUES.
Yellow,		Or,	Topaz,	Sol,	Constancy.
White,		Argent,	Pearl,	Luna,	Innocence.
Red,		Gules,	Ruby,	Mars,	Magnanimity.
Blue,		Azure,	Sapphire,	Jupiter,	Loyalty.
Green,		Vert,	Emerald,	Venus,	Love loyal.
Purple,		Purpure,	Amethyst,	Mercury,	Temperance.
Black,		Sable,	Diamond,	Saturn,	Prudence.
Orange,		Tenne,	Hyacinth,	Drn. Head,	
Murrey,		Sanguine,	Sardonyx,	Drn. Tail,	

These distinctions, however, were nowhere used but in England, being justly held in ridicule in all other countries, as a fantastic humour of our nation.

COLUMBINE. This flower is borne in the arms of the

company of Cooks. Pl. xxv., n. 4. *Argent, a chevron
sable, between three columbines, proper;* name, *Hall,* of
Coventry.

COMBATANT, that is to say, fighting, face to face.
T. 9, n. 5. *Or, lions rampant combatant, gules, langued
and armed azure;* name, *Wycombe.*

COMET, or BLAZING STAR, in heraldry, is *a star of six
points with a tail streaming from it in bend,* as the example, Pl. xviii., n. 7; according to Guillim, is not of
an orbicular shape, as other celestial bodies are, but
rather dilates in the centre like a hairy bush, and
grows thence taperwise, in the manner of a fox's tail.
Comets were supposed to prognosticate events to come.
They appear to be borne in coat-armour, of which the
aforesaid author gives us an instance; thus, *Azure, a
comet, streaming in bend, or;* name, *Cartwright.*

COMPARTMENTS. See PARTITIONS.

COMPLEMENT. A term used to signify the moon at
her full; the technical mode of blazonry being, "the
moon in her complement."

COMPONY, is when a border, pale, bend, or other
ordinary, is made up of small squares, consisting of
two metals, or colours, in one row alternately. See
Pl. v., n. 14.

COMPONY and COUNTER-COMPONY, or COUNTER-COM-
PONY only, the same when in *two* rows.

CONEY, a rabbit.

CONFRONTÉ, facing or fronting one another; a term
used by the French heralds as synonymous with *combatant.*

CONGER-EEL'S HEAD, couped, borne on a pale; name,
Gascoigne. Pl. xxxvii., n. 15.

CONJOINED, or CONJUNCT, signifies charges in arms

when joined together; viz., *gules, two lions rampant, conjoined under one head, gardant, argent;* name, *Kellum.* See Pl. xxxii., n. 22. *Seven mascles conjunct, three, three and one*   Pl. xxxiv., n. 32.

CONJOINED IN LURE is two wings joined together, with their tips downwards; as the example, Pl. x., n. 2.

CONTOURNÉ, a French term applied to animals turned to the sinister side of the shield.   Pl. xxxii., n. 23.

CONTRE signifies counter or opposite.

CONTREPOINT is when two chevrons meet in the fess points, the one rising from the base, the other inverted, falling from the chief, so that they are counter or opposite to one another.   See Pl. xxxviii., n. 17.

CONTRETREVIS, an ancient term for party per fess.

CORSLET.   See CUIRASS.

COOTE, a small water-fowl, of the duck tribe, with a sharp-pointed beak, and its plumage all black, except at the top of the head.   See Pl. xxvi., n. 17.

COPPER.   An instrument used by gold and silver wire-drawers to wind wire upon, and borne by them as part of their armorial ensign.   Pl. xxiv., n. 2.

COPPER CAKE.   See Pl. xxxvi., n. 6.   *Ermine, three copper cakes gules, and on a chief gules, a chamber proper;* name, *Chambers,* of London, Esq.

CORBIE, an heraldic term for a raven.

CORDED, signifies wound about with cords, as the example, Pl. xxxvii., n. 6.

CORMORANT.   A sharp-billed bird, in other respects much resembling a goose.   See Pl. xxxiii., n. 16.

CORNET, a musical instrument.   Pl. xxx., n. 23.

CORNISH CHOUGH is a fine blue or purple black bird, with red beak and legs.   Pl. xxxi., n. 17.

CORNUCOPIA, or Horn of Plenty, filled with fruits,

corn, &c., an emblem generally placed in the hands of the figures of Plenty and Liberality.

CORONET (Ital. *coronetta*, the diminutive of corona, a crown), when not otherwise described, is always understood to be a ducal one. For the coronets worn by the several degrees of nobility in England, &c., see CROWNS and CORONETS; and for Coronets mural, naval, &c., see MURAL, NAVAL, &c.

COST, or COTICE, is one of the diminutives of the bend, seldom borne but in couples with a bend between them. Pl. IV., n. 8.

COTICED, or COTISED, anything that is accosted, sided, or accompanied by another. See Pl. XI., n. 20. *Argent, on a bend gules, coticed sable, three pair of wings conjoined of the first;* name, *Wingfield.*

COTICE. A term used by the French when an escutcheon is divided bendwise into many equal parts. See BENDY.

COTTON-HANK, Pl. XLI., n. 6. *Azure, a chevron between three cotton hanks, argent;* name, *Cotton.*

COUNTERCHANGED is an intermixture of several metals and colours one against another. See an example, Pl. XIII., n. 15. *Quarterly or and azure, a cross of four lozenges between as many annulets, counterchanged;* name, *Peacock.* Likewise see the examples in Pl. XXXVIII., n. 19, 20, and 22.

COUNTER-COMPONÉ, composed of small squares, but never above two rows. Pl. V., n. 14.

COUNTER-EMBOWED, a dexter arm, couped at the shoulder, *counter-embowed.* Pl. XL., n. 19.

COUNTER-IMBATTLED. See the example, Pl. XL., n. 5. *Azure, a fess counter-imbattled, argent;* name, *Garnas, of* Sussex.

COUNTER-PASSANT is when two beasts are passing the contrary way to each other. Pl. IX, n. 8. *Sable, two lions counter - passant argent, collared gules;* name, *Glegg.*

COUNTER-POTENT. See POTENT.

COUNTER-PURFLEW. See PURFLEW.

COUNTER-SALIENT. See SALIENT.

COUNTER-TRIPPING. See TRIPPING.

COUNTER-VAIR, *or* and *azure:* this fur differs from vair, by having its cups or bells of the same tinctures, placed base against base, and point against point, ranged with their heads and points one upon the other, as *or* upon *or*. Pl. II., n. 5.

COUCHANT signifies a beast lying down, but with his head lifted up, which distinguishes the beast so lying from dormant. Pl. VIII., n. 20.

COUPED is when the head or any other limb of an animal, or any charge in an escutcheon that is borne, is cut evenly off. See the examples. Pl. VIII., n. 16. Pl. XXXVI., n. 14. Pl. XVIII., n. 14, n. 19.

☞ When *boar's, bears', wolves', whales',* and *otters' heads,* are couped close to the head, as example, Pl. XXXVIII., n. 2, it is termed *couped close,* to distinguish it from a boar's head couped, as Pl. XXXVIII., n. 3, and Pl. XXXIX., n. 17.

COUPED, or HUMETTÉE, A CROSS, signifies one so cut, or shortened, that the extremities reach not the outlines of the esutcheon. Pl. XXXVI., n. 14.

COUPLE-CLOSE, so termed from its enclosing by couples the chevron, of which it is a diminutive, being its fourth part. Pl. IV, n. 19. Couple-closes are always borne by pairs, one on each side of a chevron. See Plate XI., n. 16. *Sable, a chevron between two couple-*

closes, accompanied with three cinquefoils or ; name, *Renton.*

COURANT, the heraldic term for running. Pl. IX., n. 16.

COWARD, or COWED, is when a lion or other animal has its tail hanging down between its legs. Pl. XXXII., n. 13.

CRAB ; the well-known shell-fish so called, is occasionally borne in arms. *Argent, a chevron, between three sea crabs gules ;* name, *Bridger.*

CRAMPS, or CRAMPOONS, are pieces of iron, hooped at each end, and used in buildings to fasten two stones together. Pl. XXIV., n. 16.

CRAMPET, or CRAMPETTE, is the chape or metal termination at the bottom of the scabbard of a sword, by the French termed Botterolle. *Argent, three botterolles gules*, are the arms of the duchy of *Angria.* Pl. XXIV., n. 20.

CRAMPONNÉE, CROSS, so termed because it has at each end a cramp, or square piece, coming from it. Pl. XXXVI., n. 5.

CRENELLÉE. See IMBATTLED.

CRESCENT, or a half-moon, with its horns turned towards the chief of the shield ; by this position it differs from the increscent and decrescent. See Pl. VII., n. 6. *Azure, a crescent argent ;* name, *Lucy.*

CRESCENTED, A CROSS, that is, having a crescent at each end. Pl. XXXVI., n. 35.

CREST is a figure placed upon a wreath, coronet, or cap of maintenance, above the helmet or shield.* No women, except sovereign princesses, attach to their arms the helmet, mantlings, wreath, crest, or motto See Pl. XXVIII., n. 5.

* See note to p. 64.

CRESTED is when the cock, or other bird, has its comb of a different tincture from its body; it is then termed crested of such a tincture, naming it.

CRINED (Lat. *crinis*, the hair) is a term used in blazonry when speaking of the hair of a man or woman, or the mane of a horse, which, when it differs in tincture from the rest of the charge, is said to be *crined* of such a metal or colour.

CRONEL, the iron head of a tilting spear. Pl. xxxiv., n. 19. *Sable, a chevron, ermine, between three cronels of a tilting spear, argent ;* name, *Wiseman.*

CROSIER. The crook or pastoral staff of bishops and abbots, a common bearing in the arms of dioceses and monasteries. It is called *Baculis Pastoralis*, as given to them in respect of their pastoral charge and superintendence over their flock, as well for feeding them with wholesome doctrine, as for defending them from the incursions of the wolf; wherein they imitate the good and watchful shepherd, to whose crook this crosier bears a resemblance. Pl. xxvii., n. 8.

CROSS, one of the honourable ordinaries, formed by the meeting of two perpendicular with two horizontal lines, near the fess-point, where they make four right angles; the lines are not drawn throughout, but discontinued the breadth of the ordinary, which takes up only the fifth part of the field, when not charged, but if charged, the third. Pl. iv., n. 20.

CROSS-BOW, or ARBALEST. The bow is an instrument to shoot arrows from; they are of two sorts, the long-bow and cross-bow; the first discharges an arrow by the force of him who draws the bow; while the latter owes its extension to the power of a small lever, which is let off by means of a trigger. *Ermine, a cross-*

bow bent in pale gules; name, *Arblaster.* Pl. XXVII., n. 1.

CROSS CROSSLET, that is, crossed at each end. Pl.VI., n. 10.

PER CROSS. This term signifies the field to be divided into four equal parts, and to consist of metals and colours, or furs and colours, without any charge occupying the quarters; but if the quarters be charged, then it is blazoned quarterly. *Party per cross, gules and argent.* Pl. III., n. 5.

CROSS OF JERUSALEM. See JERUSALEM CROSS.

CROSSWISE, or, *in cross*, is when any charges are placed in form of a cross, five being the common number. See Pl. XXXVI., n. 17 and 18.

CROWNS AND CORONETS OF ENGLAND.

The ROYAL CROWN of GREAT BRITAIN is a circle of gold, enriched with pearls and stones, and heightened up with four crosses pattée, and four fleurs-de-lis alternately; from these rise four arch-diadems, adorned with pearls, which close under a mound, ensigned by a cross pattée. Edward IV. was the first sovereign of England that, in his seal, or on his coin, was crowned with an arch-diadem. The crown used at the last coronation was beautified and improved agreeably to the taste of the age. Pl. XLIII., n. 1.

The PRINCE OF WALES'S CORONET is a circle of gold, set round with crosses pattée, and fleurs-de-lis, but has only one arch, decorated with pearls, surmounted by a mound and cross. Pl. XLIII., n. 2. Three ostrich-feathers, *argent*, quilled *or*, enfiled with a prince's coronet of the last, with an escrol, *azure*, thereon the words *Ich dien,* I serve, Pl. 5, n. 24, is the badge or cognisance of every Prince of Wales, and is popularly supposed to have been assumed by Edward the Black Prince, after the battle of Cressy, A.D. 1346, where having, with his own hand, killed John, king of Bohemia, who served the king of France in his wars, and was his stipendiary, he took from his head such a plume and put it on his own, to perpetuate the victory. There is no authority, however, for the statement that he personally slew the brave blind old king, and strong evidence that an ostrich-feather was a family badge borne by Edward III., and all his family.

YOUNGER SONS, or BROTHERS of the BLOOD ROYAL. This coronet has a circle of gold, heightened up with four fleurs-de-lis, crosses pattée and strawberry-leaves alternately. Pl. XLIII., n. 3.

NEPHEWS of the BLOOD ROYAL differ from the younger sons or brothers, by having strawberry-leaves on the rim, as theirs have fleurs-de-lis. Pl. XLIII., n. 3.

PRINCESS ROYAL. Coronets of the Princesses of Great Britain are a circle of gold, and heightened up with crosses pattée, fleurs-de-lis, and strawberry-leaves alternately. Pl. XLIII., n. 5.

DUKE'S CORONET is a circle of gold, with eight strawberry or parsley-leaves, of equal height, above the rim. Pl. XLIII., n. 6.

MARQUIS'S CORONET is a circle of gold, set round with four strawberry-leaves, and as many pearls, on pyramidical points of equal height, alternately. Pl. XLIII., n. 7.

EARL'S CORONET is a circle of gold, heightened up with eight pyramidical points or spikes; on the tops of which are as many pearls, which are placed alternately with as many strawberry-leaves, below on the rim. Pl. XLIII., n. 8.

VISCOUNT'S CORONET is a circle of gold, having six-teen pearls on the rim. Coronets were first assigned to viscounts in the reign of King James I. Pl. XLIII., n. 9.

BARON'S CORONET, on a gold circle, six pearls, Pl. XLIII., n. 10. Coronets were assigned to barons by King Charles II., after his restoration.

The pearls on the English coronets are commonly called pearls, but they are always made of silver.

Originally the barons wore scarlet caps turned up with white: they afterwards wore caps of crimson turned up with ermine, and on the top a tassel of gold. This they used till the reign of Charles II., as before mentioned. All the above coronets have within them, when worn, a cap of crimson velvet with a gold tassel on the top, and a border of ermine, which is seen below the circlet; but the caps are now occasionally omitted in representation, which gives to the coronet a more mediæval character.

In 1665, Charles II. granted his royal warrants to the officers of arms in Scotland and Ireland, for the peers of each of those kingdoms to wear the same fashioned coronets as those of England, according to their several degrees.

The mitres of archbishops and bishops are distinguished by a plain fillet of gold. See Pl. XLIII., n. 12. Excepting that of the Palatine Bishop of Durham, which has it issuing out of a ducal coronet.

CROWNS FOREIGN, &c. PLATE XLV.

1 Celestial,	5 Charlemagne,	9 Portugal,
2 Eastern,	6 Grand Seignor,	10 Denmark,
3 Imperial,	7 France,	11 Russia,
4 Pope,	8 Spain,	12 Prussia,

CROWNS FOREIGN, &c.　Plate XLV.—*continued.*

13 Poland,	18 Dauphin,	23 Mural,
14 Persia,	19 Brunswick,	24 Civic,
15 Electoral,	20 Doge of Venice,	25 Triumphal,
16 Archduke,	21 Vallery,	26 Obsidional,
17 Duke of Tuscany,	22 Naval,	27 Chaplet,
		28 Wreath.

CROWNS FOREIGN, &c.　Plate XLIV.

1 Bohemia,	9 Waldeck,	17 Guastalla,
2 Sardinia,	10 Mecklenburg,	18 Baden,
3 Sicily,	11 Genoa,	19 Modena,
4 Holland,	12 Lorraine,	20 Holstein,
5 Orange,	13 Guelderland,	21 Hungary,
6 Hanover,	14 Mentz,	22 Sweden,
7 Palatine,	15 Catalonia,	23 Mantua,
8 Cologne,	16 Parma,	24 Valence.

These crowns are copied from the seals of the different countries.

Crowns, Vallery, Mural, &c.　See those terms.

Crusuly is the field or charge, strewed over with crosses.

Crwth, an ancient term for a violin.

Cubit Arm is the hand and arm couped at the elbow. See Pl. XL., n. 17.

Cuirass, or breast-plate of armour.　See Pl. XXVIII., n. 1.

Cuisses are those parts of armour which cover the thighs and knees, and by former heralds were called Culliers.

Cullvers, or Culliers.　See Cuisses.

Cumbent.　See Lodged.

Currier's Shave.　A tool used by curriers to thin leather; it is borne in the arms and crest of the Curriers' Company.　Pl. xxv., n. 18.

Cushions.　This charge is borne by many ancient

families. Pl. xxviii., n. 15. *Gules, three cushions ermine, buttoned and tasselled or ;* name, *Redman.*

CUTTING-IRON. A tool used by the patten-makers, and borne by them in their armorial ensign. Pl. xxxiv., n. 30.

CUTTLE-FISH, or Ink-fish. Pl. xxxiii., n. 22.

CYGNET ROYAL. This term is given to swans when they are collared about the neck with an open crown, and a chain affixed thereto. See Pl. xxxi., n. 15. The most proper blazon is, *a swan argent, ducally gorged and chained or.* When the head of a swan is a charge, it is blazoned, *a swan's neck* (not head) *erased or couped :* but this is not the custom in regard to any other species of bird.

DACRE's KNOT and BADGE. See Pl. xxxii., n. 35.

DANCETTÉ is a larger sort of indenting (being wider and deeper than that called indented), whose points never exceed three in number. Pl. iii. *Note.* See the difference in Pl. xix., n. 12. *Or, a fess dancetté sable.* N. 11, is *azure two bars indented or, a chief argent.*

DANISH AXE or HATCHET. See Pl. xxxii., n. 11, and Pl. xxix., n. 6.

DARNEL, a term for a cockle.

DAUPHIN's CROWN is a circle of gold, set round with eight fleurs-de-lis, closed at the top with four dolphins, whose tails conjoin under a fleur-de-lis. Pl. xlv., n. 18.

DEBRUISED is when a bend or other ordinary is placed over any animal, whereby it is debarred of its natural freedom. See Pl. xxxii., n. 17.

DECOLLATED, having the head cut off.

DECRESCENT shows the state of the moon when she declines from her full to her last quarter, and differs from the increscent by having the horns towards the left side of the shield. Pl. vii., n. 8. *Azure a decrescent proper ;* name, *De la Luna.*

DEFAMED signifies a creature to have lost its tail, as if it were disgraced and made infamous by the loss thereof. Pl. xxxii., n. 14.

DEGRADED. A cross is said to be *degraded* when it has steps at each end. Pl. xxxvi., n. 3. *Argent, a cross degraded sable ;* name, *Wyntworth.*

DEMI signifies the half of a thing, as a demi-lion. See Pl. viii., n. 18. *Or, a demi-lion rampant gules ;* name, *Mallory.*

DEMI-VOL is one wing. Pl. ix., n. 23.

DEMI FLEUR-DE-LIS. Pl. x., n. 8. *A demi-fleur-de-lis gules* is the crest of *Stoddyr.* See another, Pl. xxv., n. 24.

DEMI-ROSE. See Pl. xxxii., n. 29. *Or, on a fess vert, between three battle-axes gules, a fleur-de-lis or, enclosed by two demi-roses argent ;* name, *Jenynges.*

DENMARK, CROWN of, Pl. xlv., n. 10.

DETRIMENT, a term for the moon when eclipsed.

DEVOURING. See VORANT.

DEXTER signifies the right-hand side of the escutcheon ; the supporter, and everything placed on the right hand, is termed the dexter ; it is also the male side in an impaled coat of arms.

DEXTER HAND, the right hand. Pl. xxxv., n. 32. *Azure, a dexter hand couped, argent ;* name, *Brome.*

DEXTER BASE is the right side of the base, represented by the letter G. See Pl. i.

DEXTER CHIEF is the angle on the right-hand side of the chief represented by the letter A. See Pl. i.

DEXTER WING. The right wing.

DIAMOND is a precious stone, which in heraldry signifies the colour sable or black.

DIAPERED is dividing the field in panes like fretwork, and filling the same with a variety of figures, according to the fancy of the painter.   Pl. XXXVIII., n. 14.   Care must be taken that no ornament is used which can possibly be confounded with an heraldic bearing.

DIFFAMÉ.   See DEFAMED.

DIFFERENCE is certain figures added to coats of arms, to distinguish one branch of a family from another, and how distant younger branches are from the elder.   See DISTINCTION OF HOUSES.

DIMINUTIVES.   The *pale's* diminutives are the PALLET and ENDORSE; the *bend* has the GARTER, COST, and RIBBON; the *bar* has the CLOSET, BARRULET, and BAR-GEMEL; the *chevron* has the CHEVRONEL and COUPLE-CLOSE; the *bend sinister* has the SCARPE and BATON; the *bordure* has the ORLE and TRESSURE; the *quarter* has the CANTON; the *flanch* has the FLASQUE and VOIDER. See each in its respective place.

DISMEMBERED signifies a cross, or other thing, cut in pieces, and set up at a small distance, but keeping the form of the figure.   See Pl. XXXVI., n. 9.   See a lion dismembered, Pl. XXXV., n. 14.   *Or, a lion rampant gules, dismembered, within a double tressure, flory, counter-flory of the second;* name, *Maitland.*

DISPLAYED, for the wings of a bird when they are expanded, as in the example, *an eagle displayed.*   Pl. IX., n. 21.

DISTILLATORY, double-armed with two worms and bolt-receivers on fire, being part of the arms of the Distillers' Company.   Pl. XXV., n. 14.

DISTINCTIONS OF HOUSES. These differences serve to inform us from what line the bearer of each is de scended : these distinctions began about the time of Richard the Second (according to Camden Clarencieux). Pl. XLII.

FIRST HOUSE.

Fig. 1, is the label for the first son.

Fig. 2, the crescent for the second son.

Fig. 3, the mullet for the third son.

Fig. 4, the martlet for the fourth son.

Fig. 5, the annulet for the fifth son.

Fig. 6, the fleur-de-lis for the sixth son.

Fig. 7, a rose for the seventh son.

Fig. 8, a cross moline for the eighth son.

Fig. 9, a double quatrefoil for the ninth son.

By these distinctions every brother or house ought to observe his or its due difference.

SECOND HOUSE.

Fig. 1, *the crescent with the label on it* for the first son of the second son.

Fig. 2, *the crescent on the crescent* for the second son of the second son of the first house, and so on. See Pl. XLII.

☞ The distinctions made use of for differencing the several princes and princesses of the blood royal of England are generally labels, variously charged.

DISVELOPED signifies displayed ; as colours flying. or spread out, are in heraldry often said to be dis-veloped. See Pl. v., n. 1. Wyrley, noted in the life and death of the Capitaine de Bur, says, " With threaten ing ax in hand I was at hand ; and my *disvelloped* penon me before."

DOGE OF VENICE, CROWN OF, Pl. XLV., n. 20.

DOGS, of various kinds are common in heraldry. See TALBOT, ALANT, &c. *Or, a fess dancetté between three talbots passant, sable ;* name, *Carrack.*

DOLPHIN is reckoned the king of fishes, and is used in several coats of arms. The ancients invariably represent the dolphin with its back greatly incurvated. In their leaps out of the water they assume this form, but their natural shape is straight, the back being but slightly incurvated. Pl. XXVIII., n. 2. The example in blazon is termed *a dolphin naiant embowed ;* but when a dolphin appears in a coat straight, it is then termed *a dolphin extended naiant ;* when it is placed perpendicular, with its body in the form of a letter S, it is called *springing and hauriant ;* but it is most usually blazoned *a hauriant dolphin torqued. Azure, a dolphin hauriant embowed, argent ;* name, *Fitz-James.*

DORMANT signifies sleeping, with the head resting on the fore-paws. Pl. VIII., n. 19. *Or, three lions dormant in pale, sable ;* name, *Lloyd.*

DOSSER. See WATER-BOUGET.

DOUBLE DANCETTÉ, a bend ; according to Leigh, the bend double dancetté is a mark of bastardy. See Pl. XXIV., n. 13. Carter has this example, viz., *azure, a bend double dancetté, argent ;* name, *Lorks ;* but makes no mention of the mark of bastardy.

DOUBLE-HEADED (A LION). This instance is from Leigh, who says the bearer did homage to two princes (who both bore a lion rampant), for certain lands, by bearing a lion rampant with two heads, signifying the two princes he homaged. A fair example of the stories invented to account for singular charges in ancient coats, the true reason for their assumption being lost sight of. Pl. xxxii., n. 19. *Or, a lion, double-headed, azure*; name, *Sir John Mason.*

DOUBLE - TAILED, a lion rampant, double - tailed. Pl. xxxii., n. 18. *Or, a lion doubled - tailed or queued, azure;* name, *Wandesford.*

DOUBLE-FITCHY, A CROSS, each extremity having two points. Pl. xxxvii., n. 7.

DOUBLE-PARTED, A CROSS. Pl. xxxvi., n. 16. *Azure, a cross double-parted, argent;* name, *Doubler*, of Cheshire.

DOUBLE-PLUME, of ostrich-feathers, is generally composed of *five* at bottom, and *four* at top. Pl. xxxii., n. 9.

DOUBLE ROSE. See Pl. xxxvii., n. 21

DOUBLE TRESSURE, two tressures, one within the other. See Pl. xix., n. 9.

DOUBLE QUATREFOIL. The double quatrefoil is used as a distinction for the ninth brother. Pl. xlii., n. 9.

DOUBLINGS are the linings of robes or mantles of state, or the mantlings in achievements.

DOVE DISPLAYED in the glory of the sun. Pl. xxxix., n. 12. This bearing is a part of the arms of the Stationers' Company.

DOVE-TAIL, one of the partition lines, wherein two different tinctures are set within one another, in the form of doves' tails or wedges. Pl. iii.

DRAGON, an imaginary monster, used in heraldry, both in coats, crests, and supporters. Pl. viii., n. 1. *Gules, three dragons passant, in pale ermine;* name, *Blossun.*

DRAGON'S HEAD, in heraldry is the colour tenne, or orange colour. Obsolete, if ever used.

DRAGON'S TAIL, in heraldry, is the term for sanguine

or murrey, the colour of blood, or mulberry juice, also obsolete.

DRAWING-IRON, an instrument used by wire-drawers, and part of their armorial ensign.　See Pl. xxxvii., n. 25.

DUCAL CORONET.　See CROWNS and CORONETS of England.

DUCIPER, a term for a cap of maintenance.

DUN-FLY.　See GAD-FLY.

EAGLE.　The eagle was the tutelary bird and ensign of the Romans. *Azure, an eagle displayed, argent, armed gules;* name, *Cotton.*

SPREAD EAGLE signifies an eagle with two heads, as the example; but it is more heraldic to say, *an eagle with two heads, displayed.*　Pl. xxxi., n. 31.　According to Porney the reason why the Emperor of Germany bore an eagle with two necks is this: on the union of the kingdom of Romania, now a province of Turkey in Europe, its arms, which were *an eagle displayed sable,* being the same as those of the emperor, were united into one body, leaving it two necks, as they are still borne by the Emperor of Austria; but there is also the double-headed Eagle of the Emperor of all the Russias to account for.

EAGLET : when there are more than one eagle in a coat without some ordinary between them, then in blazon they are termed eaglets, or young eagles.

EARL'S CORONET.　See CROWNS and CORONETS of England.

EASTERN CROWN, so termed from its being like that formerly worn by the Jewish kings; it was made of gold, with rays about it, as the example.　Pl. xlv. n., 2.

ECLIPSED, the term used when the sun or moon is

either partially or wholly obscured, the face and rays being sable.

EEL-SPEAR, an instrument used by fishermen for taking of eels. Pl. xxviii., n. **21.** *Sable, a chevron between three eel-spears, argent ;* name, *Stratele.*

EGUISÉE, A CROSS, is that which has the two angles at the ends cut off so as to terminate in points. Pl. xxxvii., n. 3.

EIGHTFOIL, or double quatrefoil is eight-leaved grass. Sylvanus Morgan gives this as a difference of the ninth branch of a family. See Pl. xlii., n. 9.

ELECTORAL CROWN is a scarlet cap, faced with ermine, diademed with half a circle of gold, set with pearls, supporting a globe, with a cross of gold on the top. Pl. xlv., n. 15.

ELEPHANT. Pl. xxxi., n. 11. *Gules, an elephant passant argent, armed or ;* name, *Elphinstone.*

ELEVATED, as wings elevated, signifies the points of them turned upwards. See Pl. x., n. 1.

EMBATTLED. See IMBATTLED.

EMBOWED, a term for anything bent or crooked like a bow, as the dolphin. Pl. x., n. 6. A sinister arm couped at the shoulder, *embowed.* See Pl. xl., n. 18.

EMBRUED signifies a weapon, &c., that is bloody, viz., *a spear-head, embrued gules.* See IMBRUED.

EMERALD, a stone : it signifies in heraldry the colour vert or green.

EMEW of the heralds, is the bird called by the naturalists *cassowary.*

ENALURON, for a border charged with birds. The blazon would be more plain, and better understood, by naming the number; thus, *on a border azure, eight martlets or.* Pl. xxxiv., n 9.

ENDORSE is the fourth of the pale, seldom borne but when a pale is between two of them. Pl. IV., n. 4.

ENDORSED, two things placed back to back; as two lions, or two keys, *endorsed.* Pl. XL., n. 16.

ENFILED : when the head of a man, or beast, or any other charge, is placed on the blade of a sword, the sword is said to be *enfiled* with a head, &c.

ENGRAILED, a line of partition, by which ordinaries are diversified, composed of semicircles, the teeth or points of which enter the field. Pl. III. Also a bordure. See Pl. v., n. 10.

ENGROSSING-BLOCK, a tool made use of by the wire-drawers. Pl. XXIV., n. 14.

ENHANCED, is when an ordinary is placed above its usual situation, which chiefly happens to the bend and its diminutives, viz., *argent, three bendlets enhanced gules;* name, *Byron.* Pl. XXXV., n. 29.

ENGOULÉE, A CROSS, a term for crosses, saltires, &c., when their extremities enter the mouths of lions, leopards, &c. Pl. XXXVII., n. 23.

EMMANCHÉ. See MANCHÉ.

ENSIGNED, signifies borne on or over, by way of ornament; as in the example, *a man's heart gules, en-signed with a crown or.* See Pl. XIII., n. 2.

ENTÉ signifies grafted or ingrafted. This term is used in blazoning the fourth grand quarter of his late Majesty's arms, viz., *Brunswick and Lunenburgh impaled with Saxony ente-en-pointe,* that is, grafted in point.

ENTOYER, for a bordure charged with dead or arti-ficial things, to the number of eight. Pl. XXXVIII., n. 13. The most approved method is to say, *argent, a border sable charged with eight plates,* mentioning their number.

ENTRAILED, A CROSS. Pl. xxxvII., n. 20. Leigh says, the colour need not be named, for it is always sable. *Or, on a chevron, sable, a fleur-de-lis accompanied by two stags' heads caboshed, between three crosses, entrailed of the second;* name, *Carver.* See Pl. xxxvII., n. 20.

ENURNEY, for a bordure charged with beasts. Pl. xxxvIII., n. 10. The same may be observed here as before to the term entoyer, viz., that the more intelligible blazon is, *argent, a border gules, charged with eight lions passant of the first.*

ENVELOPED. See ENWRAPPED.

ENWRAPPED, viz., a child's head couped below the shoulders, *enwrapped* about the neck with a snake: some say *enveloped.* Pl. xvIII., n. 21.

EPAULIER, a shoulder-plate of armour.

ERADICATED, a term for a tree or plant torn up by the root. See Pl. xIII., n. 22.

ERASED is when the head or limb of any creature is violently torn from the body, so that it appears jagged. Pl. vIII., n. 17. *Argent, a lion's head erased, gules ;* name, *Govis.*

Note. When *boars', bears', wolves', whales',* and *otters' heads* are erased close to the head, as the example, Pl. xxxvIII., n. 4, it is termed *erased close,* to distinguish it from a head erased, as the boar's head, Pl. xxxvIII., n. 5, which exhibits a portion of the neck.

ERECT signifies anything upright or perpendicularly elevated, as Pl. x., n. 1.

ERMINE is black spots on a white field. Pl. II., n. 1.

ERMINE, A CROSS, or four ermine-spots in cross. Pl. vI., n. 13.

ERMINES is white spots on a black field. Pl. II.

ERMINITES is the field white, and the spots black, with one red hair on each side.

ERMINOIS is the field gold, and the spots black. Pl. II., n. 3.

The French say, *d'or semé d'hermines de sable.*

ESCALLOP-SHELL was the pilgrims' ensign in their expeditions and pilgrimages to holy places : they were worn on their hoods and hats, and were of such a distinguishing character that Pope Alexander the Fourth, by a bull, forbade the use of them but to pilgrims who were truly noble. They are of frequent use in armoury. Pl. XXVII., n. 2. *Sable an escallop-shell argent ;* name, *Travers.*

ESCARBUNCLE, a precious stone, resembling a burning coal in its lustre and colour. *The ancient heralds drew it as in the plate, to express those rays which issue from the centre, which is the stone.* Pl. VII., n. 18.

ESCROL. See SCROLL.

ESCUTCHEON (the) represents the original shield, buckler, or target, used in war, on which, under every variety of shape, arms were formerly, and still are blazoned. When shields ceased to be employed, their form was still retained as the field on which coat-armour is depicted ; but that form has varied considerably among different nations, at different periods, and even at the same time. The oldest heraldic escutcheons are termed Norman, on account of the shape generally used by that people. They resemble a Gothic arch reversed ; the form of which became broader in the fourteenth and fifteenth centuries, and has remained so to this day, when it is again the favourite shape. The escutcheons of maids, widows, and such as are born ladies, and are married to private gentlemen, are always in the form of a lozenge or diamond; which is supposed to refer to the spindle, as emblematic of virginity.

ESCUTCHEON OF PRETENCE is that escutcheon in which a man bears the coat of arms of his wife, being an heiress; it is placed in the centre of the man's coat, and thereby shows his pretensions to her lands, by his marriage, accrued to him and the heirs of his body. See Pl. XL., n. 4.

ESCUTCHEON, POINTS OF THE, see *ante*, p. 10, and Table I.

ESPRIT, ST., CROSS OF. This cross is worn by the knights of that order in France. Pl. XXXVI., n. 22.

ESTOILE, or star, differs from the mullet by having six waved points; those of the mullet consisting of five plain points. Pl. VII., n. 2. Guillim says, if the number of points be more than six, the number must be expressed.

EXPANDED, or EXPANSED. See DISPLAYED.

EYED is a term used in speaking of the spots resembling eyes in the peacock's tail.

EYES are borne in armoury : *barry nebulé of six pieces, azure and argent on a chief of the second, three eyes gules ;* name, *De la Hay*, of Ireland.

FACÉ, a term used for FESS.

FALCHION, a kind of broad-sword. Pl. XXV., n. 10. See another, Pl. XXX., n. 17, termed an ancient English falchion.

FALCON, in heraldry, is usually represented with bells tied on his legs ; when decorated with hood, bells, virols (or rings), and leashes, then in blazon he is said to be *hooded, belled, jessed, and leashed,* and the colours thereof must be named. Pl. IX., n. 20. *Sable, a falcon with wings expanded or ;* name, *Peché,* of Sussex.

FAN. See WINNOWING BASKET.

FANG-TOOTH. See Pl. XXIX., n. 5. *Azure, three fang teeth in fess or ;* name, *Bathor.*

FER DE FOURCHETTE, A CROSS; so termed, from its having at each end a forked iron, like that formerly used by soldiers to rest their muskets on. Pl. XXXVII., n. 18,

FER DE MOLINE. See MILL-RIND.

FERMAILE, or FERMEAU, signifies a buckle.

FESS POINT is the centre of the escutcheon. See Pl. I., letter E.

FESS, one of the honourable ordinaries, and contains a third of the field; some authors say it was a belt of honour, given as a reward by kings, &c., for services in the army. Pl. IV., n. 13.

FESS BRETESSED has the same indents as *counter-embattled ;* but the example has both sides equal to each other. Pl. XL., n. 6. *Or a fess bretessed gules ;* name, *Crebott,* of Sussex.

PER FESS is when the field or charge is equally divided by a horizontal line. *Party per fess or and azure ;* name, *Zusto,* of Venice. Pl. III., n. 3.

PER FESS and PALE signifies the field to be divided into three parts by the fess line, and the pale line, from the fess point to the middle bass point. Pl. XXXVIII., n. 30.

FESSE TARGET, an ancient term for an escutcheon of pretence.

FESSELY, an ancient term for *party per fess.*

FESSWAYS, or FESSWISE, implies any charge placed or borne in fess, that is, in a horizontal line across the field, or if a crest, on the wreath.

FETLOCK, or FETTERLOCK a horse fetlock. Pl. XXV., n. 15.

FETTERED. See SPANCELLED.

FIELD is the surface of the escutcheon or shield, which contains the charge or charges, and must be the first thing mentioned in blazoning.

FIGURED, a term sometimes used in blazoning those bearings which are depicted with a human face, as Pl. XIII., n. 25.

FILE. See LABEL.

FILLET is an ordinary, which, according to Guillim, contains the fourth part of a chief.

FIMBRIATED, A CROSS, having a narrow bordure or hem, of another tincture. See Pl. XXXVII., n. 2.

FIRE, FLAMES OF. *Argent, a chevron voided, azure, between three flames of fire proper;* name, *Wells.* Pl. XIII., n. 26.

FIRE-BALL, grenade or bomb, inflamed proper. Pl. XXVII., n. 14.

FIRE-BEACON, a machine formerly used to give notice of the approach of an enemy, and to alarm the country. This is by some ancient heralds termed a rack-pole beacon. See Pl. XXVII., n. 4. Pl. XXXIV., n. 16.

There is another figure also termed by some ancient writers a fire-beacon; but Edmondson thinks it (see the example, Pl. XXXVIII., n. 8,) should be blazoned, *a fire-chest :* such chests made of iron, and filled with fire, anciently used to warm the inside of large halls.

FIRE-BRAND, viz., a fire-brand inflamed proper. Pl. XXXV., n. 27.—Fire-brands in armoury are generally represented *raguly.*

FIRE-BUCKET, Pl. XXX., n. 20. *Argent three fire-buckets sable ;* name, *Taine.*

FIRME, a term for a cross pattée throughout. See Pl. XXXIX., n. 9.

FISH-HOOK, Pl. xxx., n. 15.   *Sable, a chevron, be tween three fish-hooks argent ;* name, *Medville.*

FISH-WHEEL, Pl. xxxii., n. 30.   *Or, between a chevron, three fish-wheels sable ;* name, *Foleborne.*

FITCHY, FITCHÉE, or FITCHED, a term used for crosses, when the lower branch ends in a sharp point (French *fichée,* fixed); supposed to have been first so sharpened to enable the primitive Christians to fix the cross in the ground for devotion; viz., *a cross-crosslet fitchy,* as Pl. vi., n. 11.

FITCHY (DOUBLE), is a cross, each extremity of which has two points.   Pl. xxxvii., n. 7.

FLANCHES.   The flanch is composed of an arched line, drawn from the upper angle of the escutcheon to the base point of one side, and so on to the other, the arches almost meeting in the middle of the field. Flanches are never borne single, but in couples, and always in the flanks of the shield.   Pl. v., n. 2.   *Ermine, a star of eight rays or, between two flanches sable ;* name, *Sir John Hobart,* of Norfolk.

FLANK is that part of an escutcheon which is between the chief and the base.

FLASQUES are like the flanch, but smaller, and not so circular.   Pl. xxxv., n. 6.   Gibbon affirms that the flasque and the flanch are one and the same.

FLAX-BREAKER.   See HEMP BREAK.

FLEAM, an instrument used by farriers in bleeding horses : some ancient heralds represent them as Pl. xxiv., n. 16.   Others term them crampoons, or cramps of iron, for fixing blocks of stone together.

FLEAM, an ancient lancet, formerly borne in the arms of the Company of Barber-Surgeons.   Pl. xxxiii., n. 7.

FLEECE, the woolly skin of a sheep suspended from the middle, by a ring in a collar or band. See GOLDEN FLEECE.

FLESH-POT, a three-legged iron pot. See Pl. XXVII., n. 15. *Argent, three flesh-pots gules, with two handles;* name, *Mounbowchier.*

FLEXED, or FLECTED, signifies bowed or bent, as the example, Pl. XIII., n. 21, viz.: *three dexter arms conjoined at the shoulders, and flexed in triangle or, with the fists clenched proper;* name, *Tremaine.*

FLEUR-DE-LIS : by some this emblem is supposed to represent the lily, or flower of the iris or flag; but it has only three leaves, by which it certainly differs from the lily of the garden, that having always five : others suppose it to be the top of a sceptre; some the head of the French battle-axe; others, the iron head of a javelin used by the ancient French. Dr. Orwade says, many deceased antiquaries, as well as some of the present day, have thought, and do think, that it was originally meant to represent the flower from which it derives its name.* Pl. XXVII., n. 19. *Azure, a fleur-de-lis argent;* name, *Digby.*

FLEURY, A CROSS. This cross is differenced from the cross-flory, by its having a line between the ends of the cross and the flowers, which that has not. Pl. XXXVI., n. 32.

FLOAT, an instrument used by the bowyers, and borne as part of their armorial ensign. Pl. XXIV., n. 10.

FLOOK, an Irish term for a large *flounder.*

FLORY signifies flowered with the French lily.

* It appears first heraldically on the seals and coins of Louis VII. of France, and was most probably a rebus signifying "Fleur de Louis."—ED,

FLORY, A CROSS, is one the extremities of which end in fleurs-de-lis: it differs from the patonce, by having the flowers at the ends circumflex, and turning down. Pl. VI., n. 3. *Azure, a cross-flory argent ;* name, *Florence.*

FLOTANT, to express anything flying in the air, as a banner-flotant.

FLYING FISH. This fish, if we except its head and flat back, has, in the form of its body, a great resemblance to the herring. The scales are large and silvery; the pectoral fins are very long; and the dorsal fin is small, and placed near the tail, which is forked. Pl. XXXIII., n. 8.

FORCENÉ signifies a horse rearing or standing on his hinder legs. Pl. XXVI., n. 4.

FORMÉE. See P ATTÉE.

FOREIGN CROWNS. See CROWNS, FOREIGN.

FOUNTAIN: we find fountains borne by *Stourton* of Stourton, being *a bend between six fountains,* in signification of six springs, whereof the river Stoure, in Wiltshire, hath its beginning, and passeth along to Stourton, the head of that barony. The fountain in ancient heraldry was always drawn as a roundle, barry wavy of six, argent and azure.

FOURCHÉE, A CROSS, signifies forked at the ends, or divided. Pl. XXVII., n. 8. *Per pale, or and vert, a cross fourchée gules;* name, *Sir John Hingham.*

FOX. Pl. XXVI., n. 15.

FRACTED, broken asunder; as, a globe *fracted.*

FRAISIER, in French, signifies a strawberry-plant. This word is used by the heralds of Scotland in blazoning the coat of *Fraser,* in allusion to the family name. It is by other heralds termed a *cinque-foil.*

FRENCH CROWN is a circle, decorated with stones,

and heightened up with eight arched diadems, arising from as many fleurs-de-lis, that conjoin at the top under a fleur-de-lis, all of gold. Pl. XLV., n. 7.

FRET, a figure resembling two sticks lying saltire-wise, and interlaced· within a mascle, by some termed Harington's Knot (being also the coat of Harington; *argent a fret sable*), and by others the Herald's True Lover's Knot. Pl. v., n. 6. *Sable a fret or ;* name, *Maltravers.*

FRETTED, A CROSS, fretted and pointed in form of five mascles. Pl. XXXVI., n. 13.

FRETTED IN TRIANGLE. Pl. XXXI., n. 28. *Azure, three trouts, fretted in triangle, heads or, tails argent;* name, *Trowtebeck.*

FRETTY. See the example, Pl. v., n. 24.

FRUCTED, a term given in blazon to all trees bearing fruit.

FURCHY, or FOURCHÉE, signifies forked.

FURNISHED, a term applied to a horse when bridled, saddled, and completely caparisoned.

FURS are used as the artificial trimming or furring of robes and garments of the nobility, and likewise as an ornament in coat-armour. See further of FURS, *ante,* p. 12.

FUSIL, derived from the French word *fusée,* a spindle; it is longer and more acute than the lozenge. Pl. VI., n. 18. *Ermine, three fusils in fesse sable;* name, *Pigot.*

FUSIL, or a spindle of yarn. Pl. XXXIV., n. 14.

FUSILLY is when the field or charge is filled with fusils. Pl. XXXVIII., n. 28. *Fusilly argent and gules* is the arms of *Grimaldi de Monaco,* in Genoa.

GADS are plates of steel and borne as part of the arms of the Ironmongers' Company. Pl. XXIV., n. 11.

GAD-BEE, or GAD-FLY : this fly is by some called the *dun-fly,* by others the *horse-fly,* and is that which in summer so much torments cattle. *Sable, three gad-bees volant, argent ;* name, *Burninghill.* Pl. XXVI., n. 23.

GALLEY. See LYMPHAD.

GAL-TRAPS, or CALTRAPS, by some supposed to be a corruption of *cheval-*trap, and by others thought to have been named *gal* or *gall-*traps, from their application to the purpose of galling horses, are implements used in war, to prevent or retard the advance of cavalry. They are made of iron, with four points, so formed that, whichever way they are placed, one point will always be erect. These implements being strewed on the ground over which the enemy's cavalry has to pass, have been found effectually to retard, if not prevent, any pursuit of a retreating army. They are frequently met with in the armorial ensigns of cavalry officers, as in those of Farrington, bart., whose ancestor was general of artillery. Pl. VII., n. 3. *Argent, three gal-traps, sable ;* name, *Trapps.*

GAMB, so termed when the whole fore-leg of a lion, or other beast, is borne in arms. See Pl. XIII., n. 1. If it is couped or erased near the middle joint, then it is called a paw. See Pl. XIV., n. 22.

GARB, a sheaf of wheat or any other grain : if the blazon is "a garb" only, wheat is always understood ; in other cases the kind of grain must be expressed, as "a garb of oats," &c. Pl. VII., n. 14.

GARDANT, signifies full-faced, looking right forward. Pl. IX., n. 1.*

---

* It is now too late to attempt the correction of the terms *gardant* and *regardant.* It is quite clear that the former is only an abbreviation of the latter, a lion regarding, or locking at you.

GARLAND. See CHAPLET.

GARNISHED signifies ornamented, and is a term applied to ornaments set on any charge whatsoever.

GARTER, the half of a bendlet. Pl. IV., n. 7.

GAUNTLET, a glove plated with steel, that covered the hand of a cavalier, when armed *cap-à-pie*, at first without separation of the fingers, in which early form it is seen in charges. Pl. XXXIV., n. 21, and Pl. XXIX., n. 24. In blazon, the word *dexter* or *sinister* must be expressed, as the charge may happen to be.

AT GAZE, when a beast of chase, as the hart, is depicted as affrontée, or full-faced. Pl. IX., n. 13.

GED, a Scotch term for the fish called a pike. *Azure, three geds hauriant argent ;* name, *Ged.*

GEMELLS, and GEMEWS. See BAR-GEMELS.

GEM-RING, a ring set with a gem or precious stone.

GENET, a small animal of the fox species, but not bigger than a weasel, occasionally met with in heraldry.

GENOUILIER, a piece of armour that covers the knees.

GERATTIE, an ancient term for powderings.

GILLY-FLOWER, properly July flower, is a species of aromatic carnation. Pl. XXIV., n. 12. *Argent, three gilly-flowers, slipped proper ;* name, *Jorney.*

GIMBAL-RINGS. Pl. XXX., n. 8. *Argent, on a bend sable, three triple gimbal-rings or ;* name, *Hawberke*, of Leicestershire. Sylvanus Morgan says, it would be more heraldic to say, *three annulets interlaced in triangle.*

GIMMAL, or GEMMOW RING, is a ring of double hoops

Regardant is now only applied to a lion looking behind him; an attitude which would be more correctly described by *Retrogardant*, as we, indeed, find the Latin for it, *Retrospiciens.*

made to play into each other, and so to join two hands, and thus serves for a wedding-ring, which pairs the parties. The name is derived from *Gemellus*, Latin; *Jumeau*, French.

GIRAFFE. See CAMELOPARDALIS.

GIRON. See GYRON.

GLAIVE, or GLEAVE. See JAVELIN.

GLAZIERS' NIPPERS, or grater, a tool used by glaziers, and part of the arms of the Glaziers' Company. Pl. xxxiii., n. 4.

GLIDING; this term is used for serpents, snakes, or adders, when moving forward fesswise.

GOBONY, or GOBONATED, is the same as *compony*, viz., it is always of one row of squares and no more. Pl. v., n. 13.

GOLDEN FLEECE is the skin of a sheep, with its head and feet, hung up at its middle by a ring in a collar, all gold, as the example, Pl. xxvi., n. 8 : it is worn by the knights of that order in Spain, instituted by Philip, Duke of Burgundy.

GOLPS are roundles of the purple tincture. Pl. viii., n. 15.

GONFANNON, the banner, standard, or ensign of the Roman Catholic Church, anciently always carried in the Popes' armies. The gonfannon is borne as an armorial figure, or common charge, by families abroad, on account of some of the family having been gonfannoniers, *i. e.*, standard-bearers to the church, as the *Counts of Auvergne*, in France. *Or, a gonfannon gules, fringed vert.* Pl. xxxiv., n. 28.

GORGE, a term in Leigh for a water-bouget.

GORGED, a term used to describe a lion or other animal having a crown by way of collar to its neck.

GORGET, a piece of armour for the neck.

GRADIENT, a term applied to a tortoise walking.

GRAIN-TREE. Pl. XXXIII., n. 20. Three sprigs of this tree is the crest of the Dyers' Company.

GRAND SEIGNIOR'S CROWN is a turban, enriched with pearls and diamonds. Pl. XLV., n. 6.

GRAPPLING-IRON. Pl. XXXII., n. 28. *Azure, a chevron or, between three grappling-irons of three flukes, double-ringed at the top ;* name, *Stewins.*

GRASSHOPPER. Amongst the Athenians grasshoppers were so much esteemed, that they wore gold ones in their hair, to denote their national antiquity, or that, like the Cicadæ, they were the first-born of the earth. Among the Egyptians, the hieroglyphic of music. Pl. XXVII., n. 5.

GRAY, a term for a badger. See BADGER.

GREAVE, that part of armour that covers the leg from the knee to the foot.

GREY-HOUND. See Pl. XXIX., n. 20.

GRICES, young wild boars; sometimes boars are bla-zoned *Grices,* in allusion to the bearer's name, *Grice.*

GRIDIRON. Pl. XXXV., n. 19. *Argent, a chevron be-tween three gridirons, sable ;* names, *Laurence* and *Scott.*

GRIECES signifies steps, viz., a cross on three grieces. See Pl. XXXVI., n. 19.

GRIFFIN, an imaginary animal, compounded of the eagle and the lion. As a charge, it is common on ancient arms. Guillim blazons it *rampant,* alleging that any fierce animal may be so blazoned as well as the lion; but *segreant* is the term generally used instead of rampant. Pl. XXXV., n. 13. *Argent, a griffin segreant azure, beaked or ;* name, *Culcheth.*

GRIFFIN, MALE: this chimerical creature is half an

eagle and half a lion, having large ears, but no wings, and rays of gold issuing from various parts of its body. Pl. xxxv., n. 2.

GRINGOLLÉE, A CROSS, a term for crosses, saltiers, &c., whose extremities end with the heads of serpents. Pl. xxxvii., n. 12.

GRITTIE, a term for a shield composed equally of metal and colour.

GOIDON, or GUIDHOMME. A small standard sometimes called an ANCIENT.

GULES signifies the colour red, and in engraving is represented by perpendicular lines. Pl. ii. Ghul, in the Persian language, signifies a rose, or rose-colour, and the heraldic term is supposed to have been imported from the East.

GUN-STONE, an ancient term for a pellet.

GURGES, or a whirlpool. This is the arms of the family named *Gorges.* See Pl. xxv., n. 6. The whirlpool is always borne proper, therefore there is no occasion for naming the field, because the whole is *azure* and *argent*, and takes up all the field, representing the rapid motion of the water turning round.

GUTTY, or guttée, from the Latin *gutta*, a drop, is said of a field, or bearing, filled with drops. See Pl. viii. n. 8, and page 27.

GUZES are roundles of the sanguine murrey or blood colour.

GYRON, a Spanish word signifying a gore, gusset, or triangular piece of cloth. Pl. v., n. 1. Menestrier gives examples of gyrons in the arms of *Giron* in Spain, of which family are descended the *Dukes* of *Ossone*, who carry three *gyrons* in their arms clearly to symbolise their *name ;* but which, he says, represent three triangular pieces of stuff, or gussets, of the coat-armour of Alphonsus the Sixth, King of Spain, who, fighting in battle against the Moors, had his horse killed, and, being in danger was rescued, and remounted, by *Don Roderico de Cissneres*, who cut off three triangular pieces, or gussets, of the king's coat-armour, which he kept as a testimony, to show the king afterwards that he was the man who saved him : for which the king advanced him to honour, graced his armorial bearing with three gyrons, Pl. 6, n. 1 ; and adorned it with a horse for a crest, to perpetuate to posterity the relief he gave the king, another example of the practice of inventing stories to account for heraldic charges. *Note.* When there is only one gyron in a coat, you may blazon thus, *argent, a gyron sable*, without mentioning the point from whence it issues, the dexter chief point being the usual fixed place. But if it stand in any other part of the shield, it must then be expressed.

GYRONNY is where a field is divided into six, eight, ten, or twelve triangular parts, of two different tinctures, and the points all uniting in the centre of the field ; gyrons signify unity, because they are never borne single. Pl. v., n. 23. *Gyronny of eight, argent and sable;* name, *Mawgyron.*

HABECK, an instrument used by the clothiers in dressing cloth, two of them differing from each other in form, as Pl. xxv., n. 9. That on the dexter is copied from the tool, which is invariably made in that form ; the other, on the sinister, shows the form in which it is painted in the arms of the Clothiers' Company.

HABERGEON, a short coat of mail, consisting of jacket without sleeves. Pl. xxiv., n. 17.

HAIE. See WEARE.

HALF-BELT. Pl. xxiv., n. 3. *Gules, two half-belts and buckles, argent;* name, *Pelham.*

HALF-SPEAR, a term for a spear with a short handle. Pl. xxiv., n. 18.

HALF-SPADE. *Azure, three half-spades or, the sides of the spade to the sinister.* Pl. xxv., n. 16; name, *Davenport.*

HAND DEXTER, the *right hand.* Pl. xxxv., n. 32.

HAND SINISTER, the *left hand.* Pl. xxxv., n. 33. *Argent, three sinister hands, couped at the wrist gules;* name, *Maynard.*

HARP, the well-known musical instrument, the tones of which are produced from strings struck with the fingers. It appears to have been used from the earliest antiquity among the Hebrews, Greeks, and Romans, though differing considerably in shape and in the number of its strings. The harp was the favourite musical instrument of the Britons and other Northern nations in the middle ages; and the high estimation in which it was held by the Welch and Irish is proverbial. It is naturally, therefore, very frequently met with as an armorial bearing, and is usually represented as Pl. xxxii., n. 17. The arms of the kingdom of Ireland are, *azure, a harp or, stringed argent,* now introduced into the royal achievement of Great Britain and Ireland.

HARPOON, an instrument used for spearing whales. Pl. xxv., n. 7.

HARPY, a poetical monster, feigned to have the face and breast of a virgin, and body and legs like a vulture. Pl. viii., n. 2. *Azure, a harpy with her wings disclosed, her hair flotant or, armed of the same.* This coat stands in Huntingdon church.

HARINGTON KNOT, a badge of the family of *Ha-rington*. See Pl. XXXII., n. 33. And also under FRET.

HARROWS are instruments used in husbandry. *Ermine, three triangular harrows, conjoined in the nombril point, gules, with a wreath argent and of the second, toothed or ;* name, *Harrow.* Pl. XLI., n. 11.

HART, a stag; properly one in its sixth year.

HARVEST-FLY. *Sable, a harvest-fly in pale, volant, argent;* name, *Bolowre.* Pl. XXVI., n. 22.

HAT-BAND. Pl. XXX., n. 21. *Gules, a chevron between three hat-bands argent ;* name, *Maynes.*

HATCHMENT is the coat of arms of a person dead, usually placed on the front of a house. See HATCH-MENTS, Pl. XX.

HAUBERK, a coat of mail.

HAURIANT, a term applied to fishes when represented palewise or erect, as if they were refreshing themselves by sucking in the air. Pl. X., n. 4.

HAWK, a bird of prey, and for its size a very bold and courageous bird, much used in heraldry. Pl. IX., n. 20.

HAWK'S BELL. Pl. XXXI., n. 35. *Or, on a fess azure, three hawks' bells of the first ;* name, *Planke.*

HAWK'S LURE. See LURE.

HAY-FORK. Pl. XXVIII., n. 8. *Argent, a hay-fork between three mullets, sable,* is the arms of *Conyngham.* This bearing, also called a SHAKE-FORK, is more properly termed by the French a Pal-fourchâ, *i. e.,* a Pale couped, forked, and pointed. We suspect that the appellation hay or shake fork is of popular and not heraldic origin.

HEAD IN PROFILE; the *head and side face* couped at the neck. See Pl. XL., n. 21.

HEART. The heart is blazoned a *human heart*, and sometimes *a body heart*. *Gules, a chevron argent, between three hearts or ;* name, *Frebody*. See Pl. XXIX., n. 21.

HEATH-COCK. Pl. XXXIII., n. 18.

HEDGE-HOG. *Azure, three hedgehogs or ;* names, *Abrahall* and *Herries*. Pl. XXVI., n. 6.

HELMETS. The helmet is armour for the head. The ancients used to adorn them with some kind of monstrous device, as the head, mouth, or paw of a lion, to make them appear more terrible. But the mediæval practice was to place upon them figures of animals, or other objects by which they might be known, and which they called *crests*. Pl. XLII.

The first is the helmet of a king, prince, or royal duke, and is of gold, full-faced, with six bars.

The second is the helmet of a marquis, earl, viscount, and baron, which is of steel in profile, open-faced, and with five gold bars.

The third helmet, standing directly forward, with the beaver open, and without bars, for a knight or baronet. It should be of plain steel.

The fourth is a plain steel helmet sidewise, with the beaver close, which is for all esquires and gentlemen.

If two helmets are to be placed on the top of a shield, for the crests to be thereon, they must be placed facing one another, as if two persons were looking at each other; but if three helmets are to be placed as before-mentioned, the middlemost must stand directly forward, and the other two on the side facing towards it, like two persons looking upon the third.

HERCE. See HARROW.

HIACINTH. See HYACINTH.

HEMP-BREAK, an instrument to make hemp soft and

fit for use. Pl. xxxiv., n. 10. *Argent, three hemp-breaks sable ;* name, *Hampsone* or *Hamston,* alderman of London.

HILTED, a term for the handle of a sword.

HOLY LAMB. See LAMB.

HONOUR-POINT is that point next above the centre of the shield, and is expressed by the letter D, Table I.

HORSE. Frequently met with as a charge in heraldry. *Sable, a horse argent, bridled gules ;* name, *Trott.* Pl. xxxi., n. 8.

HORSE-SHOE. This is the arms of Okeham, a town in Rutlandshire. In this town is an ancient custom, if any nobleman enters the lordship, as an homage he is to forfeit one of his horse's shoes, unless he redeem it with money. See Pl. xxix., n. 17. *Argent, six horse-shoes sable,* 3, 2, 1 ; name, *Ferrers.*

HUMETTY, or HUMETTÉE, signifies an ordinary, which is cut off, and nowhere reaches the edges of the shield. See Pl. xxxvi., n. 14.

HUNTING-HORN. See BUGLE-HORN.

HURTS are roundles of the azure-colour. Pl. viii., n. 12.

HYACINTH is a precious stone of a yellowish-red hue, and in heraldry is used to express the colour tenne. See COLOUR.

HYDRA, a fabulous creature, supposed to be a dragon with seven heads, as Pl. xxiv., n. 21. This is the crest of *Barret.*

IBEX is an imaginary beast, in some respects like the heraldic antelope, but with this difference, that it has two straight horns projecting from the forehead, serrated, or edged like a saw. Pl. xxxii., n. 4.

ICICLES are in shape the same as gutty. Various are the opinions concerning this bearing ; some term them clubs, others guttées reversed, and others icicles. See Pl. xxxv., n. 15.

IMBATTLED, or Crenellé, a term for the battlements of towers, churches, and houses, and is one of the lines of partition, Pl. iii. See an example, Pl. xl., n. 4, *a fess gules imbattled.*

IMBOWED. See EMBOWED.

IMBRUED signifies anything to be bloody, as spears' heads, when spotted with blood, as the example. *Sable, a chevron between three spear-heads argent, their points imbrued proper;* name, *Jefferies,* of Brecknockshire. Pl. xxxv., n. 35.

To IMPALE is to conjoin two coats of arms palewise: women impale their arms with those of their husbands. See Pl. xl., n. 3.

IMPERIAL CROWN is a circle of gold, adorned with precious stones and pearls, heightened with fleurs-de-lis, bordered and seeded with pearls, enclosing a sort of mitre, divided in the centre, and between the two portions an arched fillet, enriched with pearls, and surmounted of a mound, whereon is a cross of pearls. Pl. xlv., n. 3.

IMPERIALLY CROWNED, when any charge in arms, crest, or supporters, is crowned with a regal crown.

INCENSED, a term for panthers, when represented with fire *issuing* from their mouths and ears. See Pl. xxxi., n. 7.

INCREMENT. See INCRESCENT.

INCRESCENT shows the state of the moon, from her entrance into her first quarter, by having her horns towards the right side of the shield. Pl. vii., n. 7. *Ermine, three increscents, gules;* name, *Symmes,* of Daventry, in the county of Northampton.

INDENTED, one of the lines of partition, in shape the same as dancetté, but its teeth smaller, and the number not limited. See Pl. III., and *argent, a border indented azure.* Pl. v., n. 11.

INDIAN GOAT, or Assyrian goat, resembles the English goat, except that its horns are more bent, and the ears like those of a talbot. Pl. XXXIV., n. 2. These beasts are the supporters of the arms of Viscount *Southwell.*

INDORSED. This term is for wings or other charges when placed back to back. See Pl. XXXV., n. 16, viz., *two wings indorsed.* Pl. XL., n. 16., *two keys indorsed.*

INESCUTCHEON, a small escutcheon, borne within the shield, and usually placed in the fess-point. Pl. v., n. 7. *Ermine, an inescutcheon azure;* name, *Rokeley.*

INFAMED. See DEFAMED.

INFULA. See POPE's CROWN.

INGRAILED. See ENGRAILED.

INK-FISH, See CUTTLE-FISH.

INK-MOLINE, or Ink de Moline. See MILLRINE.

IN PRIDE. See PEACOCK.

INTER, the Latin for *between.*

INTERLACED; when chevronels, annulets, rings, keys, crescents, &c., are linked together, they are termed interlaced, viz., *three chevronels interlaced in base.* Pl. XXXV., n. 30. *A cross of four bastoons interlaced.* Pl. XXXVI., n. 15.

INVECTED, one of the lines of partition; the same form as engrailed, but the points of it turning inward to the charge. Pl. III. See the difference in Pl. XIX., n. 14. *Argent, a fess invected, gules, between three torteaux.* In the same place, n. 13, is *argent on a fess engrailed, gules, three leopards' faces, or.*

INVERTED. Inverted denotes anything that is turned the wrong way; particularly wings are said to be *inverted* when the points of them are down. Pl. x., n. 2.

IRON RING, a tool used by the wire-drawers, and borne as a part of their armorial ensign, Pl. xxxiv., n. 15.

ISSUANT, or ISSUING, signifies the charge to be coming out of the bottom of the chief, as the example. *Azure on a chief or, a demi-lion issuing gules;* name, *Markham.* Pl. x., n. 9.

JAMES, ST., CROSS OF, so termed because worn by the knights of that order in Spain. Pl. xxxvi., n. 23.

JAVELIN, or short spear, with a barbed point Pl. xxxiv., n. 25.

JELLOP, JELLOPED, terms occasionally used in blazonry to describe the comb of a cock, cockatrice, &c., when borne of a tincture different from that of the head.

JERSEY COMB, used by the wool-combers. Pl. xxx., n. 2. *Sable, three Jersey combs or, teeth argent;* name, *Bromley.*

JERUSALEM, CROSS OF, so termed from Godfrey of *Bouillon's* bearing argent, a cross-crosslet cantoned with four crosses, or, in allusion to the five wounds of Christ. Pl. xxxix., n. 13.

JESSANT signifies a lion or any beast rising or issuing from the middle of a fess, as Pl. xxxv., n. 26. The common method of heraldic writers is *a lion jessant of a fess.* But Edmondson is clearly of opinion that it should be blazoned *a demi-lion jessant of a fess,* as never more than half the lion appears.

This term is also used to express shooting forth, as

vegetables spring or shoot out, and occasionally to signify throwing out, as fleurs-de-lis out of a leopard's face; for instance, *sable, three leopards' faces jessant fleurs-de-lis or;* for *Morley* of Sussex. Pl. xii., n. 20. Edmondson says, an erroneous practice has long been established among heralds, when showing the leopard's face *jessant de lis*, of always turning the head bottom upwards; whereas the contrary position should be constantly observed, unless otherwise directed by the words of the blazon, viz., a leopard's face reversed, *jessant de lis.*

JESSED is a term used in blazoning a hawk or falcon, whose *jesses*, or straps of leather that tie the bells on the legs, are of a different tincture from the body.

JESSES, leather thongs, to tie the bells on the legs of the hawk and falcon. They are sometimes represented flotant, with rings at the end, as the example, Pl. xxxvii., n. 13. A hawk's leg erased at the thigh, *jessed and belled.*

JEW'S HARP. Pl. xxx., n 11, as born in the arms of Scopham.

JOINANT. See CONJOINED.

JOWLOPPED describes the gills of a cock, when of a different tincture from his head; same as JELLOPED.

JULIAN, ST., CROSS OF, by some called a saltire crossed at its extremities; by others a cross transposed. Pl. xxxvii., n. 24. *Argent, a Julian cross sable,* for *Julian,* of Lincolnshire.

JUPITER, one of the planets; in heraldry it signifies the colour azure, and in engraving is expressed by horizontal lines.

KEYS INDORSED. Pl. xl., n. 16. Example, *two keys*

indorsed, the bows interlaced sable ; name, *Masquenay,* or *Mackenay.*

KING-FISHER. This beautiful bird is occasionally met with in armorial bearings. Pl. xvi., n. 2, *or three king-fishers proper ;* name, *Fisher.*

KNOTS. Various kinds of knots are borne as badges by several families. The principal varieties are—

BOUCHIER'S KNOT. Pl. xxxii., n. 32.

BOWEN'S KNOT. Pl. xxxviii., n. 7.

DACRE'S KNOT. Pl. xxxii., n. 35.

HARINGTON'S KNOT ; this is the usual heraldic fret, and is a common bearing. Pl. xxxii., n. 33.

LACY'S KNOT. Pl. xxxvii., n. 11.

STAFFORD'S KNOT. Pl. xxxii., n. 31.

WAKE'S KNOT. Pl. xxxii., n. 34.

LABEL. Used to difference the arms of the eldest son from the younger ones. Pl. v., n. 3. See Pl. x., n. 1, in the distinction of houses.

LABELS are also ribbons that hang down from a mitre or coronet.

LACY'S KNOT. See Pl. xxxvii., n. 11.

LAMB, or Holy Lamb, passant, with a staff, cross and banner, is a typical figure of Our Saviour, who is understood to be that Lamb mentioned in the Apocalypse of St. John. Pl. xxxi., n. 25.

LAMBEAUX, A CROSS, is a cross-pattée at the top, and issuing out at the foot into three labels. Pl. xxxvi., n. 21. *Gules, a cross lambeaux argent ;* this is a German coat ; name, *Rudetzker.*

LAMBREQUIN is a mantle or hood, intervening between the helmet and crest, and always represented flotant ; also a name formerly given to the points of a label.

LAMP, Pl. XXVIII., n. 12. *Gules, a chevron, between three lamps argent, with fire proper;* name, *Farmer.*

LANCE, or tilting-spear, *argent on a quarter, a lance in bend or;* name, *Knight.* See Pl. XXXIV., n. 6.

LANGUED (French *langué,* of *langué,* the tongue) is a term for the tongues of beasts and birds, when of a different tincture from that of the charge. All beasts and birds (except they are tinctured gules) are langued gules; but when the beast is gules, he must be langued and armed azure. This rule is never to be deviated from, except in cases only where the blazon directs that the beast should be langued of any other colour or metal; and then such colour or metal must be expressed. If a beast or bird is to be represented in coat-armour, without either tongue or claws, you must say, when blazoning, *sans langue and arms.*

LARMES, the French for *tears ;* see GUTTÉE.

LATTICE. See TRÉILÉE.

LAUREL is frequently met with as a bearing, as well in wreaths and branches, as in sprigs and leaves.

LAVERPOT, or ewer, as borne in the arms of the Founders' Company. Pl. XXXIV., n. 6.

LAZARUS, ST., CROSS OF, worn by the knights of that order. Pl. XXXVI., n. 24.

LEASH, a tierce, or three of a kind; as three bucks, hares, &c.; also a leathern thong, by which falconers held the hawk on their hand : a term also applied to the line attached to the collar of a greyhound or other dog.

LEATHER-BOTTLE, as borne in the arms of the Bottle-makers' and Horners' Company. Pl. XXX., n. 5.

LEGS IN ARMOUR, *three legs in armour, conjoined in the fess point, spurred and garnished or :* this is the arms of the Isle of Man. See Pl. XL., n. 1. Nisbet says, "three legs of men, the device of the Sicilians, **the** ancient possessors of the Isle of Man."

LENTALLY, an ancient term for *party per bend.*

LEOPARD. This well-known animal is rarely seen entire as a charge in ancient coats, and its name is given to the lion in certain attitudes. See LION. Pl. XXXI., n. 30, presents us with a modern example. *Sable, three leopards rampant argent, spotted sable;* name, *Lynch.* It is, however, probably, from the name, that the Lynx was the animal originally represented in this coat.

LEOPARD'S FACE. When the heads of leopards are erased or couped at the neck, as Plate XXXV., n. 22, they are blazoned by the word *head,* viz., *a leopard's head erased:* but if no part of the neck appears, and the position of the head is *gardant,* as Pl. XXXV., n. 21, it is then blazoned a *leopard's face,* without mentioning the word *gardant,* which is always implied.

LEOPARD LIONÉ. See LION LEOPARDÉ.

LEVEL. Pl. XXVII., n. 24. *Azure, three levels with their plummets or;* name, *Colbrand.*

LEVER, a name sometimes given to the cormorant.

LILIES OF THE FLAG are those borne in the arms of the kingdom of France. See FLEUR-DE-LIS.

LIMBECK, or STILL. Heralds term it an antique limbeck; this example is part of the Pewterers' arms, Pl. XXXIII., n. 12.

LINED, having a line affixed to the collar of a dog or other animal, which are frequently *collared* of one tincture, and *lined,* or chained, of another. The term is also applied to the inner covering or lining of a mantle, robe, cap, &c.

LINES. See PARTITION LINES.

LION. The true heraldic lion, according to French authors, is always to be represented in profile, or, as the ancient heralds say, showing but one eye and one ear. His attitude, also, should always be rampant or ravaging. When passant and full-faced, they blazoned him a leopard, *vide* Lion Leopardé : in England, however, the lions in the royal and other achievements have always been blazoned as lions, however depicted since the time of Henry III., in whose reign they were called " *Leopards.*"

LION OF ENGLAND. This term is used when speaking of a canton, or augmentation of arms. In such case, instead of saying *on a canton gules, a lion passant gardant or*, as an augmentation, you say, he bears *on a canton a lion of England*, which hath the same signification.

LION LEOPARDÉ. This is a French term for what the English call a *lion passant gardant.* The word *leopard* is always made use of by the French heralds to express in their language, a lion full-faced, or *gardant.* Thus, when a lion is placed on an escutcheon in that attitude which we call *rampant gardant*, the French blazon it *a lion leopardé ;* when he is passant only, they call him *leopard lioné.*

LION OF ST. MARK. A winged lion, as borne in the arms of the republic of Venice, viz., *a lion sejant gardant and winged or, his legs encircled with a glory, holding in his fore-paws an open book, wherein is written, Pax tibi Marce, evangelista meus ; over the dexter side of the book, a sword erect, all proper.* Pl. XXXII., n. 24.

LION-POISSON, or *sea-lion*, so termed as the upper part is of a lion, and the hinder part ends in a fish's tail, with webbed feet; this is borne by *Inhoff* of Germany. This example was copied from the family seal. Pl. xxxii., n. 20.

LION-DRAGON, the upper half a lion, and the other going off like the hinder part of a dragon. Pl. xxxii., n. 21. *Or, a lion-dragon gules, armed, langued, and crowned of the first;* name, *Bretigni. Party per chevron, gules or, three lion-dragons ducally crowned and counterchanged;* name, *Easton.*

LIONS CONJOINED, under one head; see TRICORPORATED, and Pl. xxxii., n. 22.

LITVIT'S SKIN, a pure white fur.

LIZARD, a small animal of the crocodile species, generally painted green. Pl. xxviii., n. 6.

LOBSTER. In blazon the term *upright* is given to all shell-fish when borne as the example, because they, wanting fins, cannot properly be termed *hauriant.* Pl. xxxi., n. 32.

LOCHABER-AXE. The ancient arms of the Highlanders: see Pl. xxxvi., n. 8; and two more in Pl. xxix., n. 18.

LODGED, a term for the buck, hart, &c., when resting or lying on the ground. This term is used for beasts of chase as couchant is for those of prey. Pl. ix., n. 17. Pl. xiv., n. 18. *Argent, on a mount proper, a stag lodged, gules;* name, *Harthill.*

LONG BOW, *bend in pale, gules;* name, *Bowes.* See Pl. xxix., n. 14.

LOZENGE, a four-cornered figure, resembling a pane of glass in old casements. Pl. vi., n. 17.

LOZENGES, CROSS OF. Pl. xxxvi., n. 17. *Gules, a cross of lozenges, flory or;* name, *Fotherby.* Pl. xxxix. n. 15.

LOZENGY is when the field or charge is covered with lozenges. Pl. v., n. 21. *Lozengy, argent and gules;* name, *Fitzwilllam.*

LUCY, an old term for the fish called a pike. Pl. xxix., n. 7.

LUMIERES are the eyes.

LUNA is the Latin for the moon: in blazoning by the planets, it is used in heraldry instead of argent.

A LURE, two wings conjoined with their tips downwards, joined with a line and ring, used by falconers to decoy their hawks, by casting it up in the air like a fowl. Pl. xxxi., n. 34. *Gules, a lure, stringed and braced argent;* name, *Wavre.*

LURE also signifies two wings conjoined and inverted, which, with the tips downward, are said to be *in lure.* Pl. x., n. 2.

LUTRA. See OTTER.

LYMPHAD is an old-fashioned ship with one mast, and rowed with oars. Pl. xxxiv., n. 4.

LYRE, a musical instrument. See Pl. xxxvi., n. 28.

MADDER BAG. See Pl. xxxviii., n. 1.

MAIDEN'S HEAD, a term for the head and neck of a woman, couped below the breast, the head wreathed with a garland of roses, and crowned with an antique coronet. See Pl. xxvi., n. 2.

MAIL, armour for the body and arms, composed of small close rings, termed *mail,* or *ring armour,* as if woven in a loom. The rings composing this armour were woven together in different ways: the ancient sort were not very complex; but those of later times had the work done in so curious a manner, that ornament was combined with strength, preventing the effects of sword or lance. Mail, when painted or engraved, is made like the scales of fish, which are the best resemblance of the *mail*. See Pl. XXIV., n. 17.

MALLET. Pl. XXX., n. 24. *Gules, a chevron between three mallets or ;* name, *Soame.*

MALTA, CROSS OF, so called because worn by the knights of that order. Pl. XXXVI., n. 25.

MANACLES, or handcuffs. Pl. XXXIV., n. 29.

MANCHE, or MAUNCH, a sleeve of the fashion of the 12th century. Pl. VII., n. 13.

MANCHET, a cake of bread not unlike a muffin.

MANED, the term used in blazoning the mane or neck-hair of horses, unicorns, tigers, or other animals, when their manes are of a different tincture from the body.

MAN TIGER, or MANTICORA, an imaginary monster, with body like a lion, face like a man, and horns on the head, like those of an ox. Pl. XLI., n. 9.

MANTLE. Pl. XXXIX., n. 24.

MANTLINGS are ornamented foliage-work for the adorning of helmets in paintings of coats of arms.

MARCASSIN, a young wild boar, distinguished from the old by its tail being drawn as hanging down ; whereas the old boar's is curled, with the end only pointing downward.

MARINED, a term used for an animal which has the lower part of its body like a fish. See Pl. XXXII., n. 20. Pl. XXXI., n. 29.

MARINE-WOLF, or Seal. It resembles a quadruped in some respects, and a fish in others. Seals are common on most of the rocky shores of Great Britain ; they feed on most sorts of fish, and are seen searching for their prey near shore ; their head in swimming is always above water ; they sleep on rocks surrounded by the sea; they are extremely watchful, and never sleep long without moving; but, if disturbed by anything, take care to tumble over the rocks into the sea. Pl. xxvi., n. 11. *Argent, a chevron engrailed gules, between three marine wolves naiant sable, finned of the first, langued of the second;* name, *Fennor.*

MARK, ST. See LION OF ST. MARK.

MARKS OF CADENCY. See DISTINCTION OF HOUSES.

MARQUIS'S CORONET. See CROWNS AND CORONETS OF ENGLAND.

MARS, the name of one of the planets; in heraldry signifies the colour gules, and in engraving is represented by perpendicular lines.

MARTLET (very frequent in armories all over Europe). This bird (known as the house-martin) is frequently seen under the cornices of houses, with feet so short and wings so long, that should it settle on a level it could not easily rise; therefore, it alights on high places, that it may drop on the wing. See Pl. vii., n. 15. This bird is represented in heraldry without feet, and given for a difference to the fourth son. Pl. xxvii., n. 4; also Pl. xiii., n. 17.

MASCALLY, *argent and gules, counterly;* names, *Pogeis* and *Pegg.* See Pl. xxxix., n. 8.

MASCLE, from *Macula,* the mesh of a net. This figure is of a lozenge form, and perforated, as the example. It differs from the *fusil* in being shorter and broader, and always *voided.* Pl. vi., n. 19. *Argent, a mascle, gules.*

MASCLES, conjunct, *argent, seven mascles conjunct, three, three, and one, gules.* Pl. xxxiv., n. 32.

MASCLES, CROSS OF. Pl. xxxvi., n. 12.

MASONED, a term applied to plain strokes, representing the cement in stone buildings. Pl. xxxviii., n. 27.

MATCH, as used by artillerymen to fire cannon, is a kind of rope, twisted and prepared in a peculiar manner. It is made of hempen tow, spun on the wheel, like cord, but very slack; and is composed of three twists, boiled in a preparation of saltpetre, &c. Pl. xxviii., n. 4. *Argent, on a fess gules, between two matches kindled proper, a martlet or;* name, *Leet.*

MATCHLOCK, a peculiar kind of gun-lock fired by a match, formerly much used. Pl. xxv., n. 12. *Argent, a chevron between three matchlocks, sable;* name, *Leverage.*

MEMBERED, the term used in blazoning the beak and legs of a bird, when of a different tincture from the body.

MERCURY, one of the planets, in heraldry signifies the colour purple.

MERILLION, an instrument used by the hatband-makers, and borne as part of their arms. Pl. xxxiv., n. 1.

MERMAID, a fictitious sea animal, half a woman and half a fish, used in armories, as represented in the example. Pl. xiv., n. 4. *Argent, a mermaid gules, crined or, holding a mirror in her right hand, and a comb in her left;* name, *Ellis.*

MESLÉ, an ancient term for a field composed equally of metal and colour, as gyronny, paly, bendy, &c.

MI-COUPY, and MIPARTÉE, a French term when the half of the shield is divided per fess and per pale.

MIDDLE-BASE is the middle part of the base, represented by the letter H, Table 1.

MIDDLE-CHIEF is the middle part of the chief, represented by the letter B, Table 1.

M

MILL-PIC, an instrument used by mill-wrights. Pl. XXVIII., n. 17. *Sable, on a chevron between three mill-pics, argent, as many mullets gules;* name, *Mosley.* See another shape, Pl. XXXVII., n. 5.

MILL-CLACK, represented as the example. Pl. XXXVII., n. 23.

MILL-RIND, or RINE, is the iron fixed to the centre of a mill-stone, by which the wheel turns it; termed in French, *fer-de-moline,* or mill-iron.

MILL-STONE, charged with a mill-rine, Pl. XXXIII., n. 11. *Azure, three mill-stones argent :* name, *Milverton.*

MILL-RINE, A CROSS; so termed, as its form is like the mill-rind, which carries the mill-stone, and is perforated as that is. Pl. VI., n. 14 and 15.

MINIVER, MENU-VAIR, a white fur, said to be the belly part of the skin of the Siberian squirrel.

MITRE is a round cap, pointed and divided at the top, from which hang two pendants, fringed at both ends. The mitres used by all archbishops and bishops are surrounded at bottom with a plain fillet of gold, Pl. XLIII., n. 12; excepting that of the palatinate bishop of Durham, which issues out of a ducal coronet.* See Pl. XLIII., n. 11. These ornaments are never actually worn in England, except by the Roman Catholic prelates, but merely depicted on coats of arms. In Germany several families bear the mitre for their crest, to show that they are advocates for, or feudatories of, ancient abbeys, or officers of bishops.

MOLE, the little animal so called, when used in heraldry is represented as Pl. XXVI., n. 12. *Argent,*

---

* It has been considered that archbishops have the right of using the ducal coronet; but, according to the best authorities, it belongs solely to the arms of the see of Durham.

three moles sable, their snouts and feet gules; name,
Nangothan.

MOLE-HILL, as the example, Pl. XXIV., n. 19.

MOLINE, A CROSS, not so wide or so sharp as that
which is called ancred. T. 6, n. 2. *Argent, a cross
moline gules;* name, *Undal.* The cross moline is used
as a distinction for the eighth brother. See DISTINCTION
OF HOUSES.

MONKEY, the well-known animal so called, when
used in heraldry is represented as in nature; but if
collared, the collar is placed round the loins, instead
of the neck, as shown in the example, Pl. XXVI., n. 14.

MOOR-COCK, an heraldic representation of the male
of the black game, or large black grouse. *Argent, a
moor-cock sable;* name, *Moore.* Pl. XXVI., n. 19.

MORION, a steel cap or helmet for the head, anciently
worn by foot-soldiers, and variously shaped; see Pl.
XXVIII., n. 24; and another in Pl. XXIX., n. 22. This is
borne by the *Earl of Cardigan.** *Argent, a chevron
gules, between three morions azure.*

MORSE. See SEA-LION.

MORTAR, Pl. XXX., n. 23. *Sable, a mortar and pestle
gules;* name, *Wakerly.*

MORTCOURS are lamps used at funerals; they are
borne as part of the Wax-Chandlers' arms. Pl. XXXIV.,
n. 31.

MORTIER, a cap of state formerly worn in France by
some of the judicial dignitaries, as the President of
the Chamber of Deputies, the Chancellor, and the Chief
Justice.

MORTNÉ is a term Colombière has applied to a lion
that has neither tongue, teeth, nor claws, which, he

* And is a chapeau or Knight's cap, not a morion.—ED.

says, is borne by *Leon*, an ancient barony in Brittany. Pl. XXVI., n. 1. The term signifies, literally, *still-born*, and is used by French heralds to describe an animal divested of its natural means of defence and sustenance.

MOTTO, a word or short sentence, inserted in a scroll, under, and sometimes over, a coat of arms. Mottoes are frequently allusive to the name of the bearer, and more frequently to the bearings; and in general are short quaint sayings, of the nature of an axiom or epigraph, expressive of the predominant passion, moral or religious sentiment, of the first adopter, or of some action for which he was distinguished. They are not strictly hereditary, like the arms, but may be varied or relinquished at pleasure. By the rules of heraldry, mottoes are not permitted to women, unless they are sovereigns.

MOUND (from the French *monde*, Latin *mundus*, the world) is a name given to a ball or globe, which forms part of the regalia of an emperor or king. It is an emblem of sovereign authority and majesty, and is surmounted by a cross, usually the cross pattée, in all Christian countries. Pl. XXVII., n. 18.

MOUNT, a hillock, or elevation of ground, usually arched, and blazoned *vert*.

MOUNTAIN CAT. See Pl. XXVI., n. 16.

MOUNTED, a term applicable to a horse bearing a rider; also frequently used to describe a cross placed upon steps.

MOURN, a term for the blunted head of a tilting-spear.

MOUSSUE, A CROSS, for a cross rounded off at the ends. Pl. XXXVII., n. 20.

MULLET, supposed to be the rowel of a spur, and should consist of five points only; whereas stars consist of six, or more. T. 7, n. 1. *Argent, a mullet gules ;* name, *Haye.* Some have confounded stars and mullets together, which mistake is easily rectified by allowing mullets to consist of five points only, and stars of six, eight, or more. Bara says, mullets differ from stars by being always pierced in the middle ; Gibbon says, all French authors take the mullet for the rowel of a spur, which *molette* signifies in their language; and they affirm it must be always pierced.

Mr. Nisbet says, he ordinarily takes mullets for stars in blazon, when they accompany celestial figures, *as those in the arms of Baillie ;* but when they accompany military instruments, and other pieces of armour, for spur-rowels : as also when they have no such figures with them, but are alone in the shield, consisting only of five points, as in the arms of Sutherland, Douglas, &c.

MURAILLÉ, a term used to express any ordinary that is walled, as Pl. XLI., n. 12. *Azure, on a pale muraillé with three pieces on each side, or, an indorse sable ;* name, *Sublet.*

MURAL CROWN was made of gold, with battlements on the edge of its circle, and was given by the Romans to him who first mounted the wall of a besieged town or city, and fixed the standard belonging to the army. Pl. XLV., n. 23.

MURREY. See SANGUINE.

MUSCHETOR signifies an ermine-spot, without those three spots over them that are used in ermine.

MUSIMON, a beast which is said to be engendered between a goat and a ram. Pl. XL., n. 20.

MUSION, an ancient term for a cat.

MUZZLED : the bear is generally so represented in heraldry.

NAIANT, swimming, applied to fish when borne horizontally across the field in a swimming posture. Pl. x., n. 3.

NAISSANT, coming out, applied to a lion, or other creature, that seems to be coming out of the middle of an ordinary or charge, as Pl. xxxv., n. 26.

NARCISSUS, a flower consisting of six petals, each resembling the leaf of the cinquefoil. Pl. xxxiv., n. 8.

NAVAL CROWN. Claudius, after surprising the Britons, invented this as a reward for service at sea; it was made of gold, and consisted of prows of galleys and sails placed upon the rim or circle, alternately. It is now formed of the sterns and square sails of ships, instead of prows, placed alternately on the circle or fillet. Pl. xLv., n. 22.

NEBULÉ, one of the partition lines, signifies clouded, and is used when the outlines of an ordinary or partition line run arched in and out, or waved so as to resemble clouds, as Pl. iii.

NOMBRIL-POINT, or navel-point, is that part of the escutcheon marked with the letter F, under the fess-point. Pl. i.

NOVA SCOTIA, badge of. See BADGE.

NOWED signifies tied or knotted, and is said of a serpent, wyvern, or other creature, whose body or tail is twisted like a knot. See Pl. xxxv., n. 17.

OAK. This tree is variously borne, as an emblem of strength, constancy, and long life : *or, on a mount in base, an oak acorned proper ;* name, *Wood.* Pl. xviii., n. 12.

OBSIDIONAL CROWN, or garland ; it was composed of

grass, or twigs of trees, interwoven as the example; it was by the Romans given as a reward to him who held out a siege, or caused it to be raised, repulsing the enemy, and delivering the place. Pl. XLV., n. 26.

OGRESS. See PELLET.

OLIVE CROWN, or Garland. It was given by the Greeks to those who came off victorious at the Olympic games. Pl. XXIX., n. 4.

OLIVE TREE is the emblem of peace and concord; *or, a fess gules, between three olive-branches, proper;* name, *Roundel.*

OMBRÉ, a French term for shadowed.

ONDÉE or UNDÉE, the French term for wavy.

ONGLÉ (Lat. *ungulatus*), a term used by French heralds in blazoning the talons or claws of birds or beasts, which they describe as onglé of such a colour.

OPINICUS: a fictitious beast of heraldic invention; its body and fore legs like those of a lion; the head and neck like those of the eagle; to the body are affixed wings, like those of a griffin; and it has a tail like that of a camel. Pl. XXXII., n. 6. The opinicus is the crest to the arms of the Barber-surgeons. It is sometimes borne without wings.

OR signifies gold, and, in engraving, is represented by small dots all over the field or charge. Pl. II.

ORB. See MOUND, and REGALIA OF ENGLAND.

ORDINARIES are any of those figures which, by their ordinary and frequent use, are become peculiar to the science: such as the *cross, chief, pale, fess, inescutcheon, chevron, saltire, bend,* and *bar.* Pl. IV.

ORIFLAM, or ORIFLAMME, a name given to a standard or banner borne by the kings of France, in honour of St. Denis. The Oriflamme borne at Agincourt was an oblong red flag with five points or tails. The French infantry in later times had a banner so named, which was charged with a saltire, wavy with rays or flames issuing from the centre crossways.

ORLE signifies a border or selvage within the shield, at some distance from the edges. Pl. v., n. 4. *Azure, an orle argent;* name, *Sir John Spring.* In-orle signifies things placed regularly within the escutcheon, in the nature of an orle, near the edges. Pl. xxxv. n. 4. Martlets, trefoils, &c., when in-orle, are always eight in number. The phrase *in-orle* is also frequently used to describe any two bearings so depicted as to meet, or nearly meet, in the form of an arch; as, " two branches of laurel in *in-orle*."

ORLE, of three pieces, sable: this example is taken from Upton, to show that this ordinary is borne of many pieces. Pl. xxxix., n. 17.

ORLE and BORDURE, sable, an orle within a bordure argent. Pl. xxxix., n. 18.

OSTRICH, the largest of all birds, is frequently borne in coat armour. From the idle story of its being able to digest iron, this bird is, in heraldry, usually painted with a horse-shoe in its mouth. Pl. xxxi., n. 24.

OSTRICH FEATHERS are always drawn with their tops turned down, as Pl. xxxii., n. 8. If in coat-armoury an ostrich-feather is white, and the quill part gold, or any other colour different from the feather, it is blazoned, *penned, shafted, or quilled, of such a colour.*

OSTRICH FEATHERS IN PLUME: if three feathers are placed together, as in Pl. xxxii., n. 8, they are termed *a plume,* and their number need not be mentioned in the blazoning; but if there are more than *three,* the number should be expressed; for example, *a plume of five ostrich feathers.* If there is more than one row of feathers, those rows are termed in blazon *heights ;* for example, *a plume of ostrich feathers in two heights,* by some termed a *double plume,* at Pl. XXXII., n. 9. Where the plume is composed of nine feathers, in two heights, they should be placed *five* in the *bottom row,* and *four* in the *top row ;* if there are three heights, then the plume should consist of twelve feathers : viz., *five, four,* and *three.* They are termed *a triple plume.* See Plate XXXII., n. 10.

OTTER, the amphibious animal so called. Pl. XXVI., n. 10. *Argent, a fess between three otters sable ;* name, *Lutterel. Loutre,* being French for otter.

OUNCE, or LYNX. See LEOPARD.

OVER-ALL is when one charge is borne over another. See Plate XIV., n. 13. *Three bars wavy azure, over-all a lion rampant of the first ;* name, *Bulbeck.*

OWL. This bird, in heraldry, is always represented full-faced. Pl. XXXI., n. 16.

PADLOCK : *sable, three padlocks argent ;* name, *Lovett.* Pl XXIV., n. 1.

PALE is an honourable ordinary, consisting of two perpendicular lines drawn from the top to the base of the escutcheon, and contains one-third of the middle part of the field. Pl. IV., n. 2. The pale is like the palisades used about fortifications, and formerly used for the enclosing of camps ; every soldier was obliged to carry one, and to fix it according as the lines were drawn for the security of the camp.

IN PALE is when things are borne one above another, perpendicularly, in the nature of a pale. See Pl. X., n. 16.

PER PALE, so termed when the field or charge is

equally divided by a perpendicular line, as Pl. III., n. 1. *Party per pale, or and sable*; name, *Searle.*

PALET. See PALLET.

PALL, an archiepiscopal ornament sent from Rome to metropolitans, and appropriated to archbishops: it is made of the wool of white lambs, and resembles the letter Y in shape. It consists of pieces of white woollen stuff, three fingers in breadth, and embroidered with crosses. See Pl. XXXVI., n. 10.

PALLET is a diminutive of the pale, containing one half of the breadth of the pale. See Pl. IV., n. 3.

PALLISADO. See VALLARY.

PALLISSE is like a range of palisades before a fortification, and is so represented on a fess, rising up a considerable length, and pointed at the top with the field appearing between them. Pl. XXXIX., n. 16.

PALMERS' STAFF. See Plate XXXV., n. 3.

PALM-TREE. See Pl. XXXIX., n. 2. The Egyptians represented the year by a palm-tree, and the month by one of its branches; because it is the nature of this tree to produce a branch every month.

PALY is when the field is divided into four or more even number of parts, by perpendicular lines, consisting of two different tinctures, interchangeably disposed. *Paly of six, or and azure*; name, *Gurney*. Pl. V., n. 17.

PALY-BENDY is by lines perpendicular, which is paly, and by others diagonal athwart the shield, from the dexter to the sinister, which is called bendy. Pl. XXXVIII., n. 22. *Paly bendy sinister of six, or and azure, a canton, ermine*; name, *Buck*, of Yorkshire. See Plate XXXVIII., n. 21.

PANTHER in heraldry, when depicted with fire issuing from his mouth and ears, is termed *incensed*. The panther is always represented full-faced or *gardant*. Pl. XXXI. n. 7.

PAPAL CROWN. See POPE.

PAPILLONÉ is a field divided into variegated specks, like those on a butterfly, but ranged like the scales of a fish. Pl. XXXVIII., n. 25.

PARROT. Pl. XXVIII., n. 7. Parrots are frequent in the arms of the ancient families of Switzerland; occasioned by two great factions in the year 1262, which were distinguished by their ensigns; the one having a red standard with a white star, and the other a white standard with a green parrot; and the families that were concerned in those factions bore in their arms either stars or parrots.

PARTITION LINES are such as party-per-pale, party-per-bend, party-per-fess, party-per-chevron, party-per-cross, party-per-saltire; by which is understood a shield divided or cut through by a line or lines, either perpendicular, diagonal transverse, &c., as in example, Pl. III. Why lines are used in heraldry, is to difference bearings which would be otherwise the same; for an escutcheon charged with a chief engrailed differs from a chief wavy as much as if the one bore a cross and the other a saltire.

PARTY signifies parted or divided, and is applied to all divisions of the field, viz.:—

PARTY-PER-PALE is the field divided by a perpendicular line. Pl. III, n. 1. *Party-per-pale, argent and gules;* name, *Walgrave.*

PARTY-PER-PALE and CHEVRON signifies the field to be divided into four parts, by two lines; one is a pale line, the other a line in form of a chevron. Pl XXXVIII., n. 31.

PARTY-PER-PALE and BASE is the field divided into three parts by the pale line, and a horizontal one in base. Pl. XXXVIII., n. 32.

PASCHAL LAMB. See HOLY LAMB.

PASSANT-GARDANT, for a beast walking full-faced, looking right forward. Pl. IX., n. 1. Carter says, *Gules, a lion passant-gardant, or,* was the coat-armour of the dukes of Aquitaine, and was joined with the coat of the kings of England by the marriage of Henry II. with Eleanor of Aquitaine, being before two lions, the posture and colours one and the same. The supposition has probability in its favour; but it is unsupported by any known authority.

PASSANT-REGARDANT signifies a beast walking and looking behind him. Pl. IX., n. 12.

PASSION, or CROSS of the Passion, is like that of Calvary, but has no steps.

PASSION-NAIL. See Plate XXXVI., n. 31.

PATERNAL signifies, in heraldry, the original arms of a family.

PATERNOSTER, A CROSS; one which is made of beads. Pl. XXXVI., n. 7.

PATONCE, A CROSS, is flory at the ends, and differs from that which is so called, inasmuch as the cross flory is circumflex and turns down; whereas this extends to a pattée form. Pl. VI., n. 4. *Vert, a cross patonce, or ;* name, *Boydell.*

PATRIARCHAL CROSS, so called from its being appropriated to patriarchs, as the triple cross is to the Pope, Pl. XXXVI., n. 20. Morgan says the patriarchal cross is crossed twice, to denote that the work of redemption which was wrought on the cross extended to both Jews and Gentiles.

PATTÉE, A CROSS, is small in the centre, and so goes on widening to the ends, which are very broad. Pl. VI., n. 6,

PATTÉE, a cross pattée throughout, *i.e.*, extending to the edges of the field. See Plate XXXIX., n. 9. Some authors term it *cross pattée entire.*

PATTES are the paws of any beast.

PAVILION. See TENT.

PAW. See GAMB.

PEACOCK, when borne affronté, with its tail spread, is termed *in pride*, as Pl. XXXV., n. 11; when represented with its wings close, as the example, Pl. XXIV., n. 15, it is blazoned simply a *peacock*, and it must be drawn as the example.

PEA-RISE, a term for a pea-stalk, leaved and blossomed; it is part of the crest of *St. Quintin.*

PEAN, one of the furs, the ground black, and the spots gold. Pl. XL.

PEARL, in heraldry, is used for argent, and in engraving is left white.

PEGASUS, among the poets, a horse imagined to have wings, being that whereon Bellerophon was fabled to be mounted when he engaged the Chimera ; *azure, a Pegasus, the wings expanded argent,* are the arms of the Inner Temple, London. Pl. XXXIV., n. 20.

PELICAN HERALDIC. The pelican is generally represented with her wings indorsed, her neck embowed, pecking her breast; and when in her nest feeding her young, is termed *a pelican in her piety.* Pl. VII., n. 19.

PELICAN NATURAL. In size it exceeds the swan. This bird has an enormous bag attached to the lower mandible of the bill, and extending almost from the point of the bill to the throat. See Plate XXIX., n. 13.

PELLETS are black roundles; some term them ogresses, and gun-stones. Pl. VIII., n. 13.

PEN. Pl. XXX., n. 17. *Gules, three pens argent;* name, *Cowpen.*

PENDENT signifies hanging down.

PENNON, a small flag, ending in one sharp point, or two, which used to be placed on the tops of spears, with the crest, or motto, of the bearer. Pennons are never to be charged with the *arms.*

PENNY-YARD-PENNY, so termed from the place where it was first coined, which was in the castle of Penny-yard, near the market-town of Ross, situated upon the river Wye, in the county of Hereford. Pl. XXVII., n. 16. *Azure, three penny-yard-pence proper;* name, *Spence.*

PENNONCELLE, or PENSELL, the diminutive of the PENNON.

PER, a particle generally used in heraldry before an ordinary, to denote a partition of the field, as *party per fess, pale,* &c.

PERCLOSE, or demi-garter, is that part of the garter that is buckled and nowed. See example, Pl. XXXIX., n. 23. *Or, the perclose of three demi-garters nowed azure, garnished of the first;* name, *Narboon.*

PERFLEW. See PURFLEW.

PERFORATED. See PIERCED.

PERSIA, CROWN OF. Pl. XLV., n. 14.

PETRONEL, an ancient name for a pistol.

PEWIT: see the example, Pl. XXV., n. 23.

PHEON, the iron part of a dart, with a barbed head, frequently borne in coats; its position is always with the point downwards, unless otherwise blazoned. Pl. VII., n. 4.

PHEON, A CROSS, composed of four Pheons. Pl. VI., n. 12.

PHŒNIX, an imaginary bird, famous among the ancients, who describe it in form like the eagle, but more beautiful in its plumage; and add that when advanced in age, it makes itself a nest of spices, which being set on fire by the sun, or some other secret power, it burns itself, and out of its ashes rises another. In heraldry, *a phœnix in flames proper* is the emblem of Immortality. Pl. VII., n. 20.

PIERCED, A CROSS, or any other ordinary perforated or struck through, with a hole in it, so that the field may be seen; the piercing must be particularly expressed as to its shape, whether square, round, or lozenge; viz., *argent, a cross, square-pierced, azure.* Pl. XXXVI., n. 1.

PIKE-STAFF. See the example, Pl. XXXVIII., n. 3.

PILLAR. *Or, a pillar sable, enwrapped with an adder argent;* name, *Myntur.* Pl. XXVII., n. 3.

PILE, an ordinary. Pl. IV., n. 22. Edmondson is of opinion that, when there are two, three, or more piles, issuing from a chief, and they are not expressed in the blazon to meet in a point, they should be drawn perpendicular. *Argent a pile gules; borne by the celebrated* Sir John Chandos *in the time of Edward the Third.*

PILE, PARTY-PER, transposed. This kind of bearing is rare; for the natural bearing of piles is with the points downward: another peculiarity is, that the field is divided into three distinct colours. This coat is borne by *Meinstorpe* of Holsatia. Pl. XXXVIII., n. 33.

PILE, PARTY-PER, *in point, argent, and azure.* Pl. XXXVIII., n. 24.

PILE, PARTY-PER, in *traverse, argent, and gules;* so termed, from the lines having their beginning from

the exact points of the chief and base sinister, and so
extending to the extreme line in the fess point on the
dexter side : this coat is borne by *Rathlowe* of Holsatia.
Pl. xxxviii., n. 35.

PILGRIMS' or PALMERS' STAFFS. See Plate xxxv.,
n. 3 and 10. *Azure, three pilgrims' crook-staffs or ;*
name, *Pilgrim.*

PILY-BENDY : *or and azure, a canton ermine.* Pl.
xxxv., n. 1.

PINCERS, Pl. xxviii, n. 16, *argent, a fess between three
pair of pincers gules ;* name, *Russel.*

PINE-TREE. *Argent, on a mount in base, a pine-tree
fructed proper ;* name, *Pine.*

PLACCATE, a piece of armour worn over the breast-
plate, to strengthen it.

PLATE is a round flat piece of silver, without any
impression on it. T. 8, n. 10.

PLAYING-TABLE, or backgammon tables, Pl. xxv.,
n. 8. *Azure, three pair of backgammon tables open proper,
edged or ;* name, *Pegriz.*

PLOUGH. *Azure, a plough in fess argent ;* name,
Kroge. Pl. xxvii., n. 12.

PLUMBY. See PURPLE.

PLUME. See OSTRICH FEATHERS.

PLUMMET, used by mariners to fathom the depth of
water. Pl. xxxiv., n. 11.

POINTS OF THE ESCUTCHEON. See ESCUTCHEON.

POINTS, A CROSS, of sixteen : so termed from its
having four points at each extremity. Pl. xxxvii., n. 4.

IN POINT, is when swords, piles, &c., are so borne
as to resemble the point of a pile ; that is, that the
points of such bearings almost meet in the base of the
escutcheon.

POISSON. See MARINED.

POLAND, CROWN OF. Pl. XLV., n. 13.

POMEGRANATE : the arms of the city of Granada in Spain, are *argent, a pomegranate in pale, slipt proper ;* allusive to the name. Pl. XXVII., n. 6. It was also the badge of Queen Katherine of Arragon, and is occasionally met with in English heraldry.

POMEIS, are green roundles, so termed from the French word *pomme,* an apple. Pl. VIII., n. 14.

POMELLED, signifies the round ball or knob affixed to the handle of a sword or dagger.

POMMÉ, A CROSS, signifies a cross with a ball or knob at each end; from *pomme,* an apple. Pl. VI., n. 9.

POMMETTY, A CROSS, is one the extremities of which terminate in several, or more than one, ball or knob, like those of a pilgrim's staff. Pl. XXXVII., n. 19.

POPE'S CROWN. See TIARA.

POPINJAY, a small parrot, or paroquet, with red beak and legs.

PORCUPINE. Pl. XXVI., n. 5. *Gules, a porcupine saliant argent, quilled and chained or ;* name, *Sir Simon Eyre, Lord Mayor of London,* 1445. He built Leadenhall.

PORTATE, A CROSS, so termed because it does not stand upright, as generally crosses do, but lies athwart the escutcheon in bend, as if it were carried (Lat. *portatus*) on a man's shoulder. Pl. XXXVII., n. 16.

PORTCULLIS, a falling cross-barred door, like a harrow, hung over the gates of fortified places, and let down to keep an enemy out, the perpendicular bars being spiked, both to wound the assailants and fix themselves in the ground. The portcullis is one of the distinctions of the royal house of Tudor, in allusion to their descent from the Beauforts. Pl. VII., n. 12.

N

PORTUGAL, CROWN OF, is a ducal coronet, heightened up with eight arched diadems that support a mound, ensigned with a plain cross. Pl. XLV., n. 9.

POSÉ. See STATANT.

POTENT, A CROSS, so termed by reason of the resemblance its extremities bear to the head of a crutch, which, in *Chaucer's* description of old age, is called a *potent :*—

> "So eld she was, that she ne went
> A foote, but it were by *potent.*"

Pl. VI., n. 5. *Azure, a cross potent or ;* name, *Branchley.*

POTENT-COUNTER-POTENT, *argent and azure ;* fur so termed, because it is said to resemble the heads of crutches : in blazon the colours being named, they may be tinctured with any other, as *argent, sable, &c.* Pl. II., n. 6.

POULDRON, that part of a suit of armour which covers the shoulder.

POWDERING signifies the strewing of a field, crest, or supporters, irregularly with any small figures, as escallops, martlets, fleurs-de-lis, &c. See also SEMÉ.

PRASIN, an ancient term for green; from the Greek, signifying a leek.

PRECISE MIDDLE CHIEF. See MIDDLE CHIEF.

PRECISE MIDDLE BASE. See MIDDLE BASE.

PREDOMINANT signifies that the field is but of one tincture.

PREENE, an instrument used by clothiers in dressing cloth. Pl. XXX., n. 5. *Azure, a preene or ;* name, *Preener.*

PREMIER, from the French, signifies *first ;* and is used by English heralds to signify the most ancient peer of any degree by creation.

PRESTER JOHN, or Presbyter John, is drawn as a bishop, sitting on a tombstone, having on his head a mitre, his dexter hand extended, a mound in his sinister, and in his mouth a sword fesswise ; the point to the dexter side of the field. This is part of the arms of the episcopal see of Chichester. Pl. XXXIX., n. 11.

PRETENCE. See ESCUTCHEON OF PRETENCE.

PRIDE : this term is used for turkeycocks and pea-cocks. When they extend their tails into a circle, and drop their wings, they are said to be in their pride. Pl. XXXV., n. 11.

PRIMROSE, an ancient term for the quatrefoil.

PRISONERS' BOLT. See SHACKBOLT.

PROBOSCIS is the trunk of an elephant. Pl. XXVIII., n. 20.

PROPER : this term is applied to all creatures, vege-tables, &c., when borne in coats of arms in their natural colours.

PRUSSIA, CROWN OF. Pl. XLV., n. 12.

PURFLED, trimmed or garnished, a term for the studs and rims of armour being gold : viz., *an arm in armour proper, purfled or.*

PURPURE is the colour purple, and, in engraving, is represented by diagonal lines, from the left to the right. Pl. II.

PYOT. A provincial name for a magpie.

QUADRANS, Lat. a Canton.

QUADRATE signifies square ; a cross potent quadrate in the centre, that is, the centre of the cross is square. See Pl. XXXVI., n. 29.

QUARTER, an ordinary of a quadrangular form, con-taining a fourth part of the field ; it is formed by two lines, one drawn from the side of the shield horizontally to the centre, and the other perpendicularly from the chief, to meet it in the same point. Pl. IV., n. 23.

QUARTERINGS are the partitions of a shield, containing many coats of arms. See Plate XIX., n. 19.

QUARTERLY is when a shield or charge is divided into four parts, by a perpendicular and horizontal line, which, crossing each other in the centre of the field, divide it into four equal parts, called quarters. Pl. XIII., n. 6. Pl. XIX., n. 19.

QUARTERLY PIERCED signifies a square hole in a cross, a millrine, &c., through which aperture the field is seen. See examples, Pl. XXXVI., n. 1.

QUARTERLY QUARTERED is a saltire quartered in the centre, and the branches each parted by two different tinctures alternately. See Plate XIX., n. 16.

QUATREFOIL, four-leaved grass : this, as well as the trefoil, is much used in heraldry. Pl. VI., n. 22.

QUEUE, a term for the tail of an animal.

QUILL OF YARN. See the example, Pl. XXV., n. 22.

QUINTAIN, QUINTAL, or QUINTIN, a kind of tilting-post used in a gymnastic pastime of our ancestors. There is one at Offham, in Kent; it stands upon a green in the midst of the village, and is about seven feet in length; the transverse piece is about five feet in length, the broad part of which is marked with many circles about the size of a half-crown; and at the other end is a block of wood, weighing about four or five pounds, suspended by a chain; the whole of which turns round upon a pivot upon the upright part; and the game was played as follows: a man on horseback being armed with a strong pole, of a certain length, rides with full speed within a few feet of the quintal, and making a strong thrust at that part of it where the circles are marked, it is turned round with such violence, that, unless he is very expert, he is sure to receive a blow on the head from the pendulous piece on the opposite side. Pl. XXXIII., n. 6.

QUIVER OF ARROWS, a case filled with arrows.

RACK-POLE BEACON. See FIRE-BEACON.

RADIANT, or RAYONNANT, is when rays or beams are represented about a charge; as Pl. VI., n. 16.

RAGULED is when the bearing is uneven or ragged, like the trunk or limb of a tree lopt of its branches, so that only the stumps are seen. One of the lines of partition, from its shape, is termed raguled. Pl. III., and Pl. XXXVI., n. 2.

RAGULY, A CROSS, is one which seems to be made of two trunks of trees without branches. Pl. XXXVI., n. 2. *Sable, a cross raguly, or;* name, *Stoway.*

RAINBOW is a semicircle of various colours, arising from clouds. Pl. XVIII., n. 6. *Argent, a rainbow proper;* name, *Pont.*

RAM : the male sheep. *Sable, a chevron, between three rams' heads couped, argent;* name, *Ramsey.*

RAMPANT, a term applied to describe a beast standing upright on his hinder legs. Pl. IX., n. 2.

RAMPANT-GARDANT, signifies a lion standing upright on his hinder legs, full-faced, looking right forward. Pl. IX., n. 2.

RAMPANT-REGARDANT; a term for any beast standing upright on its hinder legs, looking behind or towards its back. Pl. IX., n. 4.

RAPING, an old term for ravenous beasts when represented *feeding.*

RAVEN, a bird found in almost all countries in the world, *or, a raven proper;* name, *Corbet.* Pl. XXVI., n. 18.

RAVISSANT, a French term, used to describe the position of a wolf, or other wild beast, half raised, on the point of springing on his prey. It is also applied occasionally to all ravenous animals, when feeding on or devouring their prey.

RAY, a stream of light from any luminous body, as the sun or stars. Pl. XII., n. 30. When rays are depicted round the sun, they should be sixteen in number; when round an estoile, six only: in either case, straight and waved alternately.

RAYONNANT, A CROSS, is that which has rays of glory behind it, darting from the centre to all the quarters of the escutcheon. Pl. VI., n. 16.

REBATED is when the top or point of a weapon is broken off.

REBATEMENT. See DIFFERENCE.

REBUS, in heraldry, is generally a device, allusive to the name of the bearer: frequently, however, the painted representation is accompanied with words, or an imperfect motto: the accompanying words explaining the thing represented, and the representation aiding to make sense of the imperfect motto; as the motto, " *We must*," on a sun-dial: the meaning of which is made up by the thing itself; that is, " We must *die all*." Puerilities of this kind were anciently so much in fashion, that many instances of their use, especially during the sixteenth century, may be found even in churches. Examples: *Islip*, abbot of Westminster, sculptured in the abbey, a representation of a man slipping from a tree. *Bolton*, prior of St. Bartholomew, Smithfield, sculptured in the church a bolt or arrow pierced through a tun. *Rose Knotwing*, in a painting on glass in an old house, Islington, the representation of a rose, a knot, or twisted cord, and a wing. Peacham, in his "Compleat Gentleman," says, "Certain citizens, wanting arms, have coined themselves devices alluding to their names, which we call *rebus* : thus, Master Jugge, the printer, in many of his books, took, to express his name, a nightingale sitting in a bush with a scroll in her mouth, on which was inscribed, Jugge, Jugge, Jugge."

RECLINANT, bowed or bending backward.

RECERCELÉE. See CERCELÉE.

RECROSSED, A CROSS, is the same as a crosslet.

REED. See SLAY.

REFLECTED, or REFLEXED, curved or turned round, as the chain or line from the collar of a dog, &c., thrown over the back.

REGALIA, the ensigns of royalty.

REGARDANT, signifies an animal looking behind, having its face turned towards its back: as seeing, marking, vigilant. Pl. IX., n. 12.

REIN-GUARD, for that part of armour which guards the lower part of the back.

REIN-DEER, as drawn in armoury, is a stag with double attires ; as the example, Pl. XXXII., n. 5.

REMORA. This word, in heraldry is used to denote a serpent, in blazoning the figure of Prudence, which is represented holding in her hand a javelin entwined with a serpent proper ; such serpent is expressed by the word Remora.

RENVERSÉ, is when anything is set with the head downwards, or contrary to its natural way of being: as a chevron with the point downwards, or when a beast is laid on its back. Pl. XXVI., n. 3.

RERE-MOUSE, or BAT. *Argent, a rere-mouse displayed sable;* name, *Baxter.* Pl. XXXI., n. 18.

RESPECTING, a term for fish, or tame beasts, when placed upright one against the other. Pl. X., n. 5. For beasts of prey the term COMBATANT is used.

REST: this figure is deemed by some a rest for a horseman's lance; by others, an organ-rest, and a musical instrument, termed a clarion or claricord. It is, in many ancient examples, drawn precisely like the mouth-organ, or Pan's pipe. It is clear it could not have been a lance-rest, as it appears centuries before the introduction of that article. Pl. VII., n. 11.

RESTRIALL, an ancient term for barry, paly and pily.

RHINOCEROS. Pl. XXXI., n. 21.

RIBBON, or RIBAND, an ordinary containing the eighth part of the bend, of which it is a diminutive. Pl. IV., n. 9.

RISING, a term applied to birds when preparing to fly. Pl. IX., n. 20.

ROMPU, A CHEVRON, signifying a chevron, bend, or the like, broken. Pl. XXXVIII., n. 18. *Sable, a chevron rompu, between three mullets or;* name, *Sault.* See Plate XIII., n. 27.

ROSE, in blazon, the following (according to Guillim) should be observed, viz., *argent, a rose gules, barbed and seeded proper.* The rose is blazoned gules; the leaves are called *barbed,* and are always green, as the seed in the middle is yellow; the word *proper* should be omitted in blazoning this flower; for it could not be understood of what colour, as there are two sorts, *white* and *red.* Pl. VI., n. 24. The rose is used as a distinction for the seventh brother. See Distinction of Houses. Pl. XLII., n. 7,

The roses of England were first publicly assumed as devices by the sons of Edward III. *John of Gaunt, Duke of Lancaster,* used the red rose for the badge of his family; and his brother *Edward,* who was created *Duke of York,* anno 1385, took a white rose for his device, which the followers of them and their heirs afterwards bore for distinction in that bloody war between the two houses of *York* and *Lancaster.* The two families being happily united by Henry VII., the male heir of the house of Lancaster, marrying Princess *Elizabeth,* the eldest daughter and heiress of *Edward* IV. of the house of York, anno 1486, the two *roses* were united in one, and became the royal badge of England.

ROSELETTES, Leigh says, signify single roses, having five leaves each.

ROSE-DOUBLE. See Pl. xxxvii., n. 21.

ROUNDELS, or ROUNDLETS. See Pl. viii., n. 9 to 15.

ROUSANT, a term for a bird preparing to take wing, but whose weight of body prevents it from rising suddenly into the air, as swans, &c. When this term is applied to a swan, we are to understand that her wings are indorsed ; as the example, Pl. x., n. 10.

RUBY, a stone used in heraldry instead of gules, being of a red colour.

RUSSIA, CROWN OF. Pl. xlv., n. 11.

RUSTRE, is a lozenge pierced of a circular form in the middle. See Pl. xxxvii., n. 22. Boyer says, *rustre* is from the German *raute,* which signifies the nut of a screw.

SABLE is the colour black, and in engraving is represented by perpendicular and horizontal lines crossing each other. Pl. ii.

SACRE or SAKER, a kind of falcon; the head gray the feet and legs bluish, the back a dark brown.

SAGITTARIUS, an imaginary creature, half man and half beast; it represents one of the twelve signs of the zodiac, and is said to have been borne by King Stephen of England, who entered the kingdom when the sun was in that sign, and obtained a great victory by the help of his archers; but we have no contemporary authority for this statement, nor pictorial example of it. Pl xxxi., n. 1.

SAIL, Pl. xxx., n. 16.   *Gules, three sails argent;* name, *Cavell.* It is sometimes represented with a portion of the mast before it.

SALAMANDER, a fictitious reptile, represented like a small common lizard in the midst of flames. Pl. xxviii., n. 3.   *Azure, a salamander or, in flames proper;* name, *Cennino.*

SALIANT signifies leaping. Pl. ix., n. 6.   *Argent, a lion saliant gules;* name, *Petit.*

COUNTER-SALIANT is when two beasts on the same escutcheon are saliant; the one leaping one way, and the other another, so that they look the direct opposite ways; as the example, Pl. ix., n. 9, which should be blazoned, *two foxes, counter-saliant in saltier,* the sinister surmounted by the dexter.

SALLED or SALLET, from the Italian Celato, a steel head-piece of the fifteenth century.

SALT, or SALT-CELLARS, are vessels with salt falling from the sides, as borne in the arms of the Salters' Company; as Pl. xxxii., n. 26. Some heralds have blazoned them sprinkling salts. They were anciently drawn as the example. At coronation dinners, and all great feasts given by the nobility and gentry in ancient times, it was usual to set one of these salts in the centre of the dining-table; not only for holding salt for the use of the guests, but as a mark to separate and distinguish the seats of the superior sort of company from those of an inferior degree; it being the custom of former times to set the nobility and gentry above the salt, and the yeomanry and persons of lower rank below the salt.

SALTIRE. This cross is an ordinary which is formed by the bend dexter and bend sinister crossing each other in the centre at acute angles; uncharged, it contains the fifth, and charged, the third part of the field. Pl. IV., n. 21.

PER SALTIRE is when the field is divided into four parts by two diagonal lines, dexter and sinister, that cross each other in the centre of the field, dividing it into four equal parts, in form of a saltire. Pl. III., n. 6. *Party per saltire ermine and gules;* name, *Restwold.*

SANGUINE is the murrey colour, or dark red, and is represented in engraving by lines diagonally from the dexter to the sinister side, and from the sinister to the dexter. Pl. XLI., n. 2.

SANS-NOMBRE signifies many whole figures strewed on the field; but if part of them are cut off at the extremities of the escutcheon, as the example, Pl. XXXV., n. 31, it then is termed *Semé.*

SAPPHIRE, in heraldry, is used to express the colour azure, it being a stone of a fine sky-blue colour, and the hardest next a diamond.

SARDONYX; this stone is used in heraldry instead of sanguine, or dark-red colour.

SATURN, one of the planets, and is used instead of the colour sable.

SATYRAL, a fictitious animal, having the body of a lion, the tail and horns of an antelope, and the face of an old man. Pl. xviii., n. 9.

SATYR. See MAN-TIGER.

SCALING-LADDER. This instrument is used to scale the walls of besieged castles and cities. Pl. xiii., n. 18. *Argent, three scaling-ladders bendwise gules;* name, *Killingworth.*

SCARPE. A diminutive of the bend sinister. Pl. iv., n. 11.

SCEPTRE, a royal staff used by kings; *azure, a sceptre in pale or, ensigned with an eye.* Pl. xxvii., n. 9.

SCORPION, Pl. xxviii., n. 19. *Argent, a fess engrailed between three scorpions erect sable;* name, *Cole.*

SCOTCH SPUR, Pl. xxx., n. 19. This is the ancient way of making spurs before rowels were invented, with the buckles fixed to the heel-piece, as the example. It is the Anglo-Norman pryck-spur.

SCRIP, *argent, a chevron between three palmers' scrips, the tassels and buckles or;* name, *Palmer.* Pl. xxvii., n. 7. In the chancel at Snodland, in Kent, where Thomas Palmer, who married the daughter of Fitz-Simon, lies buried, is the following epitaph :—

> " Palmers all our faders were,
> I a Palmer lived here;
> And travell'd still, till worn wud age
> I ended this world's pilgrimage.
> On the blest Ascension day,
> In the cheerful month of May,
> A thousand with four hundred seaven,
> I took my journey hence to heaven."

Palmer (so called from a staff of a palm-tree, which they carried as they returned from the holy war), a

Pilgrim that visited holy places; yet a Pilgrim and a Palmer differed thus: a Pilgrim had some dwelling-place, and a Palmer had none; the Pilgrim travelled to some certain place, the Palmer to all, and not to any one in particular; the Pilgrim must go at his own charge, the Palmer must profess wilful poverty; the Pilgrim might give over his profession, but the Palmer might not.—*Bailey.* The dress of a Pilgrim was an under vest, with an outer robe, having half-open sleeves, showing the under-sleeves, which continued to the wrists. On his head a broad-brimmed hat, with a shell in front; on his feet sandals, or short laced boots; in his hand a staff, and by his side a scrip.

SCROGS, a term used by the Scotch heralds for a small branch of a tree.

SCROLL, or label, wherein the motto is inserted.

SCRUTTLE. See WINNOWING-BASKET.

SCUTCHEON. See ESCUTCHEON.

SCYTHE, an instrument used in husbandry. *Argent, a scythe and in fess a fleur-de-lis sable;* name, *Snyde,* or *Sneyde.* Pl. xxxv., n. 34.

SEA-DOG is drawn in shape like the talbot, but with a tail like that of the beaver; a scalloped fin continued down the back from the head to the tail; the whole body, legs, and tail scaled, and the feet webbed. Pl. xxxii., n. 7.

SEA-GULL. Pl. xxxiii., n. 17. *Azure, a chevron or, between three sea-gulls argent;* name, *Houlditch.*

SEA-HORSE; the fore part is formed like a horse, with webbed feet, and the hinder part ends in a fish's tail. Pl. xxxi., n. 3.

SEAL. See MARINE WOLF.

SEAL'S PAW, erased, Pl. xxxiii., n. 9. *Argent, a*

chevron between three seals' paws, erased, sable. These
are the arms of *Yarmouth*, in Norfolk.

SEA-LION. The upper part is like a lion, and the
lower part like the tail of a fish. See Pl. xxxii., n. 20.
When the sea-lion is drawn erect, as Pl. xxxi., n. 29, it
is blazoned, a *sea-lion, erect on his tail.*

SEA-PIE, a water-fowl of a dark-brown colour, with a
red head, and the neck and wings white. Pl. xxxii.,
n. 3. *Gules, a chevron, between three sea-pies or ;* name
Snyer.

SEAX, a scimitar, with a semicircular notch hollowed
out of the back of the blade. Pl. xxxii., n. 2. It is
said, most incorrectly, to be formed exactly like the
Saxon sword. The Saxon sword was perfectly strait.
as evidenced by the numbers found in tumuli, and by
the drawings in Anglo-Saxon MSS. The heraldic
Seax is drawn in the shape of a cutlass or falchion.

SEEDED is chiefly appled to roses, to express the
colour of their seed.

SEGREANT signifies a griffin erect on its hind-legs,
with the wings indorsed, and displayed as ready to fly
Pl. xxxv., n. 13.

SÉJANT, *sitting ;* a term applied to all beasts when
borne in that position. Pl. viii., n. 21.

SÉJANT-ADDORSED is when two beasts are sitting
back to back. Pl. ix., n. 11. *Argent, two squirrels séjant-
addorsed gules ;* name, *Samwell.*

SEMÉ is an irregular strewing without number, all
over the field. Pl. xxxv., n. 31.

SENGREEN, or house-leek, is part of the arms of Caius
College, Cambridge.

SENTIRE, an ancient term for Piles.

SERAPH'S HEAD is a child's head between three pair

of wings; the two uppermost and two lowermost are counterly crossed; the two middlemost displayed. See Plate XXXIII., n. 1.

SHACKBOLT, by some called a prisoner's bolt. Pl. XXXIV., n. 24. *Sable, three pair of shack-bolts argent;* name, *Anderton.* See one pair, Plate XXXII., n. 27.

SHAFTED is when a spear-head has a handle in it; then it is termed shafted.

SHAKE-FORK. See HAY-FORK.

SHAMROCK, a term in Ireland for the trefoil, or three-leaved grass.

SHAVE. See CURRIERS' SHAVE.

SHIELD. See ESCUTCHEON.

SHOVELLER, a species of water-fowl, somewhat like the duck. The ancient heralds drew this bird with a tuft on its breast, and another on the back of its head, as Pl. XXXII., n. 1. *Gules, a shoveller argent;* name, *Langford.*

SHRUTTLE. See WINNOWING-BASKET.

SHUTTLE; *argent, three weavers' shuttles sable, tipped, and furnished with quills of yarn;* name, *Shuttleworth.* Pl. XXVII., n. 22.

SILK-HANKS, Pl. XXX., n. 14. Such are borne in the arms of the Silk-Throwers' Company.

SINISTER signifies the left side or part of anything, and is the female side in an impaled coat.

SINISTER CANTON is the canton placed on the left side of the shield in chief.

SINISTER BEND is a bend placed from the sinister chief to the dexter base, and in size the same as the bend.

SINISTER CHIEF is the left side of the chief, expressed by the letter C, Table I., page 10.

SINISTER BASE, the left hand part of the base, represented by the letter H, Table I., page 10.

SINISTER HAND, the left hand. Pl. xxxv., n. 33.

SINOPLE signifies the colour green.

SKEIN, a Scotch term for a dagger. *Gules, a chevron, between three skeins argent, hilted and pomelled or, surmounted of as many-wolves' heads, couped close;* name, *Skein.*

SLAY, SLEA, or REED; an instrument used by weavers, and borne as part of the arms of the Company of Weavers of the city of Exeter. Pl. xxxiv., n. 18.

SLING. See Plate xxxiii., n. 19. Such a sling is part of the arms of Cawardyn; viz., *sable, a sling bendwise between two pheons' heads.*

SLIPS. See BRANCHES.

SLIPPED is a flower or branch plucked from the stock. Pl. x., n. 11.

SLUGHORN: this term is used by the Scotch heralds for what the French call *le cri de guerre*, and the English the *war-cry*.

SNAIL, sometimes termed a house-snail. Pl. xxvii., n. 13. *Sable, a fess between three house-snails argent* name, *Shelly.*

SOL, the sun. In heraldry sometimes used to press gold, in blazoning the arms of sovereigns.

SOLDERING-IRON, a tool used by the plumbers, and borne in the arms of their Company. Pl. xxxiv., n. 33.

SPADE-IRON, or the shoeing of a spade. Pl. xxxii., n. 25. *Azure, three spade-irons or ;* name, *Becton.*

SPAIN, CROWN OF. See Plate xlv., n. 8.

SPANCELLED, or fettered, is when a horse has his fore and hind legs, of the near side fettered with fetter-locks fastened to the end of a stick. Pl. XXXIII., n. 21. This is the arms of *Percivall.*

SPERVERS, a term for *tents,* as borne by the Upholders' Company.

SPHINX, a fabulous creature represented with a head, face, and breasts like a woman ; body and legs like a lion, and wings like a bird. *A sphinx passant, wings indorsed, argent crined or,* is the crest of *Asgill,* bart Pl. XXXI., n. 2.

SPIDER and WEB. *A cobweb, in the centre a spider ,* name, *Cobster,* of Lombardy. See Plate XXXIX., n. 10.

SPLENDOUR ; a term for the sun, which, when represented with a human face, and environed with rays, is blazoned *in splendour.*

SPRIGS. See BRANCHES.

SPRINGING, for beasts of chase, is the same as saliant for those of prey. Pl. IX., n. 15.

SPUR. Gilt spurs were the distinguishing mark of Knighthood ; when borne on shields they are generally represented with the rowel downwards. See SCOTCH SPUR.

SQUARE, Pl. XXX., n. 7. *Argent, a chevron between three carpenters' squares, sable ;* name, *Attow.*

SQUIRREL. Pl. XXVI., n. 24. Also Plate XXXIX., n. 7.

SRUTTLE. See WINNOWING-BASKET.

STAFFORD KNOT. See the example, Plate XXXII., n. 31. *Or, on a chevron gules, a Stafford knot argent,* the arms of *Stafford* town.

STAG, borne in heraldry in various positions : as, *trippant, courant, lodged, at bay, at gaze,* &c. : see those terms. Pl. IX., n. 14.

STARS. See ESTOILES.

STATANT, signifies an animal standing, with all feet on the ground. Pl. VIII., n. 22

STAVES OF AN ESCARBUNCLE are the eight rays that issue from its centre. See Pl. VII., n. 18.

STILTS. See the examples, Plate XXXV., n. 5. *Argent, two stilts in saltire sable, garnished or ;* the arms of *Newby,* of Yorkshire.

STIRRUP. Pl. XXVIII., n. 22. *Gules, three stirrups with buckles and straps or ;* name, *Scudamore.*

STORK. *Argent, a stork sable membered gules ;* name, *Starkey,* of Cheshire. Pl. XXXI., n. 19.

STREAMING is the stream of light darting from a comet. See Plate XVIII., n. 7.

SUFFLUE, a term for a rest or clarion.

SUN, in heraldry, is represented with a human face, environed with rays, and is termed a sun in its splendour. Pl. XXVIII., n. 5.

SUPER-CHARGÉ is one figure charged or borne upon another.

SUPER-IMBATTLED ; *azure, a fess, super-imbattled, between six estoiles or ;* name, *Tryon.* See Plate XI. n. 8.

SUPPORTERS. See page 65.

SUPPRESSED. See DEBRUISED.

SURCOAT, a loose coat, formerly worn by military men over their armour, and upon which their arms were embroidered, in order that they might be distinguished in time of battle.

SURMOUNTED is when one charge is placed over another. See Plate XI., n. 34, viz., *sable, a pile argent, surmounted of a chevron gules ;* name, *Dyxton.*

SURTOUT, a term for over-all; it signifies a small escutcheon, containing a coat of augmentation.

SWALLOW. *Or, three swallows close, proper ;* name, *Watton.* See Plate XXIX., n. 23.

SWAN. Pl. XXXI., n. 15. *Gules, a swan argent, membered or ;* name, *Leyham.*

SWEPE ; used in ancient times to cast stones into towns and fortified places of an enemy. Pl. XXXIV., n. 17. *Argent, a swepe azure, charged with a stone or ;* name, *Magnall,* one of the names for a machine of this description being *Mangonel.*

SWIVEL, two iron links which turn on a bolt. Pl. XXXIV., n. 29. Three such are borne on a chevron, in the arms of the Ironmongers' Company.

SYNAMUR. See SANGUINE.

SYPHON. See FIRE-BUCKET.

SYREN, or Mermaid.

TABARD, a short loose garment for the body, without sleeves, worn by knights in the 15th century over their armour in order to distinguish them in battle; whereon were embroidered their arms, &c. At present a tabard is worn only by heralds, on public occasions.

TABERNACLE. See TENT.

TALBOT, a sort of hunting-dog between a hound and a beagle, with a large snout, long, round, hanging, and thick ears. Pl. XXXI., n. 26. *Argent, a talbot passant, sable, gutté d'or ;* name, *Shirrington.*

TAPER-CANDLESTICK. See CANDLESTICK.

TASCES, or TASSES, a part of armour to cover the thighs.

TASSEL is a bunch of silk, or gold fringe, and is an addition to the strings of mantles and robes of state. Pl. XXVIII., n. 18. *Gules, three tassels or ;* name, *Wooler.*

TASSELLED ; that is, decorated with tassels.

TAU, A CROSS, or St. Anthony's cross ; so called because St. Anthony the monk is always painted with

it upon his habit; likewise named from the Greek letter tau. Pl. xxxvi., n. 26.

TEAZEL, the head or seed-vessel of a species of thistle; it is used by clothiers in dressing cloth, and borne in the arms of their Company. Pl. xxxiv., n. 7.

TENNE, or TAWNY, signifies orange-colour, and in engraving is represented by diagonal lines from the dexter to the sinister side of the shield, traversed by perpendicular lines. Pl. xli., n. 1.

TENT, tabernacle, or pavilion. Pl. xxxix., n. 21. *Sable, a chevron between three tents, argent;* name, *Tenton.*

TÊTE (French), signifies the head of an animal.

THATCH-RAKE. Pl. xxx., n. 4.

THUNDERBOLT, in heraldry, is a twisted bar in pale inflamed at each end, surmounting two jagged darts, in saltire, between two wings displayed with streams of fire. Pl. xxvii., n. 20.

TIARA, a cap of golden cloth, from which hang two pendants, embroidered and fringed at the ends, *semé* of crosses of gold. This cap is enclosed by three coronets: on the top is a mount of gold, with a cross of the same. When *Boniface VIII.* was elected into the See of Rome, 1295, he first encompassed his cap with a coronet: *Benedict II.,* in 1335, added a second to it: and *John XXII.,* in 1411, a third, with a view to indicate by them that the *Pope* is *sovereign priest, the supreme judge,* and the *sole legislator* amongst Christians. Pl. xlv., n. 4.

TIERCÉ is a French term for a shield divided, or ingrafted into three areas. Pl. xxxvii., n. 26 to 33. These partitions are not used by English heralds.

TIERCÉ-IN-BEND. *Ibid.,* n. 26

TIERCÉ-IN-FESS. *Ibid.*, n. 33.

TIERCÉ-IN-GYRONS, bend sinisterwise. *Ibid.*, n. 29.

TIERCÉ-IN-GYRONS ARONDI. *Ibid.*, n. 31

TIERCÉ-IN-MANTLE. *Ibid.*, n. 32.

TIERCÉ-IN-PAIRLE. *Ibid.*, n. 27.

TIERCÉ-IN-PALE. *Ibid.*, n. 28.

TIERCÉ-IN-PILE, from sinister to dexter. *Ibid.*, n. 30.

TIGER HERALDIC, so termed to distinguish it from the natural tiger. See Pl. VIII., n. 3.

TIGER NATURAL. See Pl. XXIX., n. 1.

TILLAGE, RAKE-HEAD. Pl. XXX., n. 3.

TILTING-SPEAR, a spear used at tilts and tournaments. Pl. XXIX. n. 8.

TIMBRE, signifies the helmet, when placed over the arms in a complete achievement, but, properly, is only the French name for crest.

TINCTURE is the colour of anything in coat-armour : under this denomination may be included the two metals *or* and *argent*, gold and silver, because they are often represented by yellow and white, and are themselves of those colours.

TIRRET, a modern term for manacles or handcuffs, as in the badges of the house of *Percy*. Pl. x., n. 12. See also another form, Pl. XXIX., n. 3.

TOMB-STONE. Pl. XXX., n. 10. Three such are the arms of *Tomb.*

TOPAZ, a stone of a gold colour, by some used instead of *or*.

TORN, an ancient name in heraldry for a spinning-wheel.

TORQUED, wreathed or twisted, from the Latin *torqueo.*

TORQUED, sometimes applied to a *dolphin hauriant,*

which forms a figure similar to the letter S. See
Pl. xvi., n. 18.

TORSE. See WREATH.

TORTEAUX is a roundle of a red colour. Pl. viii, n. 11.

TORTOISE; *vert, a tortoise passant argent;* name,
Gawdy. Pl. xxvi., n. 13.

TOURNÉ, a French term synonymous with REGARDANT.

TOWER; *argent, a tower sable, having a scaling-ladder
raised against it in bend sinister.* This is the arms of
Cardivar ap Dinwall, Lord of Aberser, in South Wales.
Pl. xxxix., n. 10.

TOWERED, a term applied to the towers or turrets on
walls or castles, also applied to towers when surmounted
by smaller towers or turrets; as, *azure, a tower triple-
towered or;* name, *Towers.*

TRANSFLUENT, a term for water running through the
arches of a bridge. See Pl. xxxix., n. 22.

TRANSPOSED is when bearings are placed out of their
usual situation. See Pl. xxxviii., n. 33.

TREFOIL, or three-leaved grass. Pl. vi., n. 21. *Argent,
a fess nebulé between three trefoils slipt gules;* name,
Thorp, of Gloucestershire.

TREILLÉ, or latticed; it differs from *fretty,* for the
pieces in the *treille* do not cross under and over each
other, but are carried throughout, and are always
nailed in the joints. *Argent, treillé gules, nailed or;*
name, *Bardonenche.* See Pl. xli., n. 5.

TRESSURE, allowed to be half the breadth of the orle,
and is borne flory and counterflory : it passes round the
field in the same shape and form as the escutcheon,
and is generally borne double, and sometimes treble.
Pl. v., n. 5. Pl. xix., n. 9. If a coat be impaled with
another, either on the dexter or sinister side and hath

a tressure, the tressure must finish at the impaled line, and not be continued round the coat. The double "tressure flowerie" encompasses the lion of Scotland, and is frequently met with in the arms of the Scotch nobility.

TRESTLE, or three-legged stool. Pl. xxviii., n. 14. *Gules ; a fess humetté, between three trestles argent ;* name, *Stratford.*

TREVET. Pl. xxviii., n. 13. *Argent, a trevet sable ;* name, *Trevett.* The trevet is termed from its three feet, a *tripod,* which in Greek signifies a stool of so many feet.

TREVET, triangular. Pl. xxxv., n. 12. *Argent, a triangular trevet sable ;* name, *Barkle.*

TRICORPORATED is a lion with three bodies issuing from the three corners of the escutcheon, and meeting under one head in the fess point ; this device was borne by Edmund Crouchback, Earl of Lancaster, brother to King Edward I. Pl. xxxii., n. 16.

TRIDENT, a three-pronged barbed fork, generally placed in the hand of Neptune.

TRIPARTED, divided into three parts.

TRIPARTED, a cross-flory. Pl. xxxvii., n. 9.

TRIPPANT, or TRIPPING; this term is proper for beasts of chase, as passant for those of prey; represented with one foot up, as it were on a trot. See Pl. ix., n. 14. *Argent, a stag tripping proper, attired and unguled or ;* name, *Holme.*

Counter-Tripping is when two beasts are tripping, the one passing one way, and the other another, as the example, Pl. ix., n. 10 ; also, *sable, two hinds counter-tripping in fess argent ;* name, *Cottingham.* See Pl. xxxi., n. 13.

TRIPLE PLUME. See OSTRICH FEATHERS.

TRIUMPHAL CROWN was composed of laurel, and granted to those generals who had vanquished their enemies, and had the honour of a triumph granted to them by the Roman Senate. Pl. XLV., n. 25. In after ages it was changed for gold, and not restricted to those that actually triumphed, but presented on several other accounts, as by foreign states and provinces to their patrons and benefactors.

TRON-ONNÉE, A CROSS. See DISMEMBERED.

TRUMPET. Pl. XXIX., n. 15. *Argent, a chevron engrailed, between three trumpets sable;* name, *Thunder.*

TRUNCATED, or TRUNKED, a term applied to the main stem of trees, &c., when couped, or cut off smooth. See the example, Pl. XVIII., n. 14.

TRUNDLES, quills of gold thread, used by the embroiderers, and borne in the arms of their Company. Pl. XXXIV., n. 22.

TRUSSING; the example is a falcon, his wings expanded, *trussing* a mallard. See Pl. XXXVIII., n. 23.

TURKEY. Pl. XXIX., n. 11. *Argent, a chevron sable, between three turkey-cocks in their pride proper;* name, *Yeo.*

TURKISH CROWN. See GRAND SEIGNIOR.

TURNPIKE. See the example, Pl. XXIV., n. 4: also Pl. XXXIII., n. 10, *three such, sable, on a field argent;* name, *Woolstone.*

TURNSTILE, or TURNPIKE. Pl. XXVIII., n. 11. This example is borne as a crest by *Sir Grey Skipwith,* Bart., but now blazoned as a "*reel,* proper."

TURRET, a small tower on the top of another.

TURRET. See Pl. XXIX., n. 3. *Sable, on a bend between two turrets argent, three pheons gules, on a chief or, a lion passant, between two lozenges azure;* name, *Johnson.*

TURRETED, having small turrets on the top of a wall or tower, as Pl. xxxix., n. 19.

TUSCANY, CROWN OF. Pl. xlv., n. 17.

TUSK, the long tooth of an elephant, boar, &c.

TUSKED, a term used in blazonry, when the tusks of an animal are of a different tincture from its body.

UMBRATED, signifies shadowed.

UNDÉE, or UNDY, the same as WAVED, or WAVY.

UNGULED, signifies hoofed.

UNICORN, a fabulous beast, well known as one of the supporters of the royal arms. Pl. xxxi., n. 5. *Argent, a unicorn passant gules, armed or ;* name, *Stasam.*

UNION, CROSS OF THE. This form was settled, A.D. 1707, as the badge of the union between England and Scotland, and is blazoned, *azure, a saltire argent surmounted of a cross gules, edged of the second,* as in Pl. xxxvi., n. 27. After the union with Ireland in 1801, the cross of St. Patrick *argent a saltire gules* was incorporated with these, forming, when combined, the national flag known as the union jack.

URCHIN. See HEDGE-HOG.

URDÉE. See CLECHÉE.

VAIR, a fur used for lining the mantles of officials of high rank, supposed to have been derived from sewing together the skins of a small animal of a bluish tinge on the back and white on the belly; therefore this fur is always understood to be *argent* and *azure,* unless any other metal or tincture be specified. Pl. ii., n. 4. Argent, a border vair. Pl. v., n. 16.

VAIR ANCIENT, as appears by many good MSS., was represented by lines nebulé, separated by straight lines, in fess. See the example, Pl. xl.

VAIR, A CROSS, is one composed of four pieces of

vair, their points turned to one another, in the form of
a cross. Pl. XXXVI., n. 34.

VAIR-EN-POINT is a fur with the cups ranged upon a
line counterwise, argent and azure. Pl. XL.

VALLARY-CROWN was of gold, with palisades fixed
against the rim; it was given by the general of the
army to a captain or soldier that first entered the
enemy's camp, by forcing the palisade. Pl. XLV., n. 21.

VAMBRACED, signifies an arm habited in armour. See
Pl. XXXIV., n. 34. *Gules, three dexter arms vambraced,
in pale proper;* name, *Armstrong.*

VAMPLATE, a piece of steel formed like a funnel,
placed on tilting-spears just before the hand, to secure
it, and so fixed as to be taken off at pleasure.

VANNET, a term by some French authors for the
escallop or *cockle-shell,* when represented without ears.
See Pl. XXXVIII., n. 11.

VARVELLED, or VERVELLED.   See VERVELS and
JESSES.

VENICE, CROWN OF THE DOGE OF. Pl. XLV., n. 20.

VENUS, one of the planets, used for the colour vert.

VERDOY signifies a bordure to be charged with any
kind of vegetables. The example is, *argent a bordure
azure, verdoy of eight trefoils, argent.* Pl. XXXVIII., n. 12.
It would be more heraldic to say, *argent, a border
charged with eight trefoils, argent.*

VERRY, or VAIRÉ, always consists of four distinct
colours, whose names must be mentioned in the blazon,
as thus; *verry, or, azure, sable, gules,* &c. Pl. XL.

VERT signifies the colour green: it is represented in
engraving by diagonal lines from the dexter chief to
the sinister base. Pl. II.

VERVELS, small rings fixed to the end of the jesses,

through which falconers put a string in order to fasten
the bells to falcons' legs.

VIROLLES, or VERULES, a term applied to the ornamental rings of a hunting-horn, when set round with
metal or colour different from the horn.

VOIDED is when an ordinary has nothing but an
edge to show its form : all the inward part supposed
to be cut out or evacuated, so that the field appears
through : therefore it is needless to express the colour
or metal of the voided part, because it must of course
be that of the field. Pl. xxxvii., n. 17.

VOIDERS. These figures are formed like the flanches
and flasques, yet they differ from both as being always
smaller, and not so circular. Pl. xxxv., n. 7.

Voider, according to Holme, is certainly a diminutive
of the flanch, and, by reason of its smallness, cannot
be charged. It is a bearing ; but being very rarely used
as such, several heraldic writers do not mention it.

VOL, among the French heralds, signifies both the
wings of a bird borne in armoury, as being the whole
that makes the flight. Pl. xxxv., n. 16.

DEMI-VOL is when only a single wing is borne. Pl. IX.,
n. 23.

VOLANT : thus we term any bird that is flying. Pl. IX.,
n. 22.

VORANT : a term for any fish, bird, beast, or reptile,
swallowing any other creature whole. Pl. xvi., n. 19.

VULNED signifies wounded, and the blood dropping
therefrom, as is represented on the breast of the example.
Pl. xvi., n. 5. Likewise a heart vulned. Pl. xxxv.,
n. 18. *Argent, a fess gules, between three hearts vulned,
and distilling drops of blood on the sinister side proper ;*
name, *Tote.*

WAKE'S KNOT. See the example, Pl. XXXII., n. 34.

WALLED. See MURINILLÉ.

WARDON, the name of a *pear*, so called from having been first cultivated at Wardon Abbey, Beds, which bore three such pears as its arms ; the same arms were subsequently assumed by the family of Warden, in allusion to the name.

WASTEL-CAKE, a round cake of bread.

WATER-BAGS. Pl. XXX., n. 18. *Argent, two water bags sable, hooped together or ;* name, *Banister.* These bags anciently were carried by the help of the hoop, put about the neck. This is merely a variety of the next charge.

WATER BOUGET, a vessel anciently used by soldiers to fetch water to the camp. See Pl. XXIX., n. 16 ; and Pl. VI., n. 20.

WATTLED, a term for the gills of a cock, &c., when of a different tincture from its body.

WAVY, formed like waves, having always three risings, like waves rolling ; also a line of partition. Pl. III.

WEARE, WEIR, or *dam*, in *fess.* It is made with stakes and osier twigs, interwoven as a fence against water. Pl. XXXV., n. 25. Some authors term it a *Haie.*

WEEL : this instrument is used to catch fish. Pl. XXXIV., n. 12. *Argent, a chevron ermine, between three weels, their hoops upwards, vert ;* name, *Wylley.* See another, Pl. XXXII., n. 30. *Or, a chevron between three such weels sable ;* name, *Folborne.*

WELL, as example, Pl. XXXV., n. 8. *Gules, three wells argent ;* name, *Hadiswell.* Also Pl. XXXV., n. 9, *sable, three wells argent ;* name, *Borton.*

WELL-BUCKET, *argent, a well-bucket sable, handle and*

hoops or; name, *Pemberton.* See the example, Pl. XXXVI., n. 30.

WELKE ; the name of a shell-fish. Pl. VIII., n. 7. *Sable a fess engrailed between three welkes;* name, *Shelley,* of Sussex, Bart.

WERVELS. See VERVELS.

WHARROW-SPINDLE : an instrument formerly used by women to spin as they walk, sticking the distaff in their girdle, and whirling the spindle round, pendant at the thread. Pl. XXXIV., n. 13.

WHALE'S HEAD. See Pl. XXXVIII., n. 24. *Argent, three whales' heads, sable ;* name, *Whalley.*

WHIRLPOOL. See GURGES.

WHINTAIN. See QUINTAIN.

WING OF AN IMPERIAL EAGLE. The Germans and French always represent the wings of the eagle with a small feather between the pinion feathers. See Pl. XXXVIII., n. 29.

WINDMILL-SAIL. Pl. XXXIII., n. 24. *Azure, a chevron between three windmill-sails ;* name, *Milnes.*

WINGED, the term used in blazonry when the wings are of a different tincture from the body.

WINNOWING-BASKET, for winnowing of corn. Pl. XXV., n. 17. *Azure, three fans* (or winnowing-baskets) *or;* name, *Septvans.*

WOLF. Pl. XXXI., n. 10. *Argent, a wolf passant sable ;* name, *Walsalle.*

WOOL-CARD, Pl. XXX., n. 1. *Sable, three wool-cards, or ;* name, *Cardington.*

WREATH, an attire for the head, made of linen or silk, of two different tinctures twisted together, which the ancient knights wore when equipped for tournaments ; the colours of the silk are usually taken from the principal metal and colour contained in the coat of arms of the bearer; unless the contrary be specially mentioned, the crest should always be placed upon a wreath so formed. Pl. XLV., n. 28.

WREATHED, surrounded by a wreath. Savages or wild men are always drawn wreathed around the temples and loins, generally with oak or ivy leaves. See Pl. XVIII., n. 24. Ordinaries are termed wreathed or torqued when twisted like a wreath. *Argent, a fess wreathed azure and gules ;* name, *Carmichael.*

WYVERN. See Pl. VII., n. 24. *Argent, a wyvern gules ;* name, *Drakes.*

YATES, an ancient name in armoury for *gates.*

ZODIAC, in bend sinister, with three of the signs on it, viz., Libra, Leo, and Scorpio. See Pl. XVIII., n. 1. This coat is said to appertain to the king of Spain, Columbus having first discovered South America.

ZULE, a chess rook, borne in the coat of Zulenstein.

AN ALPHABETICAL

LIST OF HERALDIC TERMS,

IN

ENGLISH, FRENCH, AND LATIN.

English.	*French.*	*Latin.*
ABATEMENT	Abatement	Diminutiones armorum
Addorsed	Addossé	
Adumbration		Adumbratio
Alerions	Aiglettes, Aiglons	Aquilæ Mutilæ
Anchored	Ancré	Anchoratus
Annulet	Annelet	Annulus, vel Annellus
Argent	Argent	Argenteus
Armed	Armé	Armatus
Armoury, Armory	Armoiries	Insignia
Attired	Acorné	
Avelane		Crux Avellana
Azure	Azur	Asureus
Bar	Barre	Vectis
Bar-Gemel	Jumelles	Jugariæ fasciolæ
Barrulet	Barelle	Barrula
Barruly	Barellé	Transverse fasciolatus
Barry	Fascé	Fasciatum
Barry Pily	Parti Emanché	Runcinatus
Barry-per-pale	Contreface	Contrafasciatus
Barbed and Crested	Barbé et Cresté	Barbula et Crista
Barnacles		Pastomides
Barnicle		Bernicla
Baton	Baston	Bacillus
Beaked	Becqué	Rostratus
Bend	Bande	Tænia
Per Bend Sinister	Contrebarré	Contravittatus
Bendy	Bandé	Bendulatus
Bendy of Six	Contrebandé	
Bend Sinister	Barre	Vitta

English.	*French.*	*Latin.*
In bend	En Bande	Oblique dextrorsus positus
Party-per-bend	Tranché	Oblique dextrorsus bipartitum
Bendlet	Bandelette	Bandula
Bezant	Besant	Bizantius nummus
Bezanty	Bezanté	
Billets	Billettes	Laterculi
Billetty	Billetté	Laterculatus
Border	Bordure	Fimbria
Bordered	Bordé	Fimbriatus
Caboshed	Cabossé	Ora obvertantia
Caltraps	Chaussé-trappes	Murices *or* Tribuli
Canton	Canton	Quadrans Angularis
Cantoned	Cantonnée	Stipatus
Charge	Charge	Figura
Charged	Chargé	Ferens
Checky	Echiqueté	Tesselatum
Chess-Rook		Lusorius Latrunculus
Chevron	Chevron	Cantherius
Per Chevron	Mantelé	Manteliatum
Chevrony	Chevroné	Cantheriatus
Chief	Chef	Summum
In Chief	In Chef	In Summo
Cinquefoil	Quinquefeuille	Quinquefolia
Cleché	Cleché	Floralus
Close	Clos	Clausum
Collared	Acollé	
Combatant	Affronté	Pugnantes
Compony	Componé	Compositus
Counter-Compony	Contre Componé	
Counterchanged	Parti de l'un en l'autre	Transmutatus
Counter-imbattled	Bretessé	Utrinque-pinnatus
Counter-quartered	Cont'-Escartelé	Contraquadrate partitus
Counter-potent	Contrepotencé	Partibulatum
Counter-Vair	Contrevaire	
Coward	Couée	
Cotice	Cotice	Tæniola
Cotised	Cotové	Utroque latere accinctus
Couchant	Couchant	Jacens
Couped	Coupé	A latere disjunctum
Combed	Cresté	
Couple-close		Cantheria
Courant	Courant	Currens
Crowned	Couronnée	Coronatus
Crescent	Croisant	Luna Cornuta

English.	*French.*	*Latin.*
Crest	Crête	Crista
Crested	Cresté	
Cross	Croix	Crux
In-Cross	En Croix	In modum crucis col-locata
Crosslet	Croisette	Crucicula
Dancette	Danché	Denticulatus
Defamed	Diffamé	
Demy	Demi	Dimidiatus
Diapered	Diapré	Duriatus
Differences	Brisures	Diminutiones armo-rum
Displayed	Eployé	Expansus
Dismembered	Dismembré	
Dismembred	Morné	Mutilatus
Dormant	Dormant	Dormiens
Doublings	Doublé	
Dove-Tail	Assemble	
Embattled	Crenelé	Pinnatus
Engrailed	Engrailé	Striatus
Engrafted	Enté	Insitus
Environed	Environé	Septus
Erased	Arraché	Lacer
Eradicated		Eradicatus
Ermine	Hermines	
Ermines	Contre Hermines	
Escalop	Coquille	Conchilium
Escarbuncle	Escarboucle	Carbunculus
Escutcheon	Ecusson	Scutum
Etoile	Etoile	Stellula
Fess	Face	Fascia
Per Fess	Coupé	Transverse sectum
Fitchy	Fiché	Figibilis
Fillet	Filet	
Fimbriated	Franché	Fimbriatus
Flanch	Flanque	Orbiculi segmentum
Flory	Florence	Liliatus
Fret	Frette	Frectum simplex
Fretty	Fretté	Frectata
Furs	Pannes	Pellis
Fusil	Fusée	Fusus
Fusilly	Fuselé	Fusillatum
Garb	Gerbe	Fascis frumentarius
Galtrap	Chaussée-trappe	Murices
Gardant	Gardante	Obverso ore
Gliding	Ondoyante	Undans
Gorged	Clariné	Cymbalatus
Gules	Gueules	Ruber

English.	*French.*	*Latin.*
Gutty	Gutté	Guttis respersum
Gyron	Gyron	Cuneus
Gyronny	Gironné	Cuneatus
Hauriant	Hauriant	Hauriens
Helmet	Casque	Galea
Horned	Accorné	
Hooded	Chapperoné	Calyptratus
Imbattled	Crenellé	Pinnatus
Indented	Danché	Indentatus
Incensed	Animé	Incensus
Indorsed	Adossé	Ad invicem tergum vertentes
Inescutcheor.	Ecusson	Scutulum
Ingrailed	Engraillé	Striatus
Invecked	Canellé	Invectus
Issuant	Issant	Nascens
Label	Lambel	Lambella
Lambrequin	Lambrequin	Pennæ
Langued	Lampasse	Lingua
Lozenge	Lozange	Rhombus
Lozengy	Lozangé	Rhombulis inter stinctus
Mantle	Manteau	Pallium
Martlet		Merula
Manche	Manche	Manica
Mascle	Macle	Macula
Masoned	Massoné	Glutinatus
Membred	Membré	Tibiatus
Millrind	Fer de moulin	Ferrum molendinarium
Montant	Montant	Resupinus
Mound	Monde	Mundus
Musseled	Emmuselé	
Mullet	Molette	Rotula Calcaris
Nebuly	Nebulé	Nubilatum
Or	Or	Aurum
Orle	Environné	Limbus
In Orle	Environné	Ad oram positus
Over all	Sur le tout	Toti superinductum
Pale	Pal	Palus
In-pale	En Pal	In Palum collocatus
Pall	Pairle	
Paly	Pallé	Palis exoratus
Palet	Vergetté	Palus minutus
Paly-per-fess	Contrepalé	Contrapalitus
Party-per-pale	Parti	Partitus
Papillone	Papellonn	Papillionatus
Passant	Passant	Gradiens

English.	French.	Latin.
Patty	Paté	Patens
Paw	Patte	
Perished	Peri	
Pheon	Fer de dard	Ferrum jacul
Pile	Pointe	Pila Pontis
Pometty	Pometté	Sphærulatus
Potent	Potence	Patibulatum
Proper	Propre	Color naturalis
Purpure	Pourpre	Purpureus color
Quarter	Quartier	Quadrans
Quarterly	Escartelé	Quadripartite
Quartering	Escarteler	Cumulationes armorum
Quarterly Quartered	Contre escartelent	
Quatrefoil	Quatrefeuille	Quatuorfolia
Rampant	Rampant	Erectus
Ranged	Rangé	Ordinatus
Rebuses	Armes parlantes	
Reversed	Renversé	
Regardant	Regardant	Retrospiciens
Respectant	Affronté	Pugnantes
Rising	Essortant	Surgens
Rompu	Rompu	Fractus
Roundle	Torteau	Tortella
Sable	Sable	Ater, or Niger
Saltier	Sautoir	Decussis
Party-per-Saltire	Escartelé en sautoir	
Saltirewise	Posé en sautoir	In decussim dispositum
Saliant	Saillant	Saliens
Scaled	Escaille	
Segreant	Segrant	Erectus
Sejant	Assis	Sedens
Seme	Semé	Sparsus
Shortened	Raccourci	Accisus
Streaming	Chevelée	
Stringed	Enguiché	Appensus
Statant	En pied	
Surmounted	Surmonté	
Tail	Queue	Cauda
Taloned	Onglé	Ungulatus
Tierce	Tierce	Tertiatum
Treille	Treillé	
Trefoil	Trefle	Trifolium
Tripping		More suo incedens
Trunked	Tronqué	Truncatus
Tusked	Defendu	
Vair	Vairé	Variegatum

English.	French.	Latin.
Vert	Vert	Viridis color
Voided	Vuidé	Evacuatus
Volant	Volant	Volans
Vorant	Engoulant	Vorans
Umbrated	Ombré	Inumbratus
Water Bouget	Bouse	Uter Aquarius militaris
Wavy	Ondé	Undulatus
Whirlpool	Tournant d'Eau	Gurges
Two Wings expanded	Vole	Ala
A Wing	Un Demi Vol	Ala simplex
Winged	Aislé	Alatus
Wreath	Torce	Tortile
Wyvern	Dragon	Viverra

Manual of Rank and Nobility.

Honour, says Cicero, is the reward of virtue, as infamy is the recompense of vice; so that he who aspires to honour should arrive at it by the way of virtue;—which the Romans expressed by so building the Temple of Honour, that there was no possibility of entering it without first passing through the Temple of Virtue.

THE KING.

The King is so called from the Saxon word *koning*, or *cuning*, from *can*, intimating power, or *ken*, knowledge, wherewith every sovereign should especially be invested.

The supreme executive power of the British dominions is vested, by the English laws, in a single person, the *King* or *Queen;* for it matters not to which sex the crown descends; the person entitled to it, whether male or female, is immediately invested with all tho ensigns, rights and prerogatives of sovereign sway. What follows, therefore, is applicable equally to queen-regnant as to king. See Queen, p. 217.

The king is styled Father of his country; and because the protection of his subjects belongs to his care and office, the militia is annexed to his crown. He is also called the *fountain of honour*, because in him is vested the power of bestowing titles and dignities.

A king is to fight the battles of his people, and to see right and justice done to them; as also, according to his coronation oath, to preserve the rights and privileges of our holy church; the royal prerogative belonging to the crown; the laws and customs of the realm; to do justice, show mercy, keep peace and unity, &c.; and he hath power of pardoning where the law condemns.

The king being *principium, caput, et finis parliamenti,* may of his mere will and pleasure convoke, adjourn, remove, and dissolve parliaments; as also to any bill that is passed by both Houses he may refuse to give his royal assent without rendering a reason; without which assent it cannot pass into a law. He may also increase the number * of the peers of the realm.

The king of England is deemed a constituent part of the supreme legislative power, and therefore is not himself bound by any general act of parliament, unless especially named. He is the generalissimo of the kingdom, with the power of raising and regulating fleets and armies—the fountain of honour, office, and privilege—head and supreme governor of the national church, the fountain of justice and general conservator of the peace of the kingdom—his majesty being supposed, in law, to be always present in all his courts, though he cannot personally distribute justice. His judges are the mirror by which the king's image is reflected.†

Besides the attribute of sovereignty, the law ascribes to the king, in his political capacity, absolute *perfection :*

* Since the union of England and Scotland, the king can neither make an English peer nor a Scotch peer; all the peers that the king of Great Britain now creates, are either of the United Kingdom or of Ireland.

† Plowden

the " *king can do no wrong ;*" which ancient and funda-
mental maxim is not to be understood as if everything
transacted by the government was of course just and
lawful, but means only two things : First, that whatever is exceptionable in the conduct of public affairs is
not to be imputed to the king ; nor is he answerable
for it personally to his people. And, 2ndly, that the
prerogative of the crown extends not to do any injury ;
it is created for the benefit of the people ; and therefore
cannot be exerted to their prejudice. Or perhaps it
means that, although the king is subject to the infirmities
and passions of other men, the constitution has pre-
scribed no mode by which he can be made personally
amenable for any wrong that he may actually do. The
law will therefore presume no wrong, where it has provided no remedy. The *inviolability of the king* is essen-
tially necessary to the free exercise of those high
prerogatives which are vested in him, not for his own
private splendour and gratification, but for the security
and preservation of the real happiness and liberty of
his subjects.

The law ascribes to the king's majesty, in his political capacity, an absolute *immortality.* The king never
dies. *Henry, Edward,* or *George,* may die; but the
king survives them all. For, immediately upon the
decease of the reigning prince in his natural capacity,
his kingship, or imperial dignity, by act of law, without
any *interregnum* or interval, is vested at once in his
heir, who is *eo instanti* king, to all intents and purposes.
And so tender is the law of supposing even a possibility
of his death, that his natural dissolution is generally
called his *demise ; demissus regis, vel coronæ :* an expression signifying merely a transfer of property.

By letters patent, his majesty may erect new coun
ties, universities, bishoprics, cities, boroughs, colleges,
hospitals, schools, fairs, markets, courts of judicature,
forests, chases, free warrens, &c.; and no forest or chase
is to be made, nor castle, fort, or tower to be built,
without his special licence. He has also power to
coin money, and to settle the denomination or value
for which the coin is to pass current.

The dominions of the kings of England were first
England, and all the sea round about Great Britain and
Ireland, and all the isles adjacent, even to the shores of
the neighbouring nations; and our law saith the sea is
of the legiance of the king, as well as the land; and as
a mark thereof, the ships of foreigners have anciently
asked leave to fish and pass in these seas, and do at
this day lower their topsails to all the king's ships of
war; and all children borne upon these seas (as it sometimes happens) are accounted natural-born subjects to
the king of Great Britain, and need not be naturalized
as others born out of his dominions.

To England, Henry I. annexed Normandy, and
Henry II. Ireland, our kings being styled only lords of
Ireland till the 33rd of Henry VIII., although they
had all kingly jurisdiction before. Henry II. also
annexed the dukedoms of Guyenne and Anjou, the
counties of Poitou, Touraine, and Maine; Edward I.
all Wales; and Edward III. the right, though not the
possession, of France; but Henry V. added both; and
his son, Henry VI., was crowned and recognised by all
the states of the realm at Paris. King James I. added
Scotland, and since that time there have been super-
added considerable parts of America, the East Indies, as
well as that almost fifth quarter of the world Australia.

Of the sacred person and life of the king our laws and customs are so tender, that it is made high treason only to imagine or intend his death : and, as he is the father of his country, so every subject is obliged by his allegiance to defend him, as well in his natural as political capacity; for the law saith, the life and member of every subject is at the service of the sovereign.

THE QUEEN.

The Queen is so called from the Saxon word *cuningine*, as the king from *koning*.

The Queen of England is either queen-regnant, queen-consort, or queen-dowager. The queen-regnant, or sovereign, is she who holds the crown in her own right; as the first (and perhaps the second) Queen Mary, Queen Elizabeth, Queen Anne, and her present Most Gracious Majesty, Queen Victoria; and such a queen has the same powers, prerogatives, rights, dignities, and duties, as if she were king.

The queen-consort is the wife of the reigning king; and she, by virtue of her marriage, is participant of divers prerogatives above other women.

She is a public person, exempt and distinct from the king ; and, not like other married women, so closely connected as to have lost all legal or separate existence so long as the marriage continues. For the queen-consort is of ability to purchase lands, and to convey them ; to make leases, to grant copyholds, and do other acts of ownership, without the concurrence of her lord, which no other married woman can do. She is also capable of taking a grant from the king, which no other wife is from her husband. The queen-consort of England has separate courts and officers distinct from the king's, not only in matters of ceremony, but even of law; and her attorney and solicitor-general are entitled to a place within the bar of his majesty's courts, together with the king's counsel. She may likewise sue and be sued alone, without joining her husband. She may also have separate property in goods as well as lands, and has a right to dispose of them by will. In short, she is in all legal proceedings looked upon as a single not as a married woman. The reason given for which is this: the wisdom of the common law would not have the king (whose continual care and study ought to be for the public good) troubled and disquieted on account of his wife's domestic affairs; wherefore it vests in his queen a power of transacting her own concerns without the intervention of the king, as if she was an unmarried woman.

The queen-consort has also many exemptions and minute prerogatives. For instance, she pays no toll; nor is she liable to any amercement in any court. But, in general, except where the law has expressly declared her exempted, she is upon the same footing with other subjects; being to all intents and purposes the king's subject, and not his equal.

Though the queen-consort is in all respects a subject, yet, in point of security of life and person, she is put on the same footing as the king. It is equally treason to compass or imagine the death of our lady the king's companion, as of the king himself. If, however, the queen be accused of any species of treason, she shall (whether consort or dowager) be tried by the peers of parliament.

A queen-dowager is the widow of the king, and as such enjoys most of the privileges belonging to her as queen-consort. But it is not high treason to conspire her death, because the succession to the crown is not thereby endangered. Yet still, *pro dignitate regali* (for sustaining the royal dignity), no man can marry a queen-dowager without special licence from the reigning sovereign, on pain of forfeiting his lands and goods. But a queen-dowager, when married again to a subject, does not lose her regal dignity, as peeresses-dowager do their peerage when they marry com moners.

Royal Titles.

THE Royal Style, as settled on the 5th of November, 1800, in consequence of the union with Ireland, which was to commence from the 1st of January, 1801, runs thus:—"Victoria, by the Grace of God, of the United Kingdom of Great Britain and Ireland, Queen, Defender of the Faith; and of the United Church of England and Ireland, on earth the supreme head." In the Latin it is differently expressed:—"Victoria, Dei Gratiâ Britanniarum Regina," &c.; the word Britanniarum, first introduced upon the above occasion, being regarded as expressive, under one term, of the incorporated kingdoms of England, Scotland, and Ireland. James I., when he ascended the throne of England, revived the title which had been laid aside by an edict of Egbert, in the commencement of the ninth century, and styled himself *King of Great Britain,* comprehending under that appellation his dominion over England and Scotland. Before the "Union of the Crowns," Britain alone was in general used in the style of our sovereigns, to signify England and Wales. Alfred, however, was called *Governor of the Christians of Britain;* Edgar, *Monarch of Britain;* Henry II., *King of Britain;* and, nearly synonymous with the latter, John was styled, *Rex Britonium.*

The title of *King of Ireland*, was first granted by the Pope to Henry II., though it was not regularly added to the royal dignities, until assumed by Henry VIII., in 1541; before that time the dominion of the English sovereigns over that island was usually expressed by the term "Lord;" and it is a fact, that our monarchs publicly denominated some of the Irish chieftains kings, while they themselves were content with the subordinate honour of "Lord." It should be remembered, however, that the title of king did not invariably denote sovereignty; and, according to the ancient feudal system, of which those Irish kings formed a part, many of the barons who were dignified with that high-sounding appellation, were in a state of vassalage. The King of Majorca was tributary to the King of Arragon; the King of Man to the King of Scotland; and the Kings of Ireland to the King of England; to which might be added other instances from the early history of this country; while even so late as the reign of Richard II. the whole of the kings of Ireland were tributary to Robert de Vere, duke of that Island.

The title of *Defender of the Faith*, still retained in the royal style, belonged anciently to the kings of England, though it had not been generally assumed by them. "We are and will be Defenders of the

Catholic Faith," is an expression to be found in writs of Richard II. Pope Leo X., in the year 1521, renewed that dignity, which was afterwards confirmed by Clement VII., in consequence of Henry VIII. having written an answer, then much esteemed, to Luther's book on the Babylonian Captivity. Upon the suppression of the monasteries, the Pope issued a bull, annulling this title; but his attempt was as futile in that respect, as was his silly effort to depose that sovereign; the English Parliament, in the 35th year of Henry's reign, established it beyond the power of change from foreign interposition, giving that monarch not only a complete confirmation of the title, but the power of exercising it. The Pope's supremacy in England was totally suppressed, and the king acknowledged *Supreme Head of the Church*, as well as of the state; thereby laying the foundation of that reformation which was afterwards so completely and happily accomplished in this kingdom.

Henry VIII. was the first King of England who assumed the title of *Majesty*, which is still retained. Before that reign the sovereigns were addressed by the style of "*My Liege*," and "*Your Grace;*" the latter of which epithets was originally conferred on Henry IV. "*Excellent Grace*," was given to Henry VI.; "*Most High and Mighty Prince*," to Edward IV.; "*Highness*," to Henry VII.; which last expression was sometimes used to Henry VIII., and sometimes "*Grace;*" until near the end of his reign, when, in matters of state, they gave way to the more lofty and appropriate appellation of "*Majesty*," being the expression with which Francis I. addressed him at their interview in 1520. The Emperor Charles V. had, the preceding year, first assumed the novel and high-sounding title of Majesty; and the polished French monarch lost not so favourable an opportunity of complimenting our then youthful Henry. Elizabeth was, however, frequently addressed as the " *Queen's Highness,*" as well as the " *Queen's Majesty.*" James I. completed the present style of " *Most Excellent Majesty,*' or " *Sacred Majesty,*" the latter being in allusion to the inviolability or sanctity of the royal person and prerogatives.

The title of her present Majesty is as follows :—

" Her most Excellent Majesty Victoria, of the United Kingdom of Great Britain and Ireland Queen, Defender of the Faith, Sovereign of the Orders of the Garter, Thistle, Bath, St. Patrick, St. Michael, St. George, and the Star of India."

The royal *arms* are as follows :—

Quarterly, first and fourth gules, three lions passant-gardant in pale, or, for *England;* second, or, a lion rampant, within a double tressure, flory-counterflory, gules, for *Scotland;* third, azure, a harp, or, stringed argent, for *Ireland;* the whole encircled with the garter and its motto.

Crest. Upon the royal helmet the imperial crown, proper, thereon a lion statant-gardant, or, imperially crowned of the first.

Supporters. Dexter, a lion rampant-gardant, or, imperially crowned proper; sinister, a unicorn, argent, armed, crined and unguled or, gorged with a coronet composed of crosses pattée and fleurs-de-lis, with a chain affixed thereto, passing between the fore-legs and reflexed over the back of the last.

Motto. DIEU ET MON DROIT is in the compartment

below the shield, with the union roses, shamrock and thistle, engrafted on one stem.

THE PRINCE OF WALES.

Since the union with Scotland, his title has been " Prince of Great Britain, but ordinarily created Prince of Wales;" and as eldest son to the King or Queen-regnant of England, he is Duke of Cornwall from his birth, as likewise Duke of Rothsay, and Seneschal of Scotland.

His mantle, which he wears at royal coronations, is doubled below the elbow with ermine, spotted diamond-wise; but the robe which he wears in parliament is adorned on the shoulders with five bars or guards of ermine, set at a distance one from the other, with gold lace above each bar.

The younger sons of the sovereigns of England are by courtesy styled princes by birth, as are all their daughters princesses; and the title of royal highness is given to all the king's children, both sons and daughters, and her present Majesty, by letters patent under the Great Seal, in February 1864, was pleased to declare her royal will and pleasure that, besides the children of the sovereigns of these realms, the children of the sons of any sovereign of Great Britain and Ireland shall have and at all times hold and enjoy the same title.

DUKE.

The title and degree of a duke is of more ancient standing in other countries than with us; for at the time of the Conquest, the king himself was Duke of Normandy, which perhaps was the reason that neither he nor his successors for several ages thought fit to raise a subject to so high a dignity.

The first duke we meet with in England, properly so called, was Edward, surnamed the Black Prince, eldest son to King Edward III., whom his father, on the 17th March, 1337, created in parliament Duke of Cornwall: by which creation the first-born sons of the sovereign of England are Dukes of Cornwall from their birth.

A duke is said to be so called from *dux*, a leader or captain, because the *duces* of the ancient Romans were leaders of an army, and chosen in the field, either by casting lots, or by the common voice; but now the dignity of duke is generally conferred by kings and princes, and descends to the heir; though in some nations sovereigns are so called, as Duke of Savoy, Brunswick, &c.

Dukes, marquesses, earls, and viscounts were formerly created by investiture with much ceremony. The creation is now simply by letters patent of the sovereign under the great seal.

A duke's mantle or robe of estate is the same as that of the prince, with this difference, that it has only *four* guards of ermine with a gold lace above each, that of the prince having *five*.

The mantle which a duke wears at the coronation of a king or queen over his surcoat, &c., is of crimson velvet, lined with white taffeta, and is doubled with ermine below the elbow, and spotted with four rows of spots on each shoulder.

All dukes' eldest sons, by the courtesy of England, are from their birth styled marquises if their fathers enjoy that title; if there is no marquisate in the family they take the next highest title; thus the eldest son of the Duke of Northumberland has the courtesy title of Earl Percy, there being no marquisate among the family honours. The dukedom of Manchester has neither marquisate nor distinct earldom, so the eldest son is Viscount Mandeville. The younger sons are all styled lords, with the addition of their Christian name, as Lord Thomas, Lord James, &c.; and all dukes' daughters are styled Ladies.

A duke has the title of grace; and in formal superscriptions or addresses is styled, most high, potent, and noble prince; and dukes of the royal blood, most high, most mighty, and illustrious princes.

For coronet, see Pl. XLIII., n. 6.

MARQUIS.

A marquis, which by the Saxons was called *markenreve*, and signified a governor or ruler of marches and frontier countries, hath been a title with us but of late years, the first being Robert Vere, Earl of Oxford, who, by King Richard II., in 1387, was created Marquis of Dublin, and from thence it became a title of honour; for, in former times, those that governed the marches were called lord marchers, and not marquises.

His robes are the same as that of a duke, except that he has only three guards and a half instead of four on the shoulder, and his coronation mantle has four rows of spots on the right shoulder and but three on the left, whereas a duke's has four rows on each.

The honour of marquis is hereditary, as is that of a duke, earl, viscount, and baron; and the eldest son of a marquis, by the courtesy of England, is called earl, or by the next highest title in the family when there is no earldom; thus the Marquis of Salisbury's eldest son is by courtesy Viscount Cranbourne. The younger sons of marquises are called lords by their Christian names, as Lord John, &c.; and the daughters of marquises are born ladies; the eldest son of a marquis ranks next beneath an earl.

EARL.

The next degree of honour is an earl, which title came from the Saxons; for in the ancient Anglo-Saxon government, earldoms of counties were not only dignities of honour, but offices of justice, having the charge and custody of the county whereof they were earls, and for assistance having their deputy, called *vicecomes*, which office is now managed by sheriffs. The first earl in Britain that was invested by girding with the sword, was Hugh de Pusay, or Pudsey, Bishop of Durham, who, by King Richard I., was created Earl of Northumberland.

An earl's robes nowise differ from a duke's or marquis's, except that a duke's mantle has four guards, a marquis's three and a half, and an earl's but three, with a gold lace: and his coronation mantle is the same as theirs, with only this difference—a duke's has four rows of spots on each shoulder; a marquis's four on the right, and but three on the left; and an earl's has but three on each. His cap is also the same, but his coronet is different; for as a duke's has only leaves, a marquis's leaves and pearls of equal height, that of an earl has the pearls much higher than the leaves. Pl. XLIII., n. 8.

After a man is created an earl, viscount, or receives any other title of honour, above the title he enjoyed before, it becomes part of his name, and not an addition only; and in all legal proceedings he ought to be styled

by that of his dignity. An earl has the title of lordship; and, being written to, is styled right honourable.

By the courtesy of England, an earl's eldest son is
born a viscount if there is such a title attached to the
name, otherwise he is called lord only, as in the case
of the Earl of Derby, whose eldest son is Lord Stanley,
and an earl's daughters are all ladies; but his younger
sons have no title of peerage.

VISCOUNT.

The next degree of honour to an earl is that of
viscount, which was anciently an office under an earl,
who, being the king's immediate officer in his county,
and his personal attendance being often required at
court, had his deputy to look after the affairs of the
county, which officer is now called a sheriff, retaining
the name of his substitution (in Latin *vicecomes*); but
about the 18th of Henry VI., 1440, it became a degree
of honour, by his conferring this title upon John Lord
Beaumont, by letters patent, with the same ceremony
as that of an earl, marquis, and duke.

The mantle of a viscount has two guards and a half,
each having a gold lace; his coronation mantle has three
rows of spots on the right shoulder, and two on the left.

His coronet, which is a circle of gold, is adorned
with twelve silver balls. Pl. XLIII., n. 9.

The title of a viscount is, right honourable and
truly noble, or potent lord.

The eldest son of a viscount has no title of peerage,
nor are his daughters ladies; but the eldest son and
daughter of the first viscount in Great Britain and
Ireland are said to be the first gentleman and gentle-
woman without a title in the kingdom.

ARCHBISHOPS AND BISHOPS.

The two archbishops have superintendence over all the churches of England, and in some respects over the other bishops; and the Archbishop of Canterbury has a kind of supereminence over the Archbishop of York; for he has power to summon him to a national synod or convocation, and is primate of all England, and next in rank to the royal family; precedes not only dukes, but all the great officers of the crown; nor does any, except the lord chancellor, or lord keeper, come between him and the Archbishop of York.

He is "*primate and metropolitan of all England,*" and has the title of grace given him, and most reverend father in God.

To the Archbishop of Canterbury it properly belongs to crown the sovereign, to consecrate a new-made bishop, and to call provincial synods : the Bishop of London being accounted his provincial dean, the Bishop of Winchester his chancellor, and the Bishop of Rochester his chaplain.

The Archbishop of York, who is "*primate of England and metropolitan of his province,*" has the honour to crown the queen-consort, and to be her perpetual chaplain : he hath also the title of grace, and most reverend father in God.

Next to the two archbishops in the episcopal college, the bishops of London, Durham, and Winchester have always the precedence, by a statute made 21 Hen. VIII. ; and all the other bishops according to the priority of their consecrations.

The Bishop of London precedes, as being bishop of the capital city of England, and provincial dean of

Canterbury, the Bishop of Durham, as Earl of Sedburg; and the Bishop of Winchester, as prelate of the order of the Garter.

All bishops (as spiritual barons) are said to be three ways barons of the realm, viz. by writ, patent, and consecration; they precede all under the degree of viscounts, having always their seat on the sovereign's right hand in the parliament-house; and being the fathers and guardians of the church, they are styled fathers in God.

As the two archbishops are called most reverend, and have the title of grace, so the inferior bishops are called right reverend, and have the title of lordship given them.

A bishop's robe, in parliament, is of fine scarlet cloth, having a long train, and is doubled on the shoulders with miniver, edged with white ermine, as is the bosom; and when he goes to the House of Lords (the sovereign being there), his train is supported by four chaplains to the door of the house; after which, by a red riband fixed to the end of the train and tied in a loop, he supports it himself, the loop being put over his right wrist; and in that form he takes his seat, having a four-square cap on his head.

BARONS.

A temporal baron is an hereditary dignity of nobility and honour next to a bishop; and of this degree there are two sorts in England, viz. a baron by writ, and a baron by patent.

A baron by writ is he unto whom a writ of summons in the name of the sovereign is directed, without a patent of creation, to come to the parliament, appointed to be holden at a certain time and place, and there to treat and advise with his sovereign, the prelates, and nobility, about the weighty affairs of the nation.

The first institutor of a baron by patent was King Richard II., who in the year 1388, the eleventh of his reign, created John Beauchamp, of Holt Castle, Baron of Kidderminster, and invested him with a surcoat, mantle, hood, cape, and verge. The newly-created baron is now brought into the House of Lords in his robes, between two peers of the same degree, and introduced by Garter King-of-arms, who carries the letters patent, the baron himself bearing the writ. A baron has but two guards and laces on each shoulder; and his coronation mantle has but two rows of spots on each shoulder.

A baron had no coronet till the reign of King Charles II., when he was adorned with a circle of gold, and six silver balls set close to the rim, but without jewels, as now borne. Pl. XLIII., n. 10.

A barony by patent goes to the heir-male, being almost universally so limited. But a barony by writ goes to the heirs-general; and in case of more female heirs than one, it becomes in abeyance, when the king may make his option, and grant it to which of them he thinks fit.

PRIVILEGES OF PEERS.

The nobility of England enjoy many great privileges, the principal of which are as follows:—

They are free from all arrests for debt, as being the king's hereditary counsellors: therefore a peer cannot be outlawed in any civil action; and no attachment lies against his person; but execution may be taken upon his lands and goods. For the same reason they are free from all attendance at court-leet, or sheriffs' torns; or, in case of a riot, from attending the *posse comitatus.*

In criminal causes they are tried by their peers, who give their verdict not upon oath, as other juries, but upon their *honour.* A court is built on purpose, in the middle of Westminster Hall, which is pulled down when their trials are over.

To secure the honour of, and prevent the spreading of any scandal upon, peers, or any great officer of the realm, by reports, there is an express law, called *scandalum magnatum,* by which any man convicted of making a scandalous report against a peer of the realm though true, is condemned to a fine, and to remain in prison till the same be paid.

BARONETS.

This title was originally instituted by King James I., the 22nd of May, 1611, by letters patent under the great seal, to feed his unpardonable profusion, although under the specious plea of assisting him in the reduction of Ulster. The whole order was designed by the founder not to exceed two hundred persons, of which, if any became extinct for want of male-heirs, no new creations should be made even to fill the vacancies. King James indeed never exceeded the number, except by four in the room of the same number who were elevated to the peerage. But the great rule of the institution was, that none should be admitted unless upon good proof that they were men for quality, state of living, and good reputation, worthy of it; and, at the least, descended of a grandfather by the father's side, that bore arms, and had also a clear revenue in lands of at least 1,000*l.* per annum.

Those who are conversant with the personal history of the kingdom, and will read over the first list, will be readily convinced that it was highly respectable. and that these requisites were complied with.

In the reign of Charles II., however, this list of baronets was increased to 888 ; and since the reign of George II., the number has been unlimited, and the qualifications necessary for admission into this order have been frequently dispensed with.

The order of baronets in Scotland was also projected by King James, for the plantation and cultivation of the province of Nova Scotia, in America; and his son, Charles I., executed his father's plan of institution, soon after his accession to the throne, the first person dignified with this order being Sir Robert Gordon, of Gordonstow, whose patent bears date May 28, 1625.

Knighthood.

THE MOST NOBLE ORDER OF THE GARTER.

ACCORDING to the most authentic accounts, this most ancient and noble order was instituted by King Edward III., anno 1350, the 24th year of his reign.*

* The patron, St. George, was a person of great renown and chivalry, who, according to the learned Selden, suffered martyrdom at Lydia, under Diocletian. His fame was so great, that many temples and monasteries were dedicated to him in the Eastern countries, whence his reputation reached England, where his memory is still annually celebrated on the 23rd day of April, commonly called St. George's day.

Respecting the pristine institution, no positive information has yet been elicited. By some writers it is
said, that the English monarch, having engaged in a
war against France, to obtain that crown, which he
claimed as descended to him in right of his mother,
thought fit to allure to his party all such brave men
as were eminent commanders and soldiers of fortune,
with the view of exciting a spirit of emulation and military genius among his nobility. To this end he erected
a round table in the castle of Windsor, in imitation of
King Arthur's at Winchester; and here the numerous
guests were exercised at tilts and tournaments and
royally entertained with magnificent feasts, to attach
them to the king's party. On his return from his
victorious expedition into France, he rewarded those
knights who had served him valiantly with this
distinguished badge or order; the total number so
honoured being twenty-six, of which the king himself
was one.

Other authors assert, that, the same king displaying
his garter as the signal of a battle which was crowned
with success (supposed to be Cressy), gave rise to this
order.

A romantic story has also obtained credence, that the
fair Countess of Salisbury, in dancing with King
Edward, let fall her garter, which the king took up,
and tied round his own leg,* at which the queen being

* There may be more truth in this tradition than has been
generally supposed. The Countess of Salisbury alluded to was
probably that celebrated beauty, Joan Plantagenet, the Fair
Maid of Kent, ultimately the wife of Edward the Black Prince,
and mother of Richard II.—*Ed.*

jealous, or the courtiers smiling, he restored it to its
fair owner, giving as a motto—

"Honi soit qui mal y pense."
"Evil be to him (or her) who evil thinks of it."

Whatever may have been its origin, this order, which
has ever been considered as the highest in rank and
dignity in the world, and with which kings and princes
of all nations have deemed it most honourable to be
invested, consists of the sovereign and twenty-five companions, called knights of the Garter. There are
besides five principal officers : the prelate, annexed to
the see of Winchester ; the chancellor annexed to
the see of Oxford ; registrar, the dean of Windsor ;
Garter king of arms ; and usher, or black rod. Of
these the *prelate* is the principal, whose office is as
ancient as the institution. William de Edynton, then
bishop of Winchester, was the first prelate ; from which
time his successors, bishops of Winchester, have continued prelates to this day. The prelate is obliged to
wear the habit of the order yearly, on the vigil and day
of St. George, whether it be in parliament, or on any
other solemn occasion and festival.

With respect to the chancellor, at the first institution
of this order the common seal was ordained to remain
in the custody of whatsoever knight companion the king
should please. But King Edward IV. finding it necessary to settle the office of chancellor of the Garter on
a person distinct from the knights companions, yet sub-
servient to them, in a chapter holden at Westminster,
the 16th of his reign, ordered that the seal should be
delivered to Richard de Beauchamp, bishop of Salisbury, during pleasure ; and not long afterwards, by

letters patent, by reason that the chapel of Windsor was within the diocese of Salisbury, the said Richard de Beauchamp was ordained chancellor for life; and it was further ordained that, after his decease, his successors, bishops of Salisbury, should always have and hold the said office of chancellor.

King Edward VI., however, in the 7th year of his reign, ordained that this high office should not be executed by an ecclesiastic, but by a knight of known extraction, sufficient abilities, and of honour untainted; whereupon Sir William Cecil, then principal secretary of state, was made chancellor of the Garter; and so this office continued, until King Charles I., by the unanimous consent of the knights companions, declared that the bishop of Salisbury and his successors should for ever have and execute the office of chancellor of the Garter, and should succeed thereto immediately upon the first vacancy: from which period the bishops of this see have continued to preside as chancellors, till recently, when, by a rearrangement of the dioceses, Windsor was transferred to the see of Oxford, and consequently the bishop of Oxford is now chancellor of the order of the Garter.

The office of registrar was constituted at the first institution. What the first registrar's name was, or who were his successors to the reign of Henry V., are not known; but from the reign of Henry V. to that of Henry VIII. they were canons of Windsor. The first dean of Windsor constituted registrar was John Vesey, in the 8th of Henry VIII.; and at a chapter holden at Whitehall, 11th Charles I., that prince was pleased to declare that the office of the dean and registrar should be united in one and the same person. For the greater honour and splendour of this most noble order, King Henry V., with the advice and consent of the knights companions, instituted the office of Garter King-of-arms, and was pleased to appoint him the principal officer within the office of arms, and chief of all the servants of arms.

The services enjoined by him relating to the order were at first performed by Windsor Herald-at-arms, an officer created with that title by Edward III. much about the time of the institution of this order.

The first person created Garter was Sir William Brugges, who in the institution of his office is called " Jartier Roy d'Armes d'Anglois ;" but his title otherwise runs " Dictus Gartier Rex Armorum." John Smart was successor to Brugges, and had this office given him by patent under the title of " Rex Armorum de Garteria ;" and John Wrythe was styled " Principalis Heraldus et Officiarius inditi ordinis Garterii Armorum Rex Anglicorum." But Sir Gilbert Dethic, leaving out " Heraldus," joined " Principalis " with " Rex," and so it has since continued " Principalis Rex Armorum " (Principal King-of-arms).

There was assigned by Queen Elizabeth a badge of gold, to be daily worn by the King-of-arms and his successors on his breast, in a gold chain or riband, and thereon enamelled the sovereign's arms with an imperial crown, and both surrounded with a princely garter ; but Sir Edward Walker, when Garter, obtained leave to impale therein St. George's arms with those of the sovereign.

The office of Usher of the Black Rod was likewise instituted by the founder, and was granted by him to William Whitehorse, Esq., for life, and was then termed

" Officium Hostiarii Capellæ Regis infra Castrum de
Windsore." In the 3rd of Henry IV. this office is
called " Officium Virgarii comitivæ de la Garter infra
Castrum Regis de Windesore."

In the next patent to John Athelbrigg, 1st Henry V.,
it is altered to " Officium Virgarii sive Osirarii, &c.
And afterwards " Officium Virgæ Bajuli coram Rege
ad Festum Sancti Georgii infra Castrum Regis de
Windesore;" and ever since it has passed in patent by
the name of " Virgæ Bajulus Virgarius," or " Niger
Virgifer." But in the constitutions of the office he has
the title given him of Hostiarius, and is also there
required to be a gentleman of name and arms; and if
not a knight at his entrance into office, he is to be
knighted by the sovereign.

As Garter was declared the principal officer of arms,
this officer was appointed chief usher in the kingdom,
and so called Gentleman Usher of the Black Rod.

In a chapter holden at Whitehall, 13th Charles II.,
this office was fixed to one of the gentlemen ushers
daily waiters at court, the eldest of whom is properly
called Gentleman Daily Waiter and Black Rod. His
employment in general, besides what relates to the
order of the Garter, is attendance in the House of
Lords, and also among the officers of the court. In the
8th of Elizabeth there was assigned him a gold badge,
to be openly worn in a gold chain or riband on his
breast, composed of one of the knots in the collar of the
garter which tie the roses together and encompass the
garter on both sides.

The first elected by King Edward into the most
noble order of the Garter was Edward, his eldest son,
surnamed the Black Prince; and the rest of his accom-

plished companions were these that follow, and who are
thus placed in their stalls :

1. The Sovereign, King Edward III.
2. Edward, Prince of Wales.
3. Henry, Duke of Lancaster.
4. Thomas Beauchamp, Earl of Warwick.
5. Piers, Captain de Beuch.
6. Ralph Stafford, Earl of Stafford.
7. William Montacute, Earl of Salisbury.
8. Roger Mortimer, Earl of March.
9. Sir John Lisle.
10. Sir Bartholomew Burghersh.
11. Sir John Beauchamp.
12. Sir John Mohun.
13. Sir Hugh Courtenay.
14. Sir Thomas Holland.
15. Sir John Grey.
16. Sir Richard Fitz-Simon.
17. Sir Miles Stapleton.
18. Sir Thomas Wall.
19. Sir Hugh Wrotesley.
20. Sir Nele Lorin.
21. Sir John Chandos.
22. Sir James Audley.
23. Sir Otho Holland.
24. Sir Henry Earn.
25. Sir Sane Daubrichcourt.
26. Sir Walter Pavely.

From this account, it appears that the persons who
were distinguished by this honour were not all of the
nobility ; but at the present day this high and most
honourable badge of distinction is generally bestowed
on members of the peerage.

In their stalls they are placed according to their
seniority, and not according to their dignities and titles
of honour : hence a knight bachelor in former days has

taken precedency of a duke, as Sir Henry Lee, knt., had precedency of the Duke of Lennox, in the time of James I.

By a chapter holden 3rd of June, 1786, a new statute was ordained, that the order should consist of the sovereign and twenty-five knights companions, exclusive of the sons of his Majesty or his successors, who had been, or might be, elected knights thereof.

Edward III. connected with the order a number of poor or alms-knights, men of rank and merit, who had not the means of living nobly; an institution which is still continued, the members of which were long known under the title of Poor Knights of Windsor. They are now called Military and Naval Knights of Windsor.

The habit and insignia of the order of the Garter are, garter, surcoat, mantle, hood, George, collar, cap, and feathers. The GARTER, of dark-blue velvet edged with gold, bearing the motto, "HONI SOIT QUI MAL Y PENSE," in letters of gold, with buckle and pendant of richly-chased gold, is worn on the left leg below the knee. Pl. xxi., n. 3. The MANTLE is of blue velvet lined with taffeta; on the left breast is embroidered the STAR. Pl. xxi., n. 4. The SURCOAT, or kirtle, is of crimson velvet lined with white taffeta. The hood affixed to the mantle is also of crimson velvet. The HAT is of black velvet lined with white taffeta, and adorned with a large plume of white ostrich feathers, with a tuft of black heron's feathers in the centre, affixed to the hat by a band of diamonds. The COLLAR is of gold, composed of twenty-six pieces (in allusion to the number of knights), each in the form of a garter, enamelled blue, with the motto. Pl. xxi., n. 1. To which is appended the BADGE, or figure of St. George on horseback. Pl. xxi., n. 2. The JEWEL (Pl. xxi.,

n. 5) is worn in common, pendent to a broad dark-blue riband, over the left shoulder.

THE MOST HONOURABLE MILITARY ORDER OF THE BATH.

KNIGHTS OF THE BATH, so called from part of the ceremony at their creation, were commonly made at the coronation of a king or queen, or at the creation of a prince or duke of the blood royal.

In the reign of Henry IV. there was a degree of knighthood specified under the express appellation of Knights of the Bath. That king, on the day of his coronation, in the Tower of London, conferred the honour on forty-six esquires, who had watched all the night before, and had *bathed* themselves. Mr. Selden thinks this order more ancient than the time of Henry IV.; and Mr. Ashmole is of opinion that the said king did not constitute, but rather that he restored, the ancient manner of making knights, for formerly knights bachelors were created by ecclesiastics with the like ceremonies; which, however, were by King Henry IV. made peculiar to the degree of knights of the Bath.

After the coronation of Charles II., who created sixty-eight knights, the order was neglected till the year 1725, when George I. was pleased to revive and re-organise it, to consist of the sovereign, grand-master, and thirty-six companions. That king allowed the chapel of King Henry VII. to be the chapel of the order, and directed that each knight's banner, with plates of his arms and style, should be placed over the several stalls, in like manner as over those of the knights of the Garter in St. George's chapel, at Windsor; and he allowed them supporters to their arms. His Royal Highness Prince William, second son to the

Prince of Wales, on this occasion was made the first knight companion; his Grace the Duke of Montague, grand-master; and the dean of Westminster (for the time being) dean of the order. The other officers are, Bath King-of-arms, a registrar, who is also secretary, a gentleman-usher of the scarlet rod, and a messenger. The office of genealogist has been recently abolished.

Several alterations have since been made. In January, 1815, it was ordained that "for the purpose of commemorating the auspicious termination of the long and arduous contests in which this empire had been engaged," the order should be composed of three classes.

The FIRST CLASS to consist of not exceeding seventy-two knights grand crosses, exclusive of the sovereign and princes of the blood. They are distinguished by the letters G.C.B. after their names.

SECOND CLASS. KNIGHTS COMMANDERS (K.C.B.) to be entitled to the distinctive appellation of knighthood, and to have the same rights and privileges as knights bachelors, taking precedence of them; they wear the BADGE pendent by a red riband, instead of collar, round the neck (Pl. xxi., n. 2), and the star embroidered on the left side. Pl. xxi., n. 4. Those persons only are eligible either to this or the first class who are not below the rank of major-general in the army, or rear-admiral in the navy, excepting twelve of the number, who may be appointed for civil or diplomatic services.

THIRD CLASS. COMPANIONS OF THE ORDER (C.B.) take precedence of esquires, but are not entitled to the appellation of knights bachelors. The BADGE (Pl. xxi., n. 2) is worn pendent by a narrow red riband to the button-hole.

The BADGE is commonly pendent by a ring to a broad red riband over the right shoulder, hanging on the left side; but on particular occasions it is worn pendent to the collar. Pl. xxi., n. 1 and 2. The SURCOATS are of red taffeta, lined with white, and girt with a white kirtle. The MANTLE is also the same as the surcoat, with the star (Pl. xxi., n. 3) on the left breast. Motto, "TRIA JUNCTA IN UNO."

THE MOST ANCIENT ORDER OF THE THISTLE

Is fancifully stated to have been instituted by king Achaius on the occasion of a bright cross, similar to that on which the patron, St. Andrew, suffered martyrdom, appearing in the heavens to him and Hurgus, king of the Picts, on the night previous to the battle gained by them over Athelstan, king of England. The date is not known of its origin, but it was revived in 1540, by James V. of Scotland; again by James II. of England, in 1679; and subsequently by Queen Anne and King George I.; since which it has been several times re-organised. The order consisted of the sovereign and twelve knights until the reign of King George IV., who, by royal warrant at his coronation, increased the number of knights to sixteen. The COLLAR has thistles and sprigs of rue and gold enamelled (Pl. xxii., n. 1), to which is appended the BADGE, n. 2. The STAR is worn on the left side (n. 3); and the JEWEL is pendent to a green riband over the left shoulder, tied under the arm, (n. 4.) Motto, "NEMO ME IMPUNE LACESSET." The officers of this order are—the dean, a secretary, an usher of the green rod, and the Lord Lyon king-of-arms.

THE MOST ILLUSTRIOUS ORDER OF ST. PATRICK

Was instituted by King George III., Feb. 5, 1783, and consists of the sovereign, grand-master, a prince of the blood royal, and fifteen knights; the lord lieutenant of Ireland, *pro tempore*, being grand-master.

The officers of the order are, the Lord Primate the Archbishop of Armagh, prelate; the Archbishop of Dublin, chancellor; the Dean of St. Patrick, registrar; a secretary; a genealogist; an usher of the black rod and Ulster king-of-arms.

The COLLAR is of pure gold, composed of six harps and five roses alternately joined together by twelve knots; in the centre is a crown, and pendent thereto by a harp is the BADGE. Pl. XXII., n. 1 and 2. The STAR is of silver embroidery, upon a circular centre *or*, a cross saltire *gu.*, surmounted by a shamrock slipped *ppr.*, each leaf charged with a crown *or*, within a circular fillet of gold, with the motto, "QUIS SEPARABIT." Pl. XXII., n. 3. The JEWEL is likewise worn pendent from a light blue riband scarfwise over the right shoulder, n. 4.

THE ROYAL HANOVERIAN GUELPHIC ORDER

Was founded by his majesty George IV., when Prince Regent, in 1815, in commemoration of the raising of Hanover into a kingdom, and for rewarding those persons who had performed any signal service to their king and country. Until his royal highness the Duke of Cumberland became King of Hanover, this decoration was at the disposal of the sovereign of Great Britain: it is now wholly Hanoverian, unde the control of the King of Hanover. The order is composed of three classes, into which civil and military men are admitted, viz., grand crosses, commanders, and knights. The BADGES of the military grand crosses, military commanders, and military knights, only differ in size according to their class. Pl XXIII., n. 2.

The BADGES of the civil grand crosses, commanders, and knights are also alike, only differing in size, having a crown upon the upper limb of the cross (without the swords), by which it is suspended, and a wreath of oak-leaves instead of laurels. It is worn on grand occasions suspended from the collar (n. 1); but on ordinary occasions it is worn pendent from a sky-blue riband scarfwise. Commanders suspend it by a sky-blue riband worn round the neck, and knights by a riband and gold buckle from the button-hole.

The STAR worn by the military grand crosses is of eight points, &c., with the motto, " NEC ASPERA TERRENT," n. 3. That worn by the civil grand crosses only differs in the omission of the swords, and a wreath of oak-leaves being substituted for laurel.

The star of the civil commanders differs from the last. See Pl. XXIII., n. 4.

That of the military commanders is the same, with the addition of the swords, and changing the oak into laurel-leaves.

THE MOST DISTINGUISHED ORDER OF ST. MICHAEL AND ST. GEORGE

Was also instituted by his majesty George IV., in 1818, in commemoration of the united states of the Ionian Islands being placed under his sovereign protectorship.

The order is composed of three classes, and consists of the sovereign, a grand-master, a first and principal knight grand cross, eight grand crosses, twelve knights commanders, and twenty-four knights, exclusive of British subjects holding high and confidential employ in the service of the united states of Malta.

The COLLAR and BADGE (Pl. XXIII., n. 1 and 2) are worn round the neck on grand occasions ; but ordinarily the badge is worn pendent from a red riband with blue edges.

The STAR worn by the knights grand crosses is of exquisite taste, and can only be understood by reference to Pl. XXIII., n. 3. That worn by the knights commanders is of a similar description, but of less beauty. Pl. XXIII., fig. 4. Motto, "AUSPICIUM MELIORIS ÆVI."

THE MOST EXALTED ORDER OF THE STAR OF INDIA (K.S.I.)

This order was instituted by her present Majesty, 23rd of February, 1861. It consists of the sovereign, a grand-master (the governor-general of India for the time being), and twenty-five knights, together with such extra or honorary knights as the crown shall from time to time appoint. The statutes provide that it shall be competent for the sovereign to confer the dignity of knight of the order upon such princes and chiefs of India as shall entitle themselves to her Majesty's favour, and on such of her Majesty's British subjects as shall render important and loyal services to the Indian Empire. The STAR, to be worn on the left breast, is formed of wavy rays of gold issuing from the centre, having thereon a star of five points in diamonds, encircled by a light-blue enamelled riband (on which the points rest) tied at the ends, and inscribed with the motto, "HEAVEN'S LIGHT OUR GUIDE," also in diamonds. (*Vide* Frontispiece.)

The COLLAR is composed of the united red and white historic roses of England, and the lotus flower of India, between them two palm branches tied together in saltire, and in the centre an imperial crown all of gold richly enamelled in their proper colours, and connected by a double chain of gold.

The BADGE worn as a pendent to the collar, or to the riband when the collar is not worn, consists of an onyx cameo of her Majesty's head in profile, set in a perforated and ornamented oval containing the motto of the order, surmounted by a star of five points all in diamonds.

The riband is of pale blue, with a white stripe towards each edge.

KNIGHTS-BANNERETS

This degree of knighthood is of very ancient date. It was conferred in England as early as the reign of Edward I., and bestowed on persons distinguished for their gallantry by the king (or his general, which was very rare), at the head of his army, drawn up in battalia, after a victory, under the royal standard displayed, attended by all the field-officers and nobility of the court then in the army.

Knights-bannerets took place before the younger sons of all viscounts and barons, and also preceded baronets, and were allowed to bear their arms with supporters, which is denied to all others under the degree of a baron, unless they be knights grand crosses of any of the established orders.

In the year 1773, at a review of the royal navy at Portsmouth, his majesty George III. conferred this honourable title on several flag-officers, viz., Admirals Pye and Sprye, and on Captains Knight, Bickerton, and Vernon. But this was not according to the original institution, viz., " by the king in person, at the head of his army, under the royal banner displayed, on occasion of some glorious victory."

KNIGHTS BACHELORS.

This honour was formerly in very high esteem; but the original institution being perverted, it is now conferred indiscriminately upon gownsmen, burghers, physicians, and others, by the sovereign's lightly touching the person, who is then kneeling, on the right shoulder with a drawn sword, and saying, "Rise, Sir ——," mentioning the Christian name.

Originally the qualifications for it were such, that no trader could be created, nor any one of a servile condition. It was then requisite that he should be brave, expert, well-behaved, and of good morals. A candidate for knighthood being approved of, he presented himself in the church, confessed his sins, had absolution given him; he heard mass, watched his arms all night, placed his sword on the altar, which was returned by the priest, who gave him his benediction; the sacrament was administered to him, and, having bathed, he was dressed in rich robes, and his spurs and sword put on. He then appeared before his chief, who dubbed him a knight, after the same manner, in fact, as the knights bachelors are at this time made. The whole ceremony then concluded with feasting and rejoicing.

Knighthood is not hereditary, but acquired. It does not come into the world with a man, like nobility; nor can it be revoked. It was anciently the custom to knight every man of rank and fortune, that he might be qualified to give challenges, to fight in the lists, and to perform feats of arms. The sons of kings, and kings themselves, with all other sovereigns, in former days had knighthood conferred on them as a mark of honour.

They were usually knighted at their baptism, or marriage, at their coronation, or before battle.*

ESQUIRE.

A title of honour above a gentleman and below a knight. This appellation, termed in Latin *armiger*, or *scutarius*, served anciently to denote such as were bearers of arms, or carried the shield ; and was accordingly considered as a title of office only, until the reign of Richard II.; though little mention is made of this, or the addition of gentleman, in ancient deeds, till the time of Henry V., when, by a statute in the first year of that monarch, it was enacted, that in all cases where process of outlawry lay, the additions of the estate, degree, or profession of the defendant should be inserted.

This statute having made it necessary to ascertain who was entitled to this degree, it was laid down as a general rule, that there were seven sorts of esquires; viz. :—

1st. Esquires of the king's body, limited to the number of four ; who kept the door of the king's bedchamber, when he pleased to go to bed, walked at a coronation, and had precedence of all knights' younger sons. They are now *disused.*

2dly. The eldest sons of knights, and their eldest sons successively.

* No British subject is allowed to wear the insignia of any foreign order, without first obtaining her Majesty's permission ; and no licence or permission subsequent to March, 1813, to wear the insignia of those orders in England, authorises the assumption of any style, appellation, rank, precedence, privilege &c., appertaining to a knight bachelor of the United Kingdom.

3dly. The eldest sons of the youngest sons of barons, and others of the greater nobility.

4thly. Such as the sovereign invests with collars of SS, as the kings-at-arms, heralds, &c., or shall grant silver or white spurs to; the eldest sons of those last-mentioned may also bear the title.

5thly. Esquires to the knights of the Bath, being their attendants on their installation; these must bear coat-armour, according to the law of arms, are esquires for life, and also their eldest sons, and have the same privileges as the esquires of the king's body.

6thly. Sheriffs of counties and justices of peace (with this distinction, that a sheriff, in regard to the dignity of the office, is an esquire for life, but a justice of the peace only so long as he continues in the commission), and all those who bear special office in the royal household, as gentlemen of the privy chamber, carvers, sewers, cup-bearers, pensioners, serjeants-at-arms, and all that have any near or especial dependence on the royal person, and are not knighted; also captains in the wars, recorded in the official lists.

7thly. Counsellors at law; bachelors of divinity, law, and physic; mayors of towns are reputed esquires, or equal to esquires (though not really so); also the pennon-bearer to the sovereign, who carries the flag or banner, whereon the royal arms, either at war or at a funeral, are painted.

Besides, this degree of esquire is a special privilege to any of the king's ordinary and nearest attendants; for be his birth gentle or base, if he serve in the place of an esquire, he is an esquire by that service; for it is the place that dignifies the person, and not the person the place: so if any gentleman or esquire shall take upon him the place of a yeoman of the king's guard, he immediately loses all his titles of honour, and is no more than a yeoman.

There is a general opinion, that every gentleman of landed property, that has 300*l.* a year, is an esquire; which is a vulgar error, for no money or landed property will give a man properly this title, unless he come within one of the above rules.

GENTLEMAN.

Gentlemen, *Generosus*, seems to be compounded of two words, the one French, (*Gentil*), *honestus vel honesta parente natus;* the other Saxon (*man*), as if one said, a man well born. Under this name are comprised all that are above yeoman and artificers; so that nobles may with strict propriety be called gentlemen. But by the custom of England, nobility is either major or minor. Major contains all titles and degrees from knighthood upwards: minor, all from knights downwards.

Gentlemen have their beginning either of blood, as being born of worshipful parents, or from having achieved, in peace or war, some honourable action, whereby they have acquired the right to bear arms. But in these days whoever studies the laws of the realm, or professes a liberal science, or who can live without manual labour, is commonly taken for a gentleman : and a king-at-arms may grant him a patent for a new coat, if there is none that of right appertains to him from his ancestors.

If a gentleman be bound apprentice to a merchant or other trade, he does not thereby lose his degree of gentility; but if a man be a gentleman by office only, and loses his office, in that case he also loses his gentility.

By the statute 5 Eliz. cap. 4, entitled "An Act touching orders for artificers, labourers, servants of husbandry, and apprentices," amongst other things it is declared, "that a gentleman born," &c., "shall not be compelled to serve in husbandry." And in time still more ancient, the gentry of England had many advantages and privileges above the vulgar :—

1. *Pro honore sustinendo;* if a churle or peasant detracted from the honour of a gentleman, he had a remedy in law, *actione injuriarum;* but if one gentle man defamed another, the combat was anciently allowed.

2. In equal crimes a gentleman was punishable with more favour than the churle, provided the crime were not heresy, treason, or excessive contumacy.

3. With many observances and ceremonial respects a gentleman was honoured by the churle or ungentle.

4. In giving evidence, the testimony of a gentleman was deemed more authentic than a clown's.

5. In election of magistrates and officers by vote, the suffrage of a gentleman took place of an ignoble person.

6. A gentleman was excused from base services impositions, and duties, both real and personal.

7. A gentleman condemned to death was not to be hanged, but beheaded, and his examination taken without torture.

8. To take down the coat-armour of any gentleman, to deface his monument, or offer violence to any ensign of a deceased noble, was deemed an insult to the person of the dead, and punishment was due accordingly.

9. A clown might not challenge a gentleman to combat, *quia conditiones impares*

For the protection and defence of this civil dignity there were three laws : the first, *jus agnitionis*, the right or law of descent for the kindred of the father's side : the second, *jus stirpis*, for the family in general : the third, *jus gentilitatis*, a law for the descent in noble families ; by which law a gentleman of blood and coat-armour only was privileged.

To make perfection in blood, a lineal descent from *Atavus, Proavus, Avus,* and *Pater* (the great-grand father's father, the great-grandfather, the grandfather, and the father), on the father's side, was required ; and as much on the mother's side ; then was a gentleman not only of perfect blood, but of ancestry also.

Anciently, none were admitted into the inns of court but such as were gentlemen of blood ; nor were the church dignities and preferments bestowed indifferently among the vulgar. The Russians, and some other nations, admit none to the study of the law but gentle-men's younger sons. The decayed families in France are supported and receive new life from the court, camp, law, and ecclesiastical preferments, by which means their church and state are in esteem and reve-rence, being filled most commonly with the best blood and noblest by birth amongst them.

The achievement of a gentleman has no difference from that of an esquire, both their helmets being close and sideways.

YEOMEN.

Yeomen are so called of the Saxon word *zemen*, which signifies common, and are properly such as have some lands of their own to live upon ; for a carn of land, or a plough-land, was in ancient time of the yearly value of five nobles, and this was the qualification of a sokeman or yeoman. In our law they are called *legales homines*, a word familiar in writs and inquests.

It appears from Lambarde's Perambulation of Kent, p. 367, that the Saxon word *telphioneman* was given to the theyne or gentleman, because his life was valued at one thousand two hundred shillings (in those days the lives of all men were rated at certain sums of money); while the term *twyhind* was applied to the churle or yeoman, because the price of his head was taxed at two hundred shillings. Which facts may be found in the etymology of the words themselves, the one called a *telphioneman*, or twelve-hundred man, and the other a *twyhind*, or a man of two hundred. " And in this estate they pleased themselves, insomuch that a man might (as he even now may) find sundry yeomen, though otherwise comparable for wealth with many of the gentle sort, that will not yet for that change their condition, nor desire to be apparelled with the title of gentry."

As in ancient times the senators of Rome were elected *à censu;* and as with us, in conferring nobility, respect is had to revenue, by which dignity and nobility may be supported and maintained; so the wisdom of this realm hath of ancient time provided, that none shall pass upon juries for the trial of any matter real or personal, or upon any criminal cause, but such as, besides their movables, have lands for estate of life, at the least to a competent value: lest from need or poverty such jurors might be corrupted or suborned.

And in all cases the law has conceived a better opinion of those that have lands and tenements, or otherwise are of worth in movable goods, than it has of artificers, retailers, labourers, or the like.

By the statute of 2 Hen. IV. cap. 27, amongst other things it is enacted, " That no yeoman should take or wear any livery of any lord upon pain of imprisonment, and to make fine at the king's will and pleasure."

As the nobility, gentry, and clergy, have certain privileges peculiar to themselves, so have the commonalty of England beyond the subjects of other monarchs.

No freeman of England can be imprisoned, ousted of his possession, or disseised of his freehold, without order of law, and just cause shown.

To him that is imprisoned may not be denied a *habeas corpus*, if it be desired ; and if no just cause be alleged, and the same be not returned upon a *habeas corpus*, the prisoner is to be set at liberty. By *Magna Charta*, 9 Hen. III., no soldier can be quartered in any house except inns, and other public victualling-houses, in time of peace, without the owner's consent. By the petition of rights, 3 Car. I., no taxes, loans, or benevolences, can be imposed but by act of parliament.

The yeomanry are not to be pressed to serve as soldiers in the wars, unless bound by tenure, which is now abolished ; nor are the train-bands compellable to march out of the kingdom, or be transported beyond sea : nor is any one compelled to bear his own arms, if he find a sufficient man as his substitute, qualified according to the act before-mentioned ; and no freeman is to be tried but by his equals, nor condemned but by the laws of the land.

The yeomen of England were famous in our forefathers' days for archery and manhood : our infantry, which so often conquered the French, and repulsed the Scots, were composed of them, as are our militia at present.

Precedency.

PERSONS of every degree of honour or dignity take place according to the seniority of their creation, and not of years, unless descended of the blood royal, in which case they have place of all of the same degree not of the blood royal.

The younger sons of the preceding rank take place of the eldest sons of the next degree, viz. the younger sons of dukes of the eldest sons of earls; the younger sons of earls of the eldest sons of barons, &c.

There have been some alterations made as to precedency, whereby all the sons of viscounts and barons are allowed to precede baronets. And the eldest sons and daughters of baronets have place given them before the eldest sons and daughters of any knights, of what degree or order soever, though superior to that of a baronet (these being but temporary dignities, whereas that of baronet is hereditary); and the younger sons of baronets are to have place next after the eldest sons of knights.

As, also, there are some great officers of state who take place (although they are not noblemen) above the nobility of higher degree; so there are some persons who, for their dignities in the church, degrees in the universities and inns of court, offices in the state or army (although they are neither knights nor gentlemen born), yet they take place amongst them. Thus all colonels and field-officers (who are honourable), as also master of the artillery, and quarter-master-general; doctors of divinity, law, physic, and music; deans chancellors, prebendaries, heads of colleges in the universities, and serjeants-at-law—are, by courtesy, allowed place before ordinary esquires. And all bachelors of divinity, law, physic and music ; masters of arts, barristers in the inns of courts; lieutenant-colonels, majors, captains, and other commissioned military officers ; and divers patent officers in the king's household—may equal, if not precede, gentlemen who have none of these qualifications.

In towns corporate, the inhabitants of cities (and herein those of the capital or metropolitan city are the first ranked) are preferred to those of boroughs, and those who have borne magistracy to all others. And here a younger alderman or bailey takes not precedency from his senior by being knighted, or as being the elder knight, as was the case of Alderman Craven, who (though no knight) had place, as senior alderman, before all the rest who were knights, at the coronation of King James. This is to be understood as to public meetings relative to the town; for it is doubted whether it will hold good in any neutral place. It has also been determined in the Heralds' Office, that all who have been lords mayor of London shall everywhere take place of all knights-bachelors, because they have been the king's lieutenants.

It was likewise adjudged in the case of Sir John Crook, serjeant-at-law, by the judges in court, that such serjeants as were his seniors, though not knighted, should have preference, notwithstanding his knighthood.

All colonels, says Guillim, are honourable, and by the law of arms ought to precede simple knights.

Women before marriage have precedency l y their father ; but there is this difference between them and the male children, that the same precedency is due to all the daughters that is due to the eldest, whereas it is not so among the sons.

By marriage a woman participates in her husband's dignities; but none of the wife's dignities can come by marriage to her husband, but are to descend to her next heir.

If a woman have precedency by creation, descent, or birth, she retains the same, though she marries an inferior. But it is observable, that if a woman nobly born marry any nobleman, as a baron, she shall take place according to the degree of her husband, though she be a duke's daughter.

A woman privileged by marriage with one of noble degree, shall retain the privilege due to her by her husband, though he should be degraded by forfeiture, &c.; for crimes are personal.

The wife of the eldest son of any degree takes place of the daughters of the same degree (who always have place immediately after the wives of such eldest sons); and both of them take place of the younger sons of the preceding degree. Thus the lady of the eldest son of an earl takes place of an earl's daughter, and both of them precede the wife of the younger son of a marquis; also, the wife of any degree precedes the wife of the eldest son of the preceding degree. Thus the wife of a marquis precedes the wife of the eldest son of a duke. This holds not only in comparing degrees, but also families of the same degree among themselves; for instance, the daughter of a senior earl yields place to the wife of a junior earl's son; though if such daughter be an heiress, she will then be allowed place before the wives of the eldest sons of all younger earls.

s

Table of Precedency among Men.

THE KING, or the Consort of the reigning Queen.[*]
The Prince of Wales.
King's or Queen-regnant's other sons.
Grandsons.
Brothers.
Uncles.
Brothers' or sisters' sons.
Sons-in-law.
[†]
Archbishop of Canterbury.
Lord High Chancellor, or Lord Keeper.
Archbishop of York.
Archbishop of Armagh, Primate of Ireland.
Archbishop of Dublin.
[‡] Lord High Treasurer.
[‡] Lord President of the Privy Council.
[‡] Lord Privy Seal.
[‡] Lord Great Chamberlain.
Lord High Constable.
[§] Earl Marshal.
[§] Lord High Admiral.
[§] Lord Steward *of the Household.*
[§] Lord Chamberlain *of the Household.*
Dukes *according to their patents.*
Eldest sons of Dukes of the Blood Royal.
Marquises *according to their patents.*
The eldest sons of Dukes.
Earls *according to their patents.*
The younger sons of Dukes of the Blood Royal.
The eldest sons of Marquises.

----

[*] By the official Gazette, under date 20th March, 1840, it was ordered that H. R. H. Prince Albert of Saxe-Coburg and Gotha, consort of her Majesty, should take rank next the Queen.

[†] Leopold, King of the Belgians, by special statute.

[‡] Being of the degree of Barons, by stat. 31 Hen. VIII.

[§] Above all of their degree, viz., Dukes to precede Dukes, Earls above Earls, &c. Stat. 31 Hen. VIII.

The younger sons of Dukes.
Viscounts *according to their patents.*
The eldest sons of Earls.
The younger sons of Marquises.
Bishop of London.
Bishop of Durham.
Bishop of Winchester.
All other Bishops according to seniority of consecration.
* Barons *according to their patents.*
Speaker of the House of Commons.
Commissioners of the Great Seal.
The Treasurer of the Household.
The Comptroller of the Household.
Master of the Horse.
The Vice Chamberlain.
Secretary of State, *being under the degree of Baron.*
The eldest sons of Viscounts.
The younger sons of Earls.
The eldest sons of Barons.
Knights of the Garter *(if not nobles).*†
Privy Councillors (*ditto*).

---

* Any peer, being principal secretary of state, shall take precedence of all other peers of his degree. But the priority of signing treaties, or instruments, by public ministers, is always enjoyed by rank of place, and not by title.

It was confirmed by stat. 5 Anne, chap. 8, That all peers of Scotland shall be peers of Great Britain, and have rank next after the peers of the same degree in England, at the date of the union, May 1, 1707. By Act 39 & 40 Geo. III. cap. 67, it is enacted, That the lords of Parliament on the part of Ireland shall have the same privileges as the lords of Great Britain ; and all the lords spiritual of Ireland shall rank next after the lords spiritual of Great Britain, and shall enjoy the same privileges, except that of sitting in the House of Lords. The temporal peers of Ireland have rank next after the peers of the same rank in Great Britain created before the union. All peerages of Ireland and Great Britain created since the union have rank according to creation, and are considered in all respects as peerages of the United Kingdom, and enjoy the same privileges, excepting those peers of Ireland who have not sittings in the House of Lords.

† Knights of the Thistle and of St. Patrick have no precedence, under the statutes of their orders, and would be placed according to their rank irrespective of their knighthood.

Chancellor of the Exchequer.

Chancellor of the duchy of Lancaster.

Lord Chief Justice of the King's Bench.

Master of the Rolls.

Lord Chief Justice of the Common Pleas.

Lord Chief Baron of the Exchequer.

Vice-Chancellor.

Judges and Barons *of the degree of the Coif of the sa.d Courts according to seniority, and*

Judges of the Court of Review.

Commissioners of the Court of Bankruptcy.

Bannerets *made under the Royal banner, in open war, and the King or Prince of Wales personally present.*

The younger sons of Viscounts.

The youngers sons of Barons.

Baronets *according to their patents.*

Bannerets *not made by the King himself in person.*

Knights *Grand Crosses* of the Bath.

Knights *Grand Crosses* of St. Michael and St. George.

Knights Commanders of the Bath.

Knights Commanders of St. Michael and St. George.

Knights Bachelors.

Companions of the Bath.

Companions of St. Michael and St. George.

Eldest sons of the younger sons of Peers.

The eldest sons of Baronets.

The eldest sons of Bannerets.

The eldest sons of Knights of the Garter.

The eldest sons of Knights Bachelors.

The younger sons of Baronets.

Esquires by creation.

Esquires by office.

Gentlemen entitled to bear arms.

Clergymen, Barristers at Law, Officers in the Navy and Army who are Gentlemen by profession.

Table of Precedency among Women.

THE QUEEN (Regnant or Consort, as the case may be).
The Queen Dowager.
Princess of Wales.
Princesses, daughters of the King or Queen Regnant.
Princesses and Duchesses, wives of the King's or Queen Regnant's younger sons.
King's or Queen Regnant's granddaughters.
Wives of the King's or Queen Regnant's grandsons.
King's sisters.
Wives of the King's or Queen Regnant's brothers.
The King's aunts
Wives of the King's uncles.
Daughters of the King's or Queen Regnant's brothers' or sisters' sons.
Wives of the King's nephews.
Duchesses.
Marchionesses.
Wives of the eldest sons of Dukes.
Daughters of Dukes.
Countesses.
Wives of the eldest sons of Marquises.
Daughters of Marquises.
Wives of the younger sons of Dukes.
Viscountesses.
Wives of the younger sons of Marquises.
Baronesses.
Wives of the eldest sons of Viscounts.
Daughters of Viscounts.
Wives of the younger sons of Earls.
Wives of the eldest sons of Barons.
Daughters of Barons.
Wives of Knights of the Garter.
Wives of Bannerets *made by the King in person.*
Wives of the younger sons of Viscounts.
Wives of the younger sons of Barons.

Wives of Baronets.
Wives of Bannerets *not made by the King in person.*
Wives of Knights *Grand Crosses* of the Bath.
Wives of Knights *Grand Crosses* of St. Michael and St. George.
Wives of Knights Commanders of the Bath.
Wives of Knights Commanders of St. Michael and St. George.
Wives of Knights Bachelors.
Wives of Companions of the Bath.
Wives of Companions of St. Michael and St. George.
Wives of the eldest sons of the younger sons of Peers.
Daughters of the younger sons of Peers.
Wives of the eldest sons of Baronets.
Daughters of Baronets.
Wives of the eldest sons of Knights of the Garter.
Wives of the eldest sons of Bannerets.
Wives of the eldest sons of Knights Bachelors.
Daughters of Knights Bachelors.
Wives of the younger sons of Baronets.
Wives of Esquires.
Wives of Gentlemen.
Wives of Clergymen, Barristers at Law, and Officers in the
Navy and Army.

The Great Officers of State, and of the Royal Household.

THE LORD HIGH STEWARD.

THE power and influence of the lord high steward, anciently the first great officer of state, were in former times so exorbitant, that after the elevation of Henry of Bolingbroke, Duke of Lancaster, to the throne, when the office came into the hands of the crown, it was not thought prudent to intrust it again in the person of a subject. Since that time, therefore, there has not been any lord high steward in England, except to officiate *pro tempore* at a coronation, or for the arraignment of a peer or peeress for a capital crime.

THE LORD HIGH CHANCELLOR.

Formerly the second, now the first, great officer of the crown, is the lord high chancellor, or keeper of the great seal, which are the same in authority, power, and precedence. They are appointed by the sovereign's delivery of the great seal to them, and by taking the oath of office. They differ only in this point that the lord chancellor has also letters patent, whereas the lord keeper has none. He is an officer of very great power, no patents, writs, or grants being valid, until he affixes the great seal thereto.

Among the many great prerogatives of his office, he has a power to judge according to equity, conscience, and reason, where he finds the law of the land defective : to collate to all ecclesiastical benefices rated under 20*l.* a year : and to perform all matters which appertain to the speaker of the House of Lords.

In ancient times this great office was most usually filled by an ecclesiastic. The first upon record after the Conquest is Maurice, in 1067, who was afterwards bishop of London.

There is no instance of the elevation of any chancellor to the peerage until the year 1603, when King James I. delivered a new great seal to Sir Thomas Egerton, and soon after created him baron of Ellesmere, and constituted him lord high chancellor of England. But until of late years the custom never prevailed, that the lord high chancellor of England should be made an hereditary peer of the realm.

THE LORD HIGH TREASURER.

This was anciently the third great office of the crown. It was then conferred by the delivery of the golden keys of the treasury : but it is now executed by five persons, who are called lords commissioners for executing the office of lord high treasurer, viz., one who is called the first lord of the treasury, and four others, who are styled lords of the treasury only, of whom one is also denominated chancellor and under-treasurer of the exchequer, although not unfrequently the offices of first lord of the treasury, and of chancellor of the exchequer have been united in the same person.

THE LORD PRESIDENT OF THE COUNCIL.

Formerly the fourth now the third great officer of state is appointed by the crown by letters patent under the great seal, *durante bene placito* (during pleasure). His duty is to attend the royal person, and to manage the debates in council; to propose matters from the sovereign at the council-table, and to report the resolutions taken thereon.

THE LORD PRIVY-SEAL.

The lord privy-seal is a place of great trust, honour, and antiquity. In the time of Edward III., and long after, this officer was called keeper of the privy-seal (or private seal) to distinguish him from the other, called keeper of the great seal. He is appointed now by letters patent, is a privy councillor by his office, and takes place next after the president of the council. He is now the fourth great officer of state, and has the custody of the privy-seal, which he must not put to any grant without good warrant under the royal signet. This seal is used by the sovereign to all charters, grants, and pardons, before they come to the great seal; but may also be affixed to other things that never pass the great seal; as, to cancel a recognizance to the crown, or to discharge a debt.

THE LORD GREAT CHAMBERLAIN.

This high office was for many successions enjoyed by the noble family of De Vere, earls of Oxford (having been granted to them by Henry I.), until the death of Henry de Vere, the eighteenth earl, without issue; when

Mary, sister and heir of Edward, father of the said
Henry, having married Peregrine Bertie, Lord Willoughby of Eresby, was mother by him of Robert Lord
Willoughby of Eresby, who made claim to the earldom
of Oxford, as also to the office of lord great chamberlain of England; whereupon, after much dispute, the
House of Lords gave judgment that he had made good
his claim to the office but not to the earldom (which
was decided in favour of the heir-male collateral); and
he was accordingly on the 22nd of November, the 2nd
of Charles I., admitted into the House of Lords with
his staff; and his descendants continued to enjoy the
same until the death of Robert Bertie, fourth duke of
Ancaster, marquis and earl of Lindsey, Lord Willoughby of Eresby, and lord great chamberlain of
England, in 1779; who dying unmarried, was suc-
ceeded in the dukedom, marquisate, and earldom, by
his uncle, Lord Brownlow Bertie; but the barony of
Willoughby fell into abeyance; and for the great
chamberlainship there were several candidates, viz. the
Lord Brownlow Bertie, then duke of Ancaster; earl
Percy, eldest son of the duke of Northumberland; the
duchess dowager of Athol, baroness Strange, of Knockyn,
and the ladies Priscilla Barbara, and Georgiana Charlotte Bertie, sisters and co-heirs of Robert, fourth duke
of Ancaster, deceased; when, after hearing all parties
in support of their respective pretensions, the House
of Peers desired the opinion of the twelve judges, who
gave it as their opinions, that the office devolved to the
ladies Priscilla Barbara, and Georgiana Charlotte Bertie,
as heirs to their brother the aforesaid duke Robert, deceased; and that they had powers to appoint a deputy to
act for them, not under the degree of a knight, who, if his

Majesty approved of him, might officiate accordingly; and agreeably to this opinion, the House gave judgment. Whereupon, Peter Burrell, Esq., husband of the said Lady Priscilla Barbara, was appointed, and received the honour of knighthood from his Majesty; after which appointment he was created lord Gwydir.

To this officer belong very many perquisites, privileges, &c., in lieu of which he usually on a coronation receives a sum of money.

When the king or queen goes to parliament, he disposes of the sword of state to be carried by what lord he pleases, at which time he goes himself before on the right hand of the sword, next the king or queen's person, and the earl marshal on the left.

Upon all solemn occasions the keys of Westminster Hall,* the court of wards, and the court of requests, are delivered to him; and the gentleman-usher of the black rod, yeoman-usher, and the door-keepers, are then under his command.

To him also belongs the fitting up of Westminster Hall for a coronation, the trial of a peer, or any public solemnity.

He has likewise certain fees from every archbishop or bishop, when they do homage or fealty to the crown: and from all peers on their creation, or doing homage or fealty.

* By the search made by the Lord Chamberlain in the cellars under the Parliament-house, Guy Vaux (or Faux) was discovered and taken.

THE LORD HIGH CONSTABLE.

This office was for many ages held by grand serjeantry. The lord high constable and the earl marshal were formerly judges of the court of chivalry, called, in the time of Henry IV., *curia militaris*, and after, the court of honour. The power of the high constable was so great, and so improper a use was oftentimes made of it, that, so early as the 13th of Richard II., a statute was passed for regulating and abridging the same, together with the power of the earl marshal. The office went with inheritance, and by the tenure of the manors of Harlefield, Newman, and Whitenhurst, in the county of Gloucester,* in the family of the Bohuns, earls of Hereford, Essex, and Northampton, and passed from the Bohuns upon the death of Humphrey, the last earl, to Thomas of Woodstock, duke of Gloucester; and from him to the issue of Edmund, earl of Stafford, whose son, Humphrey Stafford, was created duke of Buckingham, with whose great-grandson, Edward Stafford, duke of Buckingham, beheaded by Henry VIII. on Tower Hill, this office terminated. It has never since been granted to any person, otherwise than *pro tempore* for a coronation, or trial by combat.†

* The castle of Caldecot, near Chepstow, in the county of Monmouth, was the residence of the lord high constables of England, and holden by them in virtue thereof.

† The only instance that occurs of a trial by combat being ordered since the cessation of the office of lord high constable, is between Lord Reay and David Ramsay, Esq., 28th November, 1631 : the king prevented this trial. On this occasion, Robert Bertie, earl of Lindsey, was appointed lord high constable.

EARL MARSHAL OF ENGLAND.

This office is of great antiquity, and is not said to have been holden by tenure or serjeantry, as the offices of lord steward and high constable were.

Yet, in the time of Henry I., Sir William Dugdale recites, that Robert de Venvis, and William de Hastings, impleaded Gilbert Mareschall, and John his son, for the office of mareschal* to the king, but without success; which John in the 10th of Henry II., being the king's marshal, upon the difference between that king and Thomas à Becket, archbishop of Canterbury, laid claim for the king to one of the archbishop's manors, which had been long enjoyed by his predecessors. Unto John, son of this said John, King Henry II. confirmed his office of marshal; and as such, at the coronation of Richard I., he bore the great gilt spurs, and afterwards died without issue. William Mareschall† earl of Pembroke, was his brother and heir, whose five sons successively earls of Pembroke, dying without issue male, his five daughters became his heirs; of whom Maude, the eldest, married Hugh Bigod, earl of Norfolk, whose son, Roger Bigod, earl of Norfolk, after frequent solicitations, obtained the office and honour of marshal, in right of his mother, the 32nd of Henry III.; when the king solemnly gave the marshal's

* According to Camden, this office of mareschal appears to mean the office of marshal of the king's house; an office distinct from that afterwards known by the name of earl marshal of England.

† These earls of Pembroke were oftentimes called also mareschals, according to Matthew Paris, and other historians; but it does not appear that any one had this title by creation till the time of Richard II., who conferred it on Thomas Mowbray, earl of Nottingham.

rod into her hands, in regard of her seniority in
the inheritance of the Mareschalls, earls of Pembroke,
which she thereupon delivered to Earl Roger, her son,
whose homage the king received for the same; but he
dying without issue, the inheritance devolved upon
Roger, his nephew and heir, who, in the 30th of
Edward I., having no issue, constituted the king his
heir, delivered unto him the marshal's rod, upon condition to be rendered back in case of having children,
and other certain terms; and, after dying without
issue, the office thereby fell into the King's hands.
Afterwards, King Edward II. granted the same unto
Thomas de Brotherton, his brother. Brotherton died,
leaving Margery, his daughter and heir, countess of
Norfolk, during whose life King Edward III. and
Richard II. disposed of this office to divers others;
sometimes for life, sometimes during pleasure: until at
last, king Richard II. gave it by patent to Thomas
Mowbray, earl of Nottingham, who was the grandchild
of the said Margaret, who was then created earl
marshal, being the first time that the title of earl was
affixed to the office of marshal; at the same time he
had power given that he and his successors in the
office should bear in their hands a gold truncheon,
enamelled with black at each end; at the upper end
having the king's arms engraven thereon, and at the
lower end his own arms. But, by reason of the judgment given against Mowbray, duke of Norfolk, not long
before the 21st of Richard II., this honour and office
were forfeited during his life. His posterity, however,
had them restored; which they held till the 15th of
Edward IV., when the issue male failed, and the
honour, of course, expired. But Richard III. revived

it in Sir John Howard, son of Sir Robert Howard, who
had married Margaret, one of the daughters and co-heirs
of the aforesaid Thomas Mowbray, earl marshal and duke
of Norfolk; whom he also created duke of Norfolk, and
who, adhering to his master and benefactor, was slain with
him at Bosworth field. By an attainder in parliament, the
honour and office were again forfeited, and granted to
William Berkely, earl of Nottingham, in tail, who de-
ceasing soon after, issueless, Henry VIII. gave the same
for life to Henry, earl of Surrey, afterwards duke of
Norfolk, and his issue male, whence for many years it was
held for life only.   King James I., at his coronation,
granted it to the earl of Worcester for that occasion,
and at other times it was executed by commission.
But at length King James I. was pleased, by letters
patent, dated 29th August, 1622, to constitute Thomas
Howard, earl of Arundel, earl marshal for life; and
the next year (with the advice of the privy council)
granted letters patent, wherein it was declared that,
during the vacancy of the office of lord high constable
of England, the earl marshal had the like jurisdiction
in the court of chivalry, as both constable and marshal
jointly ever possessed.   And on the 19th of October,
1672, King Charles II. was pleased to grant to Henry
lord Howard, and the heirs male of his body lawfully
begotten (with a long entail to divers others of the
Howard family), the office and dignity of earl marshal
of England, with power to execute the same by deputy
or deputies, in as full and ample a manner as the same
was heretofore executed by Henry Howard, late earl of
Arundel, grandfather to the said Henry lord Howard,
or by Thomas Howard, duke of Norfolk; or by John
Mowbray, duke of Norfolk, or any other earl marshal

of England, with an allowance of 20*l.* each year, payable out of the hanaper offices.

The *College of Arms*, commonly called the *Heralds' College*, is situate on the east side of St. Bennet's Hill, Doctors' Commons, at the south-west end of St. Paul's Churchyard. It was destroyed by the dreadful fire in 1666, but rebuilt about three years after. It is a spacious brick edifice, having an arched gateway in front, leading into a handsome quadrangle. The society was incorporated by Richard III., and consists of thirteen members; viz. three kings-of-arms, six heralds, and four pursuivants, all nominated by the earl marshal, and holding their places by patent during good behaviour.

The kings-of-arms are styled respectively *Garter*, *Clarenceux*, and *Norroy*.

Garter king-of-arms, was instituted as before mentioned (see Knights of the Garter, *ante*, p. 235,) by King Henry V., and made sovereign of all the other officers of arms in England. To him belongs the correction of arms, and ensigns of arms, usurped or borne unjustly; and the power under warrant of the earl marshal, of granting arms to deserving persons, and supporters to the nobility and knights grand crosses of the Bath.

It is the office also of Garter king-of-arms to go next before the sword in solemn processions, none interposing except the marshal; when any lord enters the parliament chamber, it is his part to assign him his place, according to his dignity and degree; to carry the ensign of the order to foreign princes, and to do, or procure to be done, what the sovereign shall enjoin, relating to the order.

Clarenceux and *Norroy* are the provincial kings-of-arms; the jurisdiction of the former comprehending all England to the south of the river Trent, and that of Norroy all to the north of that river.

Clarenceux is thus named from the Duke of Clarence, the third son of King Edward III.

Norroy, signifying North Roy, or North King.

The six Heralds are *Windsor, Chester, Lancaster, York, Richmond,* and *Somerset.* They are esquires by virtue of their office.

The four Pursuivants are denominated respectively *Rouge-croix, Blue-mantle, Rouge-dragon,* and *Portcullis.*

The Earl Marshal has a secretary who receives fees upon warrants, but is not *ex officio* a member of the corporation. There is also a registrar, who is not necessarily an officer of arms, though the appointment has generally been held by one.

It is the duty of the Heralds and Pursuivants to attend in the Public Office, one of each class together, in monthly rotation. The general duties of the Kings, Heralds, and Pursuivants are to attend the sovereign on all state occasions. To publish certain royal proclamations, marshal all the royal solemnities of coronations, marriages, christenings, funerals, &c.

To grant coats armorial and supporters to the same, to such as are properly authorised to bear them; and, where no hereditary arms are known to belong to the person applying for a grant, they design a coat, crest, &c., taking care that it shall not in any way interfere with those already allowed or recorded.

Besides the Heralds' College at London, there is the *Lord Lyon* king-of-arms for Scotland, who is second king-of-arms for Great Britain; and also *Ulster* king

T

of-arms for Ireland. The officers under the former are the Lyon depute, the Lyon clerk and Keeper of the Records and his deputy, the Fiscal, the Mercer, six Heralds—Rothesay, Marchmont, Islay, Albany, Snowdon, Ross, and six Pursuivants—Dingwall, Bute, Carrick, Ormond, Kintyre, and Unicorn. In Ulster's office there are two Heralds, Cork and Dublin, four Pursuivants, one only bearing a distinctive title, viz., Athlone, and a registrar.

LORD HIGH ADMIRAL.

The ninth great officer of state is the lord high admiral. He has the management of all maritime affairs, and the power of decision in all maritime cases, civil and criminal. By him all naval officers, from an admiral to a lieutenant, are commissioned; all deputies for particular coasts, and judges for his court of admiralty are appointed.

After the union with Scotland, Prince George of Denmark was the first lord high admiral of Great Britain. He died, 29th of October, 1708, and Queen Anne acted by secretary Burchet, until November 29, 1708, when Thomas, Earl of Pembroke, was appointed to the office, with a fee of three hundred marks per annum; and he seems to have been the last person intrusted with this high post (which since his time has been constantly in commission), until the reign of George IV., when his late Majesty, William IV., then Duke of Clarence, was constituted lord high admiral, which he held during the administration of the late Mr. Canning.

SECRETARIES OF STATE.

The principal secretaries of state have been, by virtue of their office, members of the privy council ever since the reign of Queen Elizabeth; whereas, before, they only prepared business for the council board. Until towards the end of the reign of Henry VIII. there was but one secretary of state, when his Majesty thought fit to increase the number to two, both of equal rank and authority. Since then, the multiplicity of public affairs rendered necessary the addition of a third secretary, and during the present reign two more have been added, viz., secretary for war and secretary for India. These five secretaries divide among them the management of all foreign and domestic affairs, with powers of the most extensive and comprehensive nature.

THE PRIVY COUNCIL.

This noble and honourable assembly is a court of great antiquity, composed of the most eminent persons in the kingdom, to advise the sovereigns upon all emergencies; and upon their wisdom, vigilance, courage, and integrity, depend in a great measure the honour and prosperity of the nation. By their advice the crown issues proclamations, and declarations for war and peace. All the peerage are hereditary privy councillors; but of their number the sovereign has a select council, commonly called the cabinet council, and consisting of certain great officers of state (who by virtue of their office are members of it), by whom are determined such affairs as are most important and require secrecy.

LORD STEWARD OF THE HOUSEHOLD.

The chief officer for the civil government of the king's or queen's court is the lord steward of the household.

His authority is very great, and extends over many other officers. He has the sole direction of the household below stairs; is always a member of the privy council; and at the meeting of every new parliament all the members must take the oaths by law appointed before the lord steward of the household, or some one deputed by him. He has no formal grant of his office, but receives his charge from the sovereign in person by delivery of a white staff or wand, the symbol of his office. In the time of Henry VIII. his title was great master of the king's household. But from the first of Mary he was called *magnus seneschalus hospitii regis,* or the lord high steward of the king's house.

LORD CHAMBERLAIN OF THE HOUSEHOLD.

There are two officers distinguished by the name of chamberlain; the one called lord great chamberlain (already spoken of), and the other the lord chamberlain of the household.

The last has the oversight, in the royal household, of all the officers above stairs, except the precinct of the bedchamber, which is under the government of the groom of the stole. He has the supervision of the chaplains, although he be a layman; also of the officers of the standing and removing wardrobes, beds, tents, revels, music, comedians, &c.; of all physicians, apothecaries, surgeons, messengers, trumpeters, drummers, tradesmen, and artisans, retained in the royal service. To him also belongs the oversight of the charges of coronations, marriages, cavalcades, funerals; of all furniture in the parliament-house, and in the rooms for addresses to the king or queen. He carries a white staff in his hand as a badge of his office, and wears a gold key tied with a blue riband above his pocket. He is always a member of the privy council. Under him is a vice-chamberlain, who in his absence supplies his place.

MASTER OF THE HORSE.

The third great officer of the court is reckoned the master of the horse, a place of honour and antiquity, and always filled by a nobleman of the highest rank. He has authority over the equerries, pages, coachmen, footmen, grooms, farriers, smiths, &c.; and appoints all the tradesmen who work for the royal stables; he has also the management and disposal of all the king's or queen's coaches, horses, pages, footmen, and attendants, which are used by himself, with the royal arms and livery; and at any solemn cavalcade he has the honour to ride next the king or queen.

GROOM OF THE STOLE.

This officer is first lord of the bedchamber, and has the custody of the long robe or vestment worn by the sovereign on solemn occasions, and called the *stole.* He wears a gold key as the emblem of his office, and is usually a nobleman of the highest rank. Yet there is one instance of the office being in the hands of a female, viz., Sarah, Duchess of Marlborough, anno 1702, in the reign of Queen Anne.

TREASURER OF THE HOUSEHOLD.

He is an officer in the lord steward's department, next in rank to the lord steward himself. He bears a white staff, and is a privy councillor.

COMPTROLLER OF THE HOUSEHOLD,

Is the second officer under the lord high steward, and next to the treasurer of the household. He also bears a white staff, and is a privy councillor.

LORD ALMONER.

He disposes of what is termed the almonry, or royal alms, on Maundy Thursday (the Thursday in Passion-Week).

The charity bestowed upon this occasion, to each lazar (or poor person) admitted to partake of this ceremony, is woollen cloth for one suit, linen for two shifts, six penny loaves of bread, fish in wooden platters, a quart bottle of wine, and two red leathern purses, one containing as many silver pennies as the king or queen is years old, the other as many shillings as the reign has lasted.

GENTLEMEN AT ARMS.

The honourable band of gentlemen pensioners was first instituted by King Henry VIII., in 1539. It is now designated the honourable corps of gentlemen at arms. Their office is to attend the royal person upon all occasions of public solemnities; as at court, on coronations, St. George's feasts, public audiences of ambassadors, at the going to parliament, royal funerals, &c. They are properly considered as a troop of guards attendant on the king's or queen's person. They wait one-half at a time; but on certain days and extraordinary occasions they are all obliged to attend under the penalty of the cheque.

Previously to the accession of King William IV,

admission to this corps was attainable by persons of any class by purchase. That sovereign, however, made some salutary alterations, which have been still further improved by her present Majesty, and the corps is now strictly composed of gentlemen, the majority of them having held rank in the army.

The officers of the corps consist of the captain (generally a nobleman), a lieutenant, standard-bearer, and a clerk of the cheque.

YEOMEN OF THE GUARD.

These were first instituted by King Henry VII., anno 1486, as a body-guard to him, and their number at that time was fifty men; but they have since undergone several alterations, and their present establishment is 100. Eight of them are styled ushers, four superannuated yeomen, six yeomen hangers, two yeomen bedgoers. Their officers are a captain, who is generally a nobleman, a lieutenant, an ensign, a clerk of the cheque, and four exons.

On all occasions of great solemnities, or the sovereign's going publicly in state by land or water, they attend. Their dress, by gradual alteration, has at length become a conventional costume composed of a coat of the fashion of the reign of William III., a hat of the period of Charles II., and a ruff of the time of James I.

THE END.

LONDON: PRINTED BY WILLIAM CLOWES AND SONS, LIMITED,
DUKE STREET, STAMFORD STREET, S.E., AND GREAT WINDMILL STREET, W.

The Star

The Collar and Badge.

THE INSIGNIA OF THE ORDER OF THE STAR OF INDIA.

Pl. II.   TABLE 2.

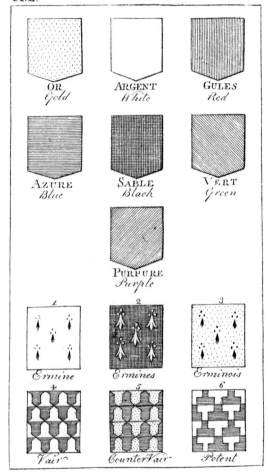

OR
Gold

ARGENT
White

GULES
Red

AZURE
Blue

SABLE
Black

VERT
Green

PURPURE
Purple

1

Ermine

2

Ermines

3

Erminois

4

Vair

5

CounterVair

6

Potent

Pl. III.

TABLE 3.

1. Party Per Pale
2. Party Per Bend
3. Party Per Fefs
4. Party Per Chevron
5. Party Per Crofs
6. Party Per Saltire

Engrailed

Invecked

Wavy

Nebule

Imbattled

Raguly

Indented

Dancette

Dove Tail

Pl IV.

TABLE 4.

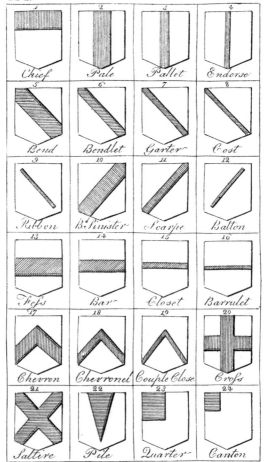

1 Chief	*2* Pale	*3* Pallet	*4* Endorse
5 Bend	*6* Bendlet	*7* Garter	*8* Cost
9 Ribbon	*10* B. Sinister	*11* Scarpe	*12* Balton
13 Fess	*14* Bar	*15* Closet	*16* Barrulet
17 Chevron	*18* Chevronel	*19* Couple Close	*20* Crofs
21 Saltire	*22* Pile	*23* Quarter	*24* Canton

Pl. V.

TABLE 5.

1 Gyron	*2* Flanches	*3* Label	*4* Orle
5 Tressure	*6* Frett	*7* Inescutcheon	*8* Chaplet
9 Border	*10* Engrald	*11* Indented	*12* Quarterly
13 Gobony	*14* Compony	*15* Checky	*16* Vair
17 Paly	*18* Bendy	*19* Barry	*20* Barry Pily
21 Lozengy	*22* Checky	*23* Gyrony	*24* Fretty

Pl. VI.　　　TABLE 6.

1 Cross	2 Moline	3 Flory	4 Patonce
5 Potent	6 Pattee	7 Avellane	8 Batonny
9 Pommee	10 Croslet	11 Croslet Fitchy	12 4 Pheons
13 4 Ermine Spots	14 Mill Rind	15 Mill Rind	16 Rayonnant
17 Lezenge	18 Fusil	19 Maicle	20 Water Bovget
21 Trefoil	22 Quarterfoil	23 Cinquefoil	24 Rose

Pl. VII.   TABLE 7

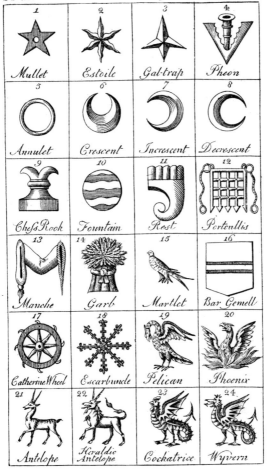

1 Mullet	2 Estoile	3 Gal-trap	4 Pheon
5 Annulet	6 Crescent	7 Increscent	8 Decrescent
9 Chess Rook	10 Fountain	11 Rest	12 Portcullis
13 Manche	14 Garb	15 Martlet	16 Bar Gemell
17 Catherine Wheel	18 Escarbuncle	19 Pelican	20 Phoenix
21 Antelope	22 Heraldic Antelope	23 Cockatrice	24 Wyvern

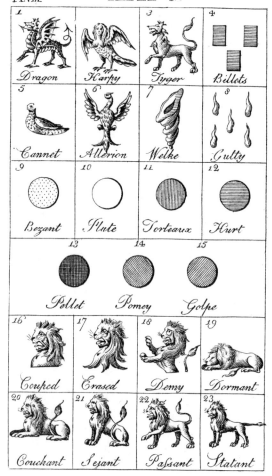

1 Dragon	*2* Harpy	*3* Tyger	*4* Billets
5 Cannet	*6* Allerion	*7* Welke	*8* Gutty
9 Bezant	*10* Plate	*11* Torteaux	*12* Hurt
13 Pellet	*14* Pomey	*15* Golpe	
16 Couped	*17* Erased	*18* Demy	*19* Dormant
20 Couchant	*21* Sejant	*22* Passant	*23* Statant

Pl. IX.   TABLE 9.

1 Passant Gardant	2 Rampant	3 Rampant Gardant	4 Rampant Regardant
5 Rampant Combatant	6 Saliant	7 Rampant Addorsed	8 Counter Passant
9 Counter-Saliant	10 Counter Tripping	11 Sejant Addorsed	12 Passant Regardant
13 at Gaze	14 Tripping	15 Springing	16 Courant
17 Lodged	18 Cabossed	19 Close	20 Rising
21 Displayed	22 Volant	23 Demy Vol.	24 Indorsed

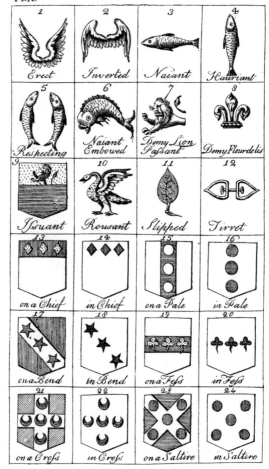

1	2	3	4
Erect	Inverted	Naiant	Hauriant
5	6	7	8
Respecting	Naiant Embowed	Demy Lion Passant	Demy Fleurdelis
9	10	11	12
Issuant	Rousant	Slipped	Tirret
13	14	15	16
on a Chief	in Chief	on a Pale	in Pale
17	18	19	20
on a Bend	in Bend	on a Fess	in Fess
21	22	23	24
on a Cross	in Cross	on a Saltire	in Saltire

PL.XI.

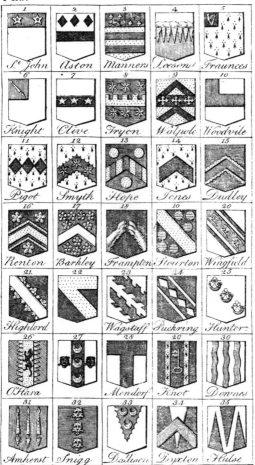

1 St. John	2 Aston	3 Manners	4 Leeson	5 Fraunces
6 Knight	7 Clive	8 Fryon	9 Walpole	10 Woodvile
11 Pigot	12 Smyth	13 Hope	14 Jones	15 Dudley
16 Renton	17 Barkley	18 Frampton	19 Stourton	20 Wingfield
21 Highlord	22	23 Wagstaff	24 Puckring	25 Hunter
26 O'Hara	27	28 Mendorf	29 Knot	30 Downes
31 Amherst	32 Snigg	33 Dallison	34 Dyxton	35 Hulse

Pl. XII.

1 Grevile	2 Packer	3 Athins	4 Berenger	5 Barker
6 Baines	7 Turner	8 Simeon	9 Rich	10 Kinnaird
11 Twisden	12 Prince	13 Hilborne	14 Newton	15 Porter
16 Drumond	17 Burnaby	18 Hildesley	19 Haydon	20 Morley
21 Arbuthnot	22 Rawlyns	23 Chute	24 Stapleton	25 Paulet
26 Ewart	27 Rawline	28 Norton	29 Gwyn	30 Aldam
31 Kagg	32	33 Weele	34 Hawkeridge	35

Pl. XIII.

1 Newdigate	2 Grafton	3 St. Clare	4 Dillon	5 Monox
6 Quarterly	7 Humphrey	8 Lowther	9 Biest	10 Tounson
11 Bourden	12 Cennino	13 Chapman	14 Shorter	15 Peacock
16 Cole	17 Washbourne	18 Shipstowe	19 Madden	20 Row—
21 Tremaine	22 Borough	23 Buocafoco	24 Villages	25 Gamin
26 Wells	27 Sault	28 Davy	29 Hoast	30 Bateman
31 Cooks	32 Douglas	33 Clarke	34 Sturgeon	35 Ambesace

Pl. XIV.

Pl. XV.

Sketch of Plate

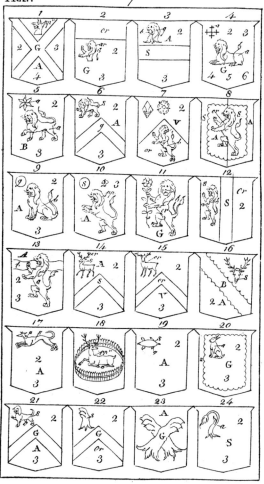

Pl. XVI.

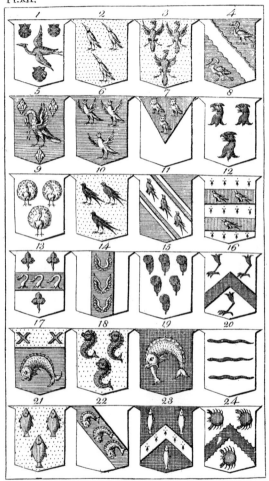

Pl. XVII.   *Sketch of Plate*

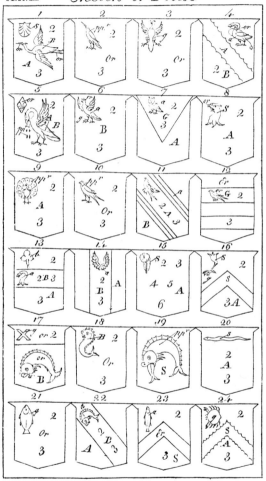

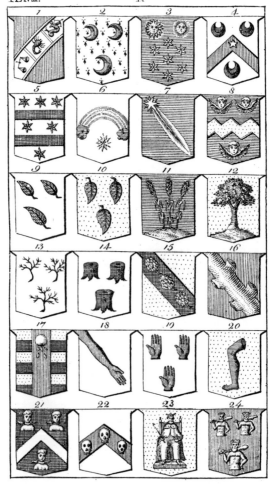

Pl. XIX.

Pl. XX.

HATCHMENTS.

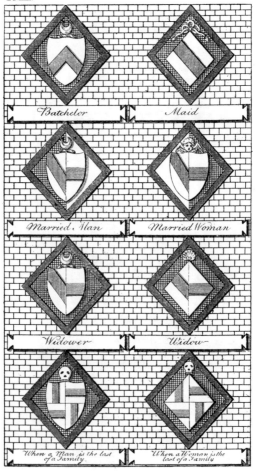

Batchelor

Maid

Married Man

Married Woman

Widower

Widow

When a Man is the last of a Family.

When a Woman is the last of a Family.

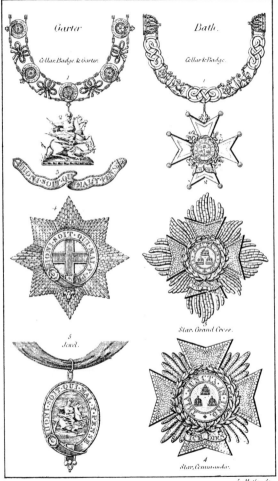

Garter.

Bath.

Collar. Badge & Garter.

Collar & Badge.

1

1

3

2

4

5
Jewel.

3
Star. Grand Cross.

4
Star. Commander.

Jos. Matlow Sc.

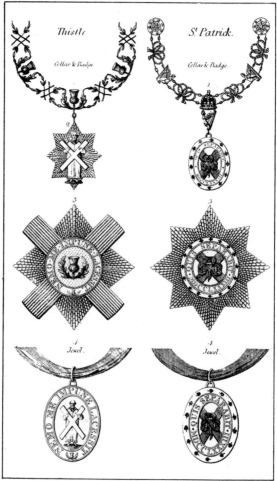

Thistle
Collar & Badge

St Patrick.
Collar & Badge

Jewel.

Jewel.

Jos Mallon Sc.

Pl. XXIII. KNIGHTHOOD.

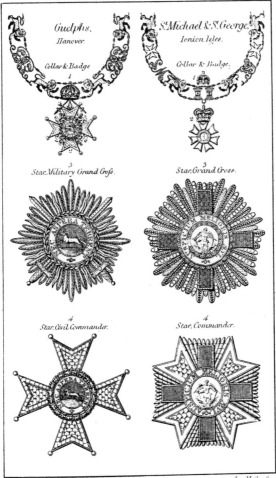

Guelphs.
Hanover.

Collar & Badge.
1

2

St. Michael & St. George.
Ionian Isles.

Collar & Badge.
1

2

3
Star, Military Grand Cross.

3
Star, Grand Cross.

4
Star, Civil Commander.

4
Star, Commander.

Jos. Mutlow sc.

Pl XXIV.

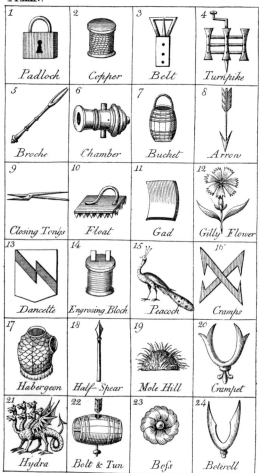

1 Padlock	2 Copper	3 Belt	4 Turnpike
5 Broche	6 Chamber	7 Bucket	8 Arrow
9 Closing Tongs	10 Float	11 Gad	12 Gilly Flower
13 Dancette	14 Engrosing Block	15 Peacock	16 Cramps
17 Habergeon	18 Half-Spear	19 Mole Hill	20 Crampet
21 Hydra	22 Bolt & Tun	23 Bess	24 Boteroll

Pl. XXV.

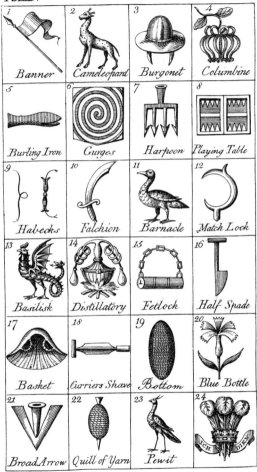

1 Banner	2 Cameleopard	3 Burgonet	4 Columbine
5 Burling Iron	6 Gurges	7 Harpoon	8 Playing Table
9 Habecks	10 Falchion	11 Barnacle	12 Match Lock
13 Basilisk	14 Distillatory	15 Fetlock	16 Half Spade
17 Basket	18 Curriers Shave	19 Bottom	20 Blue Bottle
21 Broad Arrow	22 Quill of Yarn	23 Pewit	24

Pl. XXVI.

1 Morine	2 Maiden's Head	3 Renverse	4 Forcene
5 Porcupine	6 Hedge-hog	7 Ass	8 Golden Fleece
9 Beaver	10 Otter	11 Marine Wolf	12 Mole
13 Tortoise	14 Monkey	15 Fox	16 Cata Mountain
17 Coot	18 Raven	19 Moor-cock	20 Dove
21 Bee Hive	22 Harvest-fly	23 Gad bee	24 Squirrel

Pl. XXVII

1 Cross-bow	2 Escallop	3 Pillar	4 Fire Beacon
5 Grass-hopper	6 Pomegranate	7 Scrip	8 Crosier
9 Scepter	10 Anchor	11 Cardinals Hat	12 Plough
13 Snail	14 Fire Ball	15 Flesh Pot	16 Penny-Yard penny
17 Harp	18 Mound	19 Fleur-de-lis	20 Thunderbolt
21 Battle-Axe	22 Shuttle	23 Bugle Horn	24 Level

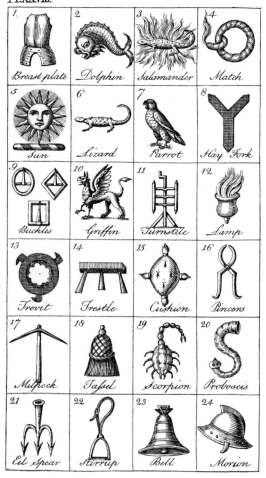

1. Breast plate	2. Dolphin	3. Salamander	4. Match
5. Sun	6. Lizard	7. Parrot	8. Hay Fork
9. Buckles	10. Griffin	11. Turnstile	12. Lamp
13. Trevit	14. Trestle	15. Cushion	16. Pincors
17. Milpeck	18. Tassel	19. Scorpion	20. Proboscis
21. Eel Spear	22. Stirrup	23. Bell	24. Morion

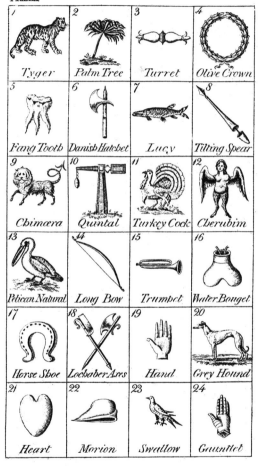

1 Tyger	*2* Palm Tree	*3* Turret	*4* Olive Crown
5 Fang Tooth	*6* Danish Hatchet	*7* Lucy	*8* Tilting Spear
9 Chimæra	*10* Quintal	*11* Turkey Cock	*12* Cherubim
13 Pelican Natural	*14* Long Bow	*15* Trumpet	*16* Water Bouget
17 Horse Shoe	*18* Lochaber Axes	*19* Hand	*20* Grey Hound
21 Heart	*22* Morion	*23* Swallow	*24* Gauntlet

Pl.XXX

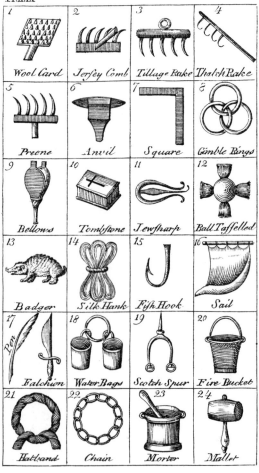

1 Wool Card	*2* Jersey Comb	*3* Tillage Rake	*4* Thatch Rake
5 Preene	*6* Anvil	*7* Square	*8* Gimble Rings
9 Bellows	*10* Tombstone	*11* Jewsharp	*12* Ball Tasselled
13 Badger	*14* Silk Hank	*15* Fish Hook	*16* Sail
17 Pen Falchion	*18* Water Bags	*19* Scotch Spur	*20* Fire Bucket
21 Hatband	*22* Chain	*23* Morter	*24* Mallet

Pl. XXXI

1 Sagittarius	2 Spinx	3 Sea Horse	4 Mermaid	5 Unicorn
6 Asis	7 Panther	8 Horse	9 Bear	10 Wolf
11 Elephant	12 Bull	13 Counter-Tripping	14 Cock	15 A Signet
16 Owl	17 Cornish Chough	18 Rere mouse	19 Stork	20 Boar
21 Rhinoceros	22 Goat	23 Camel	24 Ostrich	25 Holy Lamb
26 Talbot	27 Caboshed	28 Fretted	29 Sea Lion	30 Leopard
31 Spread Eagle	32 Lobster	33 Attire	34 Lure	35 Hawks Bell

Pl. XXXII.   Pl. 15.

1 Shoveller	2 Seax	3 Sea Pie	4 Ibex	5 Rein Deer
6 Opinicus	7 Sea Dog	8 a Plume	9 Double Plume	10 Triple Plume
11 Danish Axe	12 Broad Axe	13 Coward	14 Defamd	15 Baillotte
16 Tricorporated	17 Debruis'd	18 Double Tail'd	19 Double Headed	20 Lyon Poison
21 Lion Dragon	22 Conjoined	23 Contourne	24 of S.t Mark	25 Spade Iron
26 Salt	27 Shackbolts	28 Grappling Iron	29 Demy Rose	30 Wheel
31 Stafford Knot	32 Bourchier Knot	33 Harring Knot	34 Wake's Knot	35 Dacres Knot

Pl. XXIII.

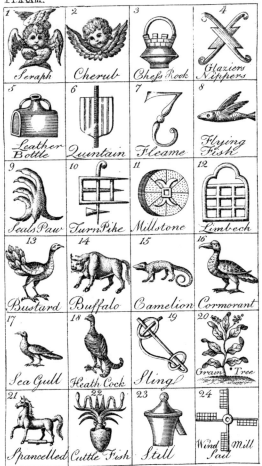

1 Seraph	2 Cherub	3 Chess Rook	4 Glaziers Nippers
5 Leather Bottle	6 Quintain	7 Fleame	8 Flying Fish
9 Seals Paw	10 TurnPike	11 Millstone	12 Limbech
13 Bustard	14 Buffalo	15 Camelion	16 Cormorant
17 Sea Gull	18 Heath Cock	19 Sling	20 Gram Tree
21 Spancelled	22 Cuttle Fish	23 Still	24 Wind Mill Sail

Pl. XXXIV. CHARGES AND THEIR NAMES.

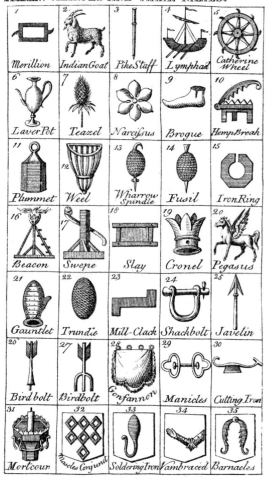

1 Merillion	2 Indian Goat	3 Pike Staff	4 Lymphad	5 Catherine Wheel
6 Laver Pot	7 Teazel	8 Narcissus	9 Brogue	10 Hemp Break
11 Plummet	12 Weel	13 Wharrow Spindle	14 Fusil	15 Iron Ring
16 Beacon	17 Swepe	18 Slay	19 Cronel	20 Pegasus
21 Gauntlet	22 Trundle	23 Mill-Clack	24 Shackbolt	25 Javelin
26 Bird bolt	27 Birdbolt	28 Confannon	29 Manicles	30 Cutting Iron
31 Mortcour	32 Mascles Conjured	33 Soldering Iron	34 Vambraced	35 Barnacles

Pl. XXXV.

1 Pily Bendy	2 Male Griffin	3 Palmers Staffs	4 in Orle	5 Stilt
6 Flasques	7 Voiders	8 Well	9 Well	10 Pilgrims Staff
11 in his Pride	12 Trevet	13 Segreant	14 Dismembered	15 Icicle
16 Vole	17 Nowed	18 Vulned	19 Grid Iron	20 Entrailed
21 Leopards face	22 Leop.d Head	23 Cornet	24 Demi Fleur de lis	25 Weare
26 Naissant	27 Fire Brand	28 Battled Embattel'd	29 Bends Enhanced	30 Chev.s Brac'ed
31 Semee of	32 Dexter H.d	33 Sinister H.d	34 Scythe	35 Imbru'd

Pl. XXXVI. CROSSES.

1	2	3	4	5
Pierced	Raguled	Degraded	Cercelee	Cramponnee
6	7	8	9	10
Copper Cake	Pater Noster	Lochaban Axe	Tron-onnee	Pall
11	12	13	14	15
Cap	Mascles	Fretted	Couped	Interlaced
16	17	18	19	20
Doub.Parted	Lozenges	Bezanty	Calvary	Patriarchal
21	22	23	24	25
Lambeaux	St.Esprit	St.James	S.Lazarus	Malta
26	27	28	29	30
Tau	Union	Lyre	Quadrate	Well Bucket
31	32	33	34	35
Pafsion Nail	Fleury	Ankred	Vair	Crefcented

PL.XXXVII. CROSSES & PARTITION LINES.

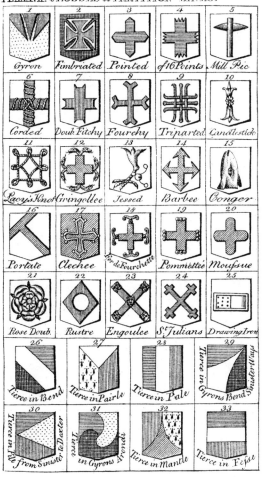

1 Gyron	2 Fimbriated	3 Pointed	4 of 16 Points	5 Mill Pic
6 Corded	7 Doub. Fitchy	8 Fourchy	9 Triparted	10 Candlestick
11 Lacy's Knot	12 Gringollee	13 Jessed	14 Barbee	15 Conger
16 Portate	17 Clechee	18 for de Fourchette	19 Pommettee	20 Mousfue
21 Rose Doub.	22 Rustre	23 Engoulee	24 St Julians	25 Drawing Iron
26 Tierce in Bend	27 Tierce in Pairle	28 Tierce in Pale	29 Tierce in Gyrons Bend Sinister Ways	
30 Tierce in Pile from Sinister to Dexter	31 Tierce in Gyrons Arondi	32 Tierce in Mantle	33 Tierce in Fesse	

Pl. XXXVIII.

BORDURES, COUNTER CHANGES & LINES.

1 Madder Bag	2 Couped Close	3 Couped	4 Ers. Close	5 Erased
6 Circular Wreath	7 Bowen Knot	8 Fire Beacon	9 Enaluron	10 Enurny
11 Vannet	12 Verdoy	13 Entoyre	14 Diaperd	15 Bendy
16 Couched	17 Contrepoint	18 Chev. Rompu	19 Barry Indented	20 Barry Bendy
21 Paly B. Sinis	22 Paly Bendy	23 Trussing	24 Whales Head	25 Papellone
26 Cockatrice	27 Masonry	28 Fusilly	29 Wing	30 P. Fesse & Pale
31 P. Pale & Chevron	32 P. Pale & Base	33 P. Pile Transposd	34 P. Pile in Point	35 P. Pile Traverse

Pl. XXXIX.

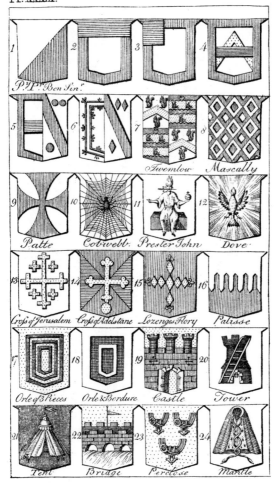

1 2 3 4

P.P.P. Bon Sin.

5 6 7 *Twemlow* 8 *Mascally*

9 *Patte* 10 *Cobwebb* 11 *Prester John* 12 *Dove*

13 *Cross of Jerusalem* 14 *Cross of Adelstane* 15 *Lozenges Flory* 16 *Palisse*

17 *Orle of 3 Pieces* 18 *Orle & Bordure* 19 *Castle* 20 *Tower*

21 *Tent* 22 *Bridge* 23 *Perclose* 24 *Mantle*

Pl. XI

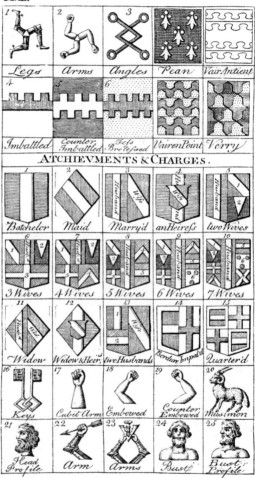

Legs	Arms	Angles	Pean	Vair Antient
Imbattled	Counter Imbattled	Fess Bretessed	Vairen Point	Verry

ATCHIEVMENTS & CHARGES.

Batchelor	Maid	Marry'd	an Heiress	two Wives
3 Wives	4 Wives	5 Wives	6 Wives	7 Wives
Widow	Widow & Heir.	two Husbands	Border Impal'd	Quarter'd
Keys	Cubit Arm	Embowed	Counter Embowed	Musimon
Head Profile	Arm	Arms	Bust	Bust Profile

Pl. XLI

1. Tenne
2. Sanguine
3. Arch
4. Charged
5. Treille
6. Cotton hank
7. Battering ram
8. Chain shot
9. Man Tiger
10. Chevronny
11. 3 Harrows
12. Muraille
13. Bishop
14. Knight of the Garter & his Lady
15. Baronet
16. Commoner & his Lady

HELMETS.

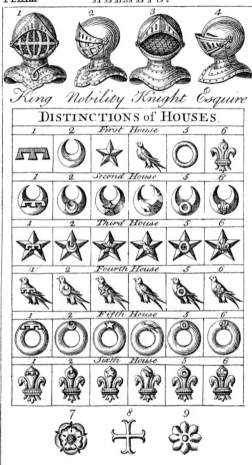

King   Nobility   Knight   Esquire

DISTINCTIONS of HOUSES.

CROWNS, CORONETS, MITRES, &c.

Crown of State

2 Prince of Wales

3 Younger Sons or Brothers

4 Nephews of the Blood Royal

5 Princess Royal

6 Duke

7 Marquis

8 Earl

9 Viscount

10 Baron

11 Bishop of Durham

12 Bishop

13 Cap of Dignity

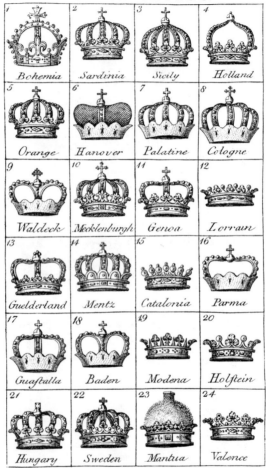

1 Bohemia	2 Sardinia	3 Sicily	4 Holland
5 Orange	6 Hanover	7 Palatine	8 Cologne
9 Waldeck	10 Mecklenburgh	11 Genoa	12 Lorrain
13 Guelderland	14 Mentz	15 Catalonia	16 Parma
17 Guastalla	18 Baden	19 Modena	20 Holstein
21 Hungary	22 Sweden	23 Mantua	24 Valence

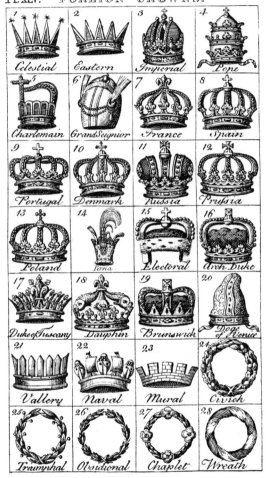

1 Celestial	2 Eastern	3 Imperial	4 Pope
5 Charlemain	6 GrandSeignior	7 France	8 Spain
9 Portugal	10 Denmark	11 Russia	12 Prussia
13 Poland	14 Persia	15 Electoral	16 Arch Duke
17 Duke of Tuscany	18 Dauphin	19 Brunswick	20 Doge of Venice
21 Vallery	22 Naval	23 Mural	24 Civick
25 Triumphal	26 Obsidional	27 Chaplet	28 Wreath